HUNTIN... R VICTIMS
1960-2006

Serial Killers
Hunting Britons and their Victims, 1960-2006

Published by
WATERSIDE PRESS
Domum Road
Winchester SO23 9NN
United Kingdom

Telephone 01962 855567 UK Landline low-cost calls 0845 2300 733
E-mail enquiries@watersidepress.co.uk
Online catalogue and bookstore www.watersidepress.co.uk

ISBN 978 1904380 33 7

Cataloguing-In-Publication Data A catalogue record for this book can be obtained from the British Library

Cover design Waterside Press. Using the names of the known victims of serial killers during the time-frame covered by the book.

Printing and binding CPI Antony Rowe Ltd, Chippenham and Eastbourne, UK.

North American distributor International Specialised Book Services (ISBS), 920 NE 58th Ave, Suite 300, Portland, Oregon, 97213-3786, USA
Telephone 1 800 944 6190 Fax 1 503 280 8832 orders@isbs.com www.isbs.com

Serial Killers

HUNTING BRITONS AND THEIR VICTIMS
1960-2006

David Wilson

WATERSIDE PRESS

About the author

David Wilson is professor of criminology at the Centre for Criminal Justice Policy and Research at the University of Central England in Birmingham. A former prison governor, he is editor of the *Howard Journal* and a well-known author, broadcaster and presenter for TV and radio, including for the BBC, C4 and Sky Television. He has written three earlier books for Waterside Press: *The Longest Injustice: The Strange Story of Alex Alexandrowicz* (with the latter) (1999), *Prison(er) Education: Stories of Change and Transformation* (with Ann Reuss) (2000) and *Images of Incarceration: Representations of Prison in Film and Television Drama* (with Sean O'Sullivan) (2004).

Serial Killers

HUNTING BRITONS AND THEIR VICTIMS 1960-2006

David Wilson

Acknowledgements

There are a variety of people that I would like to thank who have helped in different ways to ensure that I had the space, time and ability to complete this book. Most immediately I am grateful to colleagues at the Centre for Criminal Justice Policy and Research at the University of Central England in Birmingham who encouraged me at every stage of writing. In particular I am grateful to Professors John Rouse and Chris Painter who allowed me a sabbatical term, and to Professor Doug Sharp, the Director of the Centre, for his continued support. I would also like to thank Professor Mike King, Dr Azrini Wahidin, Dr Kate Williams, Gurmit Heer and James Treadwell for offering advice at various stages of the book's completion. So too Matthew Cremin, Deputy Course Director of the Masters in Criminology at UCE, and Linda Harland, the Faculty Registrar, were also both very supportive. I am particularly grateful to Professors John Muncie, Roger Hood and Keith Soothill who each read a draft or draft chapters of the book, and made perceptive comments on how to improve on the contents. I am also grateful to the librarians and staff of the university libraries of UCE and Cambridge, and of the Radzinovicz Library in Cambridge, and to Barbara McCalla.

Outside of the academy I would like to thank a variety of friends who listened patiently and at times endlessly as I would go over some detail related to the book, and who would demand—as only friends can—that I stop 'talking nonsense' (or words to that effect) and start making sense. And when I was writing about some very dark places, they reminded me that there is always light to illuminate the gloom. Chief amongst these people are the 'Thursday night' group, which includes Paul Carr, Ross Collins, Julian Cook, David Cotterill, Ian Dryer, Tim Graham, James Hole, Stuart Holton and Paul Wildman. Here too I would like to thank Paul Harrison and Martin Brunt of *Sky News*, Sarah Thackray of the BBC, Peter Harness, Jacquie Drewe and the redoubtable 'Team America'—Natasha Blake and Jessica Hanscom.

I would also like to take this opportunity to thank my family for putting up with my disappearance into my study for hours on end, especially when instead I could—perhaps should—have been attending to some more pressing domestic matter. As ever Anne Maguire and Hugo and Fleur Wilson were wonderful, charming, supportive, funny and life enhancing.

Finally, I would like to pay tribute to Roger Cruickshank who sadly died before this book reached publication. Roger shaped my thinking in so many ways that I cannot begin to imagine what life is going to be like without him.

David Wilson
June 2007

SERIAL KILLERS

CONTENTS

CHAPTER

List of tables and figures

'Very well written, *Serial Killers* tackles the subject from a fresh perspective … its conclusions will stir debate.' **Professor Roger Hood**, All Souls College, Oxford University

'This is an interesting and very readable book that usefully reflects on serial homicides in ways which go beyond the usual focus of considering the clinical characteristics of such offenders. Wilson paints on a much wider canvas reminding us that the common feature of British serial killing is the vulnerability of the victims. This leads on to the notion that the victims of serial killers not only reflect wider social relations, but also that they may be victimised because they are perceived as living outside the moral order of competitive capitalist society. The message emanating from this study of British serial killing is that Britain is inadequate in its provision of social and economic protection for the poor and vulnerable.' **Professor Keith Soothill**, Lancaster University

'This book is a timely contribution to the literature on serial killing. It provides an insight into a topic which has to date been largely ignored by academic analysis and is at the same time perceptive and accessible to a wider audience than that normally addressed in criminological discourse. In his chapter on policing Professor Wilson has been able for the first time to analyse the Byford Report into the case of the Yorkshire Ripper and in so doing he has been able to offer a new analysis on how to understand the failure of the police to stop the Ripper killings.' **Professor Douglas Sharp**, University of Central England, Birmingham

'Wilson lifts the lid on the social, institutional, political and economic contexts that make serial killing possible … Finally someone has gone beyond the sensational voyeurism of writing about serial murders and produced an accessible and perceptive analysis which will encourage all of us to begin to take this issue more seriously.' **Professor John Muncie**, Open University

This book is dedicated to the 326 known victims of British serial killers since 1960.

Introduction

As the unique amalgam, in a new genetic configuration of contributions from a man and a woman, one is born into the world, as different from other people, in much the same way as my fingerprints were different from other peoples.

The quote above comes from the serial killer, Dennis Nilsen. It is taken from his unpublished autobiography which was leaked to me, via a circuitous route in 2005, given HM Prison Service's determination that Nilsen should not be allowed to further publicise his views on how and why he became a serial killer. In many respects I agree with the Prison Service and I use this quote merely because it perfectly summarises what this book is *not* about: in other words, the relentless focus of virtually every popular or academic account on the individual psyche of those who kill and kill again. Put simply, I am not interested in Nilsen—the 'new genetic configuration'—who has been endlessly medicalised and pathologised, with every episode in his childhood, youth, army, police and civil service career poured over looking, as it were, for clues as to why he would eventually kill some 15[1] young men in the late 1970s and early 1980s.

What is true for Nilsen is also true for the other serial killers who appear in this book, where the search for why they 'did it' has been rooted in their individual psychology—the so-called medico-psychological tradition—with the implication that if we were just to look more closely at the killer's genetic make-up, his sexuality, his relationship with his father, his mother, or at his childhood more generally and so forth, we would eventually discover the root cause of his or her murderous intentions. My lack of interest stems from several practical concerns, a theoretical perspective developed over many years spent working with serial offenders, and through my work as an academic writing and teaching about them.

The practical concerns can be easily described. In my work with serial killers and other serial offenders I encountered two distinct groups. The first group—the majority of those whom I spent time with and including Dennis Nilsen—had invariably developed a very robust and self-serving view as to why they had repeatedly killed. (Consider, for example, why Nilsen wants to use the description 'unique' and 'different' at the beginning of his autobiography and what this might also imply about how he views himself. Indeed, it is also the

---

[1] Interestingly, in a letter sent to the London *Evening Standard* on 9 November 2006, Nilsen admitted to murdering the 14 year-old schoolboy Stephen Holmes, whom he claimed he had picked up in a Cricklewood pub in December 1978. Nilsen was never charged with this murder, although in December 2006 the Crown Prosecution Service decided that it would not be in the public interest to prosecute him further, given that he is currently in prison with no prospect of release. In the letter, Nilsen complained bitterly about not being allowed to publish his autobiography.

exact opposite of how his biographer describes how Nilsen came to be 'born into the world'. As such Brian Masters (1985: xiii) notes that Nilsen 'started life unremarkably enough'). Yet, time after time, the views and insights of those killers whom I worked with were more often than not socially constructed to suit the nature and circumstances of their arrest, conviction and imprisonment. All too often their explanations were rooted in the forlorn hope that, for example, there might come a day when release was possible through parole; or they were simply proffered to engineer a more favourable prison transfer; or sometimes to maintain a conception of 'self' more in keeping with their own sense of who they were and what they thought they were entitled to.

More than this, when one investigated their explanations in any depth they could have been applied more generally to each and every one of us. After all, who amongst us has not had a beloved parent, grandparent, uncle or aunt die? Who has not felt lonely, bullied or excluded as a child? Who has not been saddened by the end of a close and loving relationship with another person? Who would not like to be given a little more credit for their achievements and a little less criticism for their failings? Would these everyday—almost prosaic—life-events be enough to push us into 'killing for company', as Masters (1985) claimed in respect of Nilsen? Are these justifications enough to account for the phenomenon of serial killing? And whilst some serial killers—such as Robert Black, who abducted, sexually assaulted and killed at least three young girls in the 1980s—have undoubtedly had appalling childhoods filled with abandonment and abuse, is this justification enough to explain their crimes, especially when so many other people have had similar experiences, but have not gone on to kill and kill again?

These observations about the explanations that serial killers give for their motivation stem from working with them after they have been caught and imprisoned. However, even in the immediate aftermath of arrest—long before their trial and conviction—those serial killers who are prepared to talk regularly construct a picture that is often far removed from the reality of events. Peter Sutcliffe, for example, after his arrest for a series of attacks and murders of women in Yorkshire in the 1970s, gave a variety of interviews to detectives working on the case. He appeared forthcoming, but as the leading expert on the murders has commented: 'It is now wholly evident that he was grossly deceitful and manipulative' (Bilton, 2003: 655). Specifically, Sutcliffe—better known as the 'Yorkshire Ripper'—sought to hide any sexual motive for his crimes, and instead wanted to paint a picture of himself as simply mad, which would thus influence every aspect of his trial and his sentence.

So too Fred West, before taking his own life, left 111 pages of autobiography. However, as David Canter (2003: 62) explains, anyone hoping to discover clues in this autobiography as to why West killed would be disappointed for 'the journal ignores all of this'. Canter's observation would come as no surprise to John Bennett, the detective in charge of the West investigation. After West was arrested, his interviews with the police amounted to 145 tape recordings that translated into 6,189 pages of transcript (Souness, 1995: 278).[2] Nonetheless, since his retirement Bennett has commented: 'West's interviews were worthless except to confirm that nothing that he said could be relied upon as anything near the truth' (Bennett and Gardner, 2005: 168). Indeed, Gordon Burn, one of West's most perceptive biographers, simply dismisses him as a 'bullshitting liar', who claimed, for example, to have travelled the world with the Scottish pop singer Lulu (Burn, 1998: 136). Burn explains that West would talk 'palaver while apparently talking the truth. Laying out and simultaneously covering up' (Burn, 1998: 253).

The second group that I have encountered were the mirror opposite of the first. In short, they never talked at all about the motivation that drove them to murder and they kept their secrets well-guarded. For example, just after his conviction in April 2001 for the murder of 15 of his patients, West Yorkshire Police decided to re-interview Harold Shipman—Britain's most prolific serial killer—about the deaths of other patients whom he had attended whilst practising in Todmorden. Their videotape—which I have viewed—is very revealing and I quote here from a transcript.

Police officer: No replies are going to be given to any questions during the course of this interview and any subsequent interviews. I think it is fair to say for the purposes of the tape that we are happy that we are interviewing Harold Shipman. (Officer gets up and walks round the table to place a picture in front of the face of Shipman, who has turned to face the wall.)

Police officer: To start with, if I can try to jog your memory by showing you a photograph, that's Elizabeth Pearce. Of the three ladies there it's the elderly lady dressed in black. For the benefit of the tape Dr Shipman's eyes are closed. (Officer returns to desk and picks up two photographs.)

Police officer: Unfortunately we don't have a photograph of Mr Lingard. To try and jog your memory here is a photograph of Eagle Street and there is a photograph of

---

2 On the other hand Rosemary West said nothing of substance in her 46 police interviews between 23 April and 1 June 1994 (Souness, 1995: 278). Here it is also worth noting that Masters (1996: 334) suggests that Rose West should have been acquitted at her trial and maintains that 'there were no witnesses to the alleged crimes, no confession from the defendant, no cause of death had been established for any of the victims, no time or place of death could be accurately ascribed and on six counts there was nothing to suggest that the defendant had even met the girls she was alleged to have killed'. Whilst this is of interest, Masters consistently downplays much of the evidence against Rose West—particularly in relation to the assault on Caroline Owens and the significance of this (see *Chapter 5*). However, as with all those serial killers who appear in this book, I have accepted the judgement of the courts against them and written on the basis that their convictions are legally sound as of the time of writing.

where Mr Lingard lived. Just for the benefit of the tape, Dr Shipman's eyes are closed and he didn't look at all. (Officer returns to desk and returns with another photograph which he places again in front of the face of Shipman.)

Police officer: Just to try and jog your memory, Dr Shipman, I have here a photograph of Lily Crossley. Just for the benefit of the tape Dr Shipman's eyes are closed and he didn't look at all. (See, also, Peters, 2005: 170-171)

This final note from the police officer exactly sums up this second group of silent and uncommunicative serial killers—'just for the benefit of the tape Dr Shipman's eyes are closed and he didn't look at all'. Not only did he not look, but he also never spoke. Shipman never discussed why he killed 215 (and possibly 260) elderly people either in Todmorden, Hyde or elsewhere and ultimately, like Fred West, he chose to commit suicide in his cell—at HMP Wakefield in Shipman's case—in January 2004, rather than reveal the circumstances that led him to murder.

So, to apply Gordon Burn's phrase about Fred West more generally, we have one group of serial killers who 'lay out' and another who 'cover up'; some who talk endlessly—although not necessarily to any purpose and others who refuse to, or indeed cannot, talk at all.

FROM THE INDIVIDUAL TO THE SOCIAL

These practical concerns are thus real enough, but there is also a theoretical perspective that should stop us simply viewing serial killing from the point of view of the killer. For, as the anthropologist Elliot Leyton (1986) in *Hunting Humans* has argued, the 'individual discourse' of the medico-psychological tradition about serial killers fails to meet the challenge of causation by ignoring cultural and historical specificity. After all, dangerous and deranged individuals are a constant feature over time and between cultures. Yet, given that this is so, how are we then to explain why Britain had no serial killers during the 1920s and 1930s, whilst just across the Channel Germany had 12 (Jenkins, 1988)? Indeed, why did the late 1970s and early to mid-1980s produce so many British serial killers? For Leyton, focussing on North America, the answer to these questions of cultural and historical specificity is to argue that serial killing cannot just be understood as the result of a greater or lesser number of dangerous personalities existing in society at any one time, but rather has to be seen as the product of the socio-economic system which cannot reward the efforts of all and thus may dangerously marginalise certain people.

Leyton goes further and argues that serial killing should be viewed as a form of 'homicidal protest' (1986: 287)—a theme which is discussed more fully in the first two chapters of this book, but which in essence suggests that some people will react to challenges to their position in the economic and social structure by killing those in the challenging group. Leyton's analysis is dynamic, provocative and, as the title of this book suggests, much of what appears here is an extended argument with Leyton to see if it is possible to understand Britain's 19 serial murderers and their 326 known victims since 1960 in this way. Indeed the time-frame chosen for the book has been partly constructed around Leyton's argument, which thus helps to explain why I do not consider British serial killers from the 1940s or 1950s, such as John Reginald Christie or John George Haigh.

So, the theoretical perspective that is presented here consciously moves the discourse about serial killing away from the individual—the pathological and the medical and into the social. It argues that to truly understand why serial killers kill we need to investigate the very nature of the social structure—the society—that has created these people whom we label as serial killers. And, as is implicit in this analysis, it also suggests that the responsibility for serial killing therefore does not lie so much with the individual serial killer, but can be better found within the social and economic structure of Britain since 1960, which (generalising on a theme developed later) does not reward the efforts of all and in particular has marginalised large sections of society.

It therefore should come as no surprise that the victims of British serial killers have been exclusively confined to certain marginalised groups in our culture—the elderly, gay men, prostitutes, babies and infants, and young people moving home and finding their feet elsewhere in the country—and that women make up a significant number in all but one of these categories. It is people from within these marginalised groups who are the focus of this book, although I do not claim to be an expert on, for example, gerontology or queer theory. Instead, whilst sketching in the backgrounds to how individuals from within these groups come to be victimised I use more familiar criminological territory—such as policing initiatives or cultures to develop my argument more fully.

CRIMINOLOGICAL METHODS

In creating this focus and to make my argument a wide range of academic disciplines and research methods have been employed. Most obviously this is a book of criminology and its primary concerns are with the crimes committed by the 19 serial killers. However, it is also a book about history. By 'history' I do not mean the chronicling of ever more, spine-tingling, fetishistic detail about the crimes that were committed—the provenance of the 'true crime' genre—but rather the use of the historical realities of these crimes to make a criminological argument. In short, by looking at the wider forces that produced the victims of serial killers in Britain I am attempting to discern and thereafter interpret wider patterns and regularities in our recent past, so as more clearly to understand our present and, hopefully, better mould our future.

As for research methods, most obviously I have interviewed several serial killers both whilst working as a prison governor and now as an academic. As I have already inferred, one or two serial offenders maintain a regular correspondence with me. I have used these experiences to inform my understanding of what they did, whilst not necessarily accepting the insights that they offered as to why they thought that they had killed. Indeed my academic concerns with them were usually simply practical. In other words, what I was interested in discussing with them was how they chose their victims and whether that choice contributed to their ability to escape detection for as long as they did. Of course here it would be traditional to name those who were interviewed, but I want to resist that temptation for two reasons. Firstly, because to do so would inevitably mean that the reader would become seduced back into the individual discourse and secondly because I am less interested in the serial killers themselves than I am in their victims. To me naming them gives them a status which I would prefer to deny them.

So too I have triangulated a voluminous secondary literature about serial killing with contemporary records where these exist, most obviously in reports about these serial killers as they appeared in *The Times,* the *Guardian* or in other newspapers and which would—almost incidentally—provide details about their victims. Official inquiries after a series of deaths had occurred, such as, for example, the Allitt Inquiry, which was concerned with investigating the murder of four children and a number of serious assaults by the nurse Beverly Allitt in 1991, also proved a useful source in relation to the victims of serial killers.

More than this, primary research has been conducted with a variety of the groups that have been the targets of British serial killers—most obviously young people, gay men and the elderly. As such, I conducted research about the protection offered by the police to gay men and women in Birmingham (Wilson and McCalla, 2004) and for three years co-ordinated a research programme on behalf of the Children's Society—the results of which have been published in a variety of sources (see, in particular, Wilson, 2003; Wilson, 2004). So too as part of my research for my last book I conducted primary research with elderly men who were imprisoned (Wilson, 2005). This helped me to understand how the elderly cope in a social structure that was specifically designed for the young and mobile. Finally, I acted as a consultant on the Channel 4 TV documentary *Dressed To Kill* (2001, dir. Stuart Clarke), which told the story of the Welsh serial killer Peter Moore and which afforded me access to various materials related to that case.

All of these methods were further enhanced when I was engaged by *Sky News* to advise them on a series of murders of young women working in the sex industry in Ipswich in late 2006. As such I got to see at first-hand the police investigation of these murders and how they were reported upon by the various journalists working on the case. This proved to be an invaluable experience for a variety of reasons, but chiefly because it allowed me access to the sites where the bodies of these young women had been dumped after their murder and also to the red light area of Ipswich where the journalists involved interviewed a number of prostitutes.

As befits a book about criminology, I have drawn heavily on some texts to inform the argument which is presented. Indeed I have already drawn attention to the fact that this book can be read as an extended argument with Elliot Leyton's *Hunting Humans* (but which, in any event, might be more properly described as anthropology). However, in attempting to understand the 46-year time period that forms the backdrop to the book I am indebted to several key texts that I would like to acknowledge here.

Most immediately I have drawn inspiration from Jock Young's (1999) *The Exclusive Society* which (p.vi):

> traces the rapid unravelling of the social fabric of the industrialised world in the last third of the twentieth century, charting the rise of individualism and of demands for social equality which emerged on the back of the market forces that have permeated and transformed every nook and cranny of social life.

In attempting to understand these 'market forces' more fully I have used Will Hutton's (1996) *The State We're In* to develop a better insight into the dynamics of the economics of Thatcher's Britain after 1979, which could arguably be described as still dominating the economic life of Britain today. So too I have relied on Dominic Sandbrook's *Never Had It So Good* to sketch in the social life of Britain (if you like, the 'nooks and crannies' described by Young) at the beginning of the period under consideration here. I have also relied on Steve Hall and Simon Winlow's remarkable *Violent Night* from the end of our time period to try to understand the meaning, place and context of violence in the night time economy of Britain and to look at what happens when young people from working class communities become immersed in the consumer economy, its practices and values. I have also benefited from reading Alessandra Buonfino and Geoff Mulgan's (2006) edited collection of portraits about what it means to live in Britain called *Porcupines in Winter* and Nick Davies's (1997) *Dark Heart*. Finally it should also be acknowledged that I have written theoretically with Professor Keith Soothill of Lancaster University about Harold Shipman (Soothill and Wilson, 2005) and Professor Soothill's own work with Chris Grover (Grover and Soothill, 1999) has been particularly helpful in allowing me to understand structural explanations related to British serial killing.

In my academic work I have always tried to write in a tradition of 'accessibility' to the general reader and I hope that this book is no exception. As such, I have kept academic references to a minimum and where theory is used I hope that this is sufficiently explained so as not to dissuade the non-specialist reader from persevering. This accessibility has been consciously chosen for, as befits the desire to understand our present and mould our future, I do not believe that this can be done simply by appealing to the academy. If change is to come, I believe that this will only happen when the general reader and the wider public understand—and hopefully accept—the arguments and insights that academics take for granted.

Of course the demands of accessibility are many and varied (for me, accessibility has never implied simplicity) and in relation to a book that seeks to make a criminological argument within a historical context, this has meant that I have had to think very carefully about how to structure the materials that are presented here. So, for example, I could have chosen to handle the historical data in one or two chapters, before dealing with the criminological detail in others, but separated from the history. Whilst on one level this seemed appealing (it has the appearance of simplicity), it struck me as being unsatisfactory, suggesting as it did that the story that I wanted to tell had two separate, if connected parts. Thus, throughout, I have attempted to weave historical detail into each chapter.

The book opens with a long introductory chapter that seeks to provide an overview, both to the historical period under discussion and to the main criminological arguments. Thereafter each chapter takes its primary focus from the group that has been victimised, although where appropriate further historical detail is also provided. In short *Chapter 1* offers some broad-brush strokes, whereas the finer detail is presented in subsequent chapters. Last, but not least, a conclusion attempts to re-state and amplify the argument that has been presented.

Throughout the text, both as a means of making this argument accessible and also as a way of connecting the argument to those who read the book, I consciously use the individual narratives and biographies of the victims of serial killers—where I have been able to reconstruct them through secondary materials such as newspaper articles and from 'true crime' accounts. In this latter genre I am particularly indebted to the work of Brian Masters and Gordon Burn. As such, I try to open each chapter by building up a portrait of someone who has been victimised and attempt to tell their story to the reader, rather than setting out the story of their killer. In doing so I am trying to connect the reader to that life, in the hope that that victim does not seem distant and anonymous, but is instead humanised and, as a result, given some dignity. Yet there is also more going on here, for in trying to provide these pen pictures of people who are rarely seen within popular accounts of serial killers or in the academic discourse about serial killing, I am attempting to create a different interpretation about who it is who is victimised and in what circumstances. Indeed, as Nicci Gerrard has argued in writing about the murders of Holly Wells and Jessica Chapman in Soham, Cambridgeshire by Ian Huntley, 'in the single narrative, we extrapolate wider meanings.' She goes on:

> One life will engage our personal sympathies while a whole plethora of statistics will not. We need to imagine what it is like, need to identify in order to properly care. Through stories we impose patterns, make meanings, give beginnings and endings, because we cannot bear a world or self without them. (2004: 11)

Of course this has not always been possible. The murders of Holly and Jessica—two young, attractive, white schoolgirls in a sleepy Cambridgeshire town—attracted world-wide attention that brought in its wake a great deal of biographical detail which allowed for the re-construction of 'beginnings and endings'. However the victims of serial killers (unlike the killers themselves) have rarely garnered the same attention. Quite simply, the victims of serial killers are often those who are on the margins of society for one reason or another, who as a result have left no record from which to reconstruct their lives. They do not leave letters, diaries or autobiographies; they do not maintain websites, nor are they the subjects of television documentaries, or films. Some victims do not even have a name and are identified in police records simply by their physical characteristics, such as the colour of their hair, the condition of their teeth or perhaps a tattoo. Indeed it should come as no surprise that one of the victims that we know most about—Lucy Partington, who was murdered by the Wests— was a relative of the novelist, Martin Amis, who has since written about his cousin's life (2001). Even so other victims of the Wests were not even reported as missing to the police. In short, our lack of detail and understanding of the nature of their lives, and sometimes simply the absence of images about the victims of serial killers, has resulted in both a popular and academic over-concentration on the serial killers themselves where images and details—if not necessarily understanding—abound. If history is written by the 'winners', then the story of serial killing has been almost universally written from the perspective of those who have 'won' merely through their prosecution, conviction and imprisonment for some of the worst crimes that this country has ever witnessed.

Of course the use of biography and narrative within criminology has a long history dating back to the Chicago School and has of late gained new momentum with the work of ethnographers and cultural criminologists. Of the former, Ken Plummer (2001: 395), for example, has argued that 'to tell the story of a life may be one of the cores of culture ... these stories—or personal narratives—connect the inner world to the outer ... They make links across life phases and cohort generations revealing historical shifts in a culture'. So too Paul Willis (2000: xi) has suggested that ' "big ideas" are empty of people, feeling and experience'. He continued:

> In my view well-grounded and illuminating analytical points flow only from bringing concepts into a relationship with the messiness of ordinary life, somehow recorded.

Echoing these themes, the cultural criminologist Mike Presdee has suggested that 'biography' and 'biographical accounts' of everyday life provide 'superior accounts', explanations and descriptions of crime than the 'nurtured ignorance' produced by rational, scientific academic research. In short, when trying to understand the reality of crime and how it impacts on everyday life, we need to understand how people live and how they make sense of their lives. Thus, he suggests that '(auto)biography is the raw material; our material'. However, 'it cannot stand on its own, it needs to be 'worked on' (Presdee, 2004: 43).

I have attempted to 'work on' the lives of those who have been victimised by serial killers and see how their individual circumstances created their social vulnerability, which thereafter facilitated their murder. This 'working on' has involved many things. Crucially it has been about analysing, and in doing so making connections between individuals and the reality of their lives, so as to discern broader patterns in operation over our historical time-frame and thus create a link between those who might have been killed in the 1960s and those who were murdered many years later. So too this 'working on' involves making a criminological argument and by harnessing these individual lives to the broader patterns that can be discerned I hope to suggest something about the type of society that Britain has become between 1960 and 2006.

Some critics might suggest that 19 serial killers and their 326 victims do not make a very large 'sample' on which to build an argument.[3] In one sense this is true. However, I believe that it is possible to justify this small sample and the conclusions that can be drawn from an analysis of it for two reasons. Firstly, the serial killer 'industry' is now so large and omnipresent in academic, and especially in popular discourse that it is vitally important to start to deconstruct that industry by moving it away from the individual into the social (see also Seltzer (1998: 2) for an attempt to understand what it is about 'modern [American] culture that makes the type of person called the serial killer possible'). We have to start somewhere and the victims of serial killing seem to me to be an ideal place to start that deconstruction. Secondly, and as I argue in *Chapter 1*, serial killing is a unique phenomenon and therefore we have to use all our skills to understand that phenomenon better. Attempting to explain serial killing at the social level is not an easy task, but by analysing the serial killer's

---

[3] By way of comparison it has been calculated that since 1900 in the USA there have been 558 serial killers responsible for at least 3,850 deaths (Fox and Levin, 2005: 32).

victims we can at least begin to discern wider patterns at work in society and in doing so gain a deeper, richer understanding of how we have helped to create serial killers.

Finally, I do not discount the anger that much of the argument that is contained in this book will engender. After all, in relation to the government's (and sometimes the general public's) view of offenders—especially serial offenders—we have been completely wedded to ideas of 'personal responsibility' now for quite some time. Thus, the desire to replace the 'individual' with the 'social' in relation to serial killing will not chime well with policies that seek to blame and pathologise the individual, and exonerate the society which that individual inhabits. However, I am not trying to let the various serial killers who are presented here 'off the hook'. Nor am I trying, as Mary Midgley (1984) warns against in her philosophical essay about wickedness, to blame society for every sin. Rather, I am instead trying to demonstrate that those who want to kill repeatedly can only achieve this objective when the social structure in which they operate allows them to do so by placing value on one group to the detriment of others. For when this happens and when communities are fractured and anxious, when people feel isolated and cut off from each other, and when the bonds of mutual support have been all but eradicated as each individual believes that they have to struggle simply to survive, those who want to kill large numbers of their fellow human beings achieve their purpose.

Sadly, in this way, serial killing becomes a useful guide that reveals the limits of our current social arrangements and the inadequacy of our provision for the social and economic protection of the poor and the vulnerable. For if children, young people leaving home, gay men, prostitutes and the elderly are the prime victims of serial killers this is only because we have created a society where children, young people leaving home, gay men, prostitutes and the elderly are also generally the victims of a social and economic system that does not see value in their lives and routinely excludes them from the protection of the state.

CHAPTER 1

Serial Killing 1960-2006

CHAPTER 1

Serial Killing 1960-2006

> Sexual intercourse began
> In nineteen sixty-three
> (which is rather late for me)
> Between the end of the Chatterley ban
> And the Beatles' first LP.

> (Phillip Larkin, '*Annus Mirabilis*')

This chapter has several related introductory and interconnected aims. First, it seeks to outline in a broad-brush manner the period under discussion—the time-frame from 1960 to the end of 2006—although this is done largely through the presentation of an argument, rather than one historical 'fact' following on from another. However, the changes during this period—some of which are dramatic and pronounced—as well as the period's continuities form the backdrop to the remainder of the book. In particular I use Young's (1999) description of Britain moving from an 'inclusive' to an 'exclusive' society as a way of understanding the changes that Britain experienced. Secondly, it introduces the concept of serial killing in a British context. As such, it provides a standard, criminological definition of serial killing—so as to differentiate this phenomenon from 'mass murder' or 'spree killing'; introduces the 19 British serial killers recorded since 1960; and then provides an overview of their 326 victims.

Here it should be noted that 'British' has a very specific definition. To be included in the list that I have constructed the killer has to have been British born and raised, and to have murdered in Britain.[1] Thus, for example, I have excluded serial killers such as Michael Lupo, who killed four gay men in London in 1986, given that Lupo was born and raised in Italy. I have also excluded British born serial killers who killed abroad, such as John Scripps, who murdered in Singapore and Thailand, and who has the unenviable reputation of being the last Briton to be hanged for murder in Singapore, on 16 April 1996. I also outline the differences between those people who were murdered in Britain during this period and those who became the victims of serial killers. Finally, so as to harness this material into a criminological argument, and building on the work of Grover and Soothill (1999), I outline Leyton's (1986) concept of 'homicidal

---

[1] Nonetheless, I have included Michael Copeland in my list despite the fact that he killed one of his victims in Germany, whilst stationed there with the British Army. He killed his other two victims in England.

protest' in serial killing and consider whether this is appropriate in relation to the British experience. The chapter starts by attempting to chart the broad changes that Britain was to go through during the period under discussion.

FROM INCLUSION TO EXCLUSION

Dominic Sandbrook (2005), in his comprehensive account of Britain from the Suez Crisis of 1956 to the Beatles topping the charts in 1963, opens his first chapter with an account of the 1960 prosecution of Penguin Books for their publication of D. H. Lawrence's *Lady Chatterley's Lover*, under the terms of the Obscene Publications Act 1959. However, as a revisionist historian, Sandbrook is in a sense poking fun at those other historians who use the trial as a way of attempting to chart the changes that Britain experienced in the 1960s. For Sandbrook this was not a question of a new, frank, open Britain challenging the old, established order, and he uses different contemporary reactions to the Lady Chatterley case to suggest that British history in the 1960s was 'much more complicated, diverse and contradictory than it has often been given credit for' (2005: xvi).

In short, British history in the 1960s was not just about radical transformation—there was just as much conservatism and conformity, and Sandbrook argues that too much is made of change, and not enough attention is paid to continuity. He suggests that Britain in the 1950s was 'one of the most conservative, stable and contented societies in the world,' where eight out of ten people lived in towns and cities and just one person in every 100 worked on the land. Even so Britain was still a 'profoundly unequal society' and Sandbrook notes that 'poverty had not disappeared' (2005: 29-30). Nonetheless the vast majority of people continued to go happily about their business, in large part because of the foundations of the Welfare State laid down by Clement Atlee's Labour Government of 1945-1951—known by some historians as the 'post-war settlement'. By this they mean that there was a political commitment from both the left and the right to full employment; state-funded social security; a national health service; free education; health and unemployment benefits; a mixed, part private, part public economy; and recognition of trades unions. However, as our time-period develops, the political consensus between the Conservatives and Labour that had maintained this post-war settlement begins to break down, and with the coming to power of Margaret Thatcher's government in 1979, shatters irrevocably. And, as such, radical changes took place in virtually every sphere of British life.

The Left Realist criminologist, Jock Young, has been at the forefront of attempts to understand and make sense of these changes. In doing so Young is in part trying to explain the rise in crime that Britain experienced in the last third of the twentieth century, but he is also making a much broader argument. In particular he argues that Britain had been, at the beginning of our time period:

> a consensual world with core values centring around work and the family. It was an inclusive world; a world at one with itself, where the accent was on assimilation whether of wider swathes of society (lower working class, women or youth), or immigrants entering into a monocultural society. It was a world where the modernist project was deemed within a breath of success. (Young, 1999: 3)

However, by the end of the period—largely as a result of changes initiated during the late 1970s, British society had become characterised by

> a great deal of material and ontological precariousness, and which responds to deviance by separation and exclusion. Such a process is driven by changes in the material basis of advanced industrial societies, from Fordism to post-Fordism and represents the movement into late modernity. (Young, 1999: 26)

In these two small paragraphs Young begins to outline a rich and provocative argument about the changes that Britain has experienced more generally, the rise in crime particularly and the causes of both. Thus, there is a move from 'modernity' to 'late modernity', from 'Fordism' to 'post-Fordism' and from 'inclusion' and 'assimilation' to 'separation and exclusion'. Young is also suggesting that this exclusion is the product of 'material and ontological precariousness', and that the basis for this precariousness are changes in the 'material bases of advanced industrial societies.' Thus, the key here is the labour market, and the changes in how, who and how many people are employed.

Employment, or perhaps more accurately unemployment, based on changes in how work was done (or, as it might be termed more academically, the move from Fordism to post-Fordism), and by which group (increasingly women, or men on part-time contracts) begins to alter the basis on which society generally is organized, and more particularly how individual people come to view themselves, and how they are viewed by others. Added to this, as Young argues, echoing Robert Merton (1938) and Emile Durkheim (1933), both of whom also suggested that the basis for crime had to be seen as emanating from the social structure of society itself, the fact that:

> the market brings together wide swathes of the population ... it creates the practical basis of comparison. It renders visible inequalities of race, class, age and gender. It elevates a universal citizenship of consumption, yet excludes a significant minority from membership. (Young, 1999: 47)

Young maintains that the inclusion that characterised the early part of the period was founded on collective values—created by the simple fact that everyone's labour was needed, and thus there was a need to include everyone.

However, as the market society developed it engendered a culture of individualism, which had 'undermined the relationships and values necessary for a stable social order and hence gives rise to crime and disorder' (Young, 1999: 50). In short, individualism had created a culture of 'every person for themselves' and left in its wake an 'underclass' whose labour was no longer needed, and who could effectively be excluded from society and left to fend for themselves (Young, 1999: 49, 50). Thus exclusion from the market facilitated exclusion from society.

However, Young is not arguing that the 'inclusive' society of the earlier period under discussion was somehow 'better' than the 'exclusive' society that characterised the later period. Indeed, he argues that both were 'failures'. In the former the failures came from the demands for conformity and homogeneity; in the latter, whilst the exclusive world granted diversity and difference, it cast difference in 'essentialist terms', which was always 'prone to demonisation' (Young, 1999: 148). By 'essentialism' Young means that individuals or groups are separated from each other on the basis of their culture or nature, and that this is a technique of exclusion, rather than one of inclusion. Thus society becomes characterised by greater choice, but less 'embeddedness and greater disjointedness, which makes for ontological insecurity' (Young, 1999: 192). Civil society becomes more segmented, and people become more wary, appraising and less tolerant of each other. Indeed Young uses this insight and his argument more generally about the universality of citizenship through consumption, to suggest a basis for understanding the growth of crime in Western societies. In doing so he also reveals the impossibility of the criminal justice system ever being able to halt the rise in crime or engender social cohesion.

In relation to the failures of the inclusive and exclusive societies we might also develop Young's argument by suggesting, for example, that as well as the changes that he identifies, there are also continuities. Specifically, there are continuities with regard to power relations beyond those of class. Here I am suggesting that if we accept that social power is not limited to capitalist relations, we can gain some insight into why so many women were murdered by serial killers throughout the period under discussion by remembering that Britain was a capitalist and a patriarchal society. Patriarchy remains a constant in British culture over our time-frame, as do homophobia, poverty and the vulnerability of the elderly, although clearly the move from an inclusive to an exclusive society exacerbated these vulnerabilities. Often this was simply a consequence of removing the social and economic protection that had been afforded to those groups who were vulnerable, largely because some theorists saw this protection as merely contributing to, for example, idleness or immorality (see, for example, Murray, 1990, 1994; Lilley, 1993).

All of this can be given further depth by considering the insights offered by the political and economics journalist, Will Hutton. In his book *The State We're In* (ed.1995), written just before New Labour came to power in 1997, Hutton suggests that Britain had become 'a world of us and them' where 'individuals are compelled to look out for themselves', and where 'the growth in inequality has been the fastest of any industrialised state' (Hutton, 1995: 2, 9, 18). Hutton noted that by 1995 one in four of the adult male population were unemployed or idle, and that unemployment had increased six-fold since the first oil crisis of 1973; that one in three children were living in poverty; and that 'the state is doing all that it can to wash its hands of future generations of old people' (Hutton, 1995: 199). Like Young, the key to understanding all of this was for Hutton the state of the British economy after 1979, and in particular the British 'messianic *laissez-faire* philosophy, seeing its future as a low-cost, de-regulated producer in a free market world with low social overheads and a minimalist welfare state' (Hutton, 1995: 58). Hutton's suggestion was that Thatcherism's ascendancy had allowed capitalism to be 'left to its own devices' and other areas of social and economic life had to be harnessed to facilitate capitalist goals. Thus, for example, in 1979 there were five million members of 'closed shops' (trade unions of which membership was a condition of employment), but by 1993 these had been abolished; in 1979 13.3 million people had been union members, but by 1993 this figure had dropped to nine million, with only 31 per cent of employed workers belonging to a union—the lowest level since 1946, and Hutton saw the Miners' Strike of 1984-1985 as the 'seminal act in the drama of labour decline' (1995: 82, 94). I suggest that it is no coincidence that 1986 produced more serial killers than at any other point in British history. So too, during this period qualifications for unemployment benefit and income support became tougher; the state pension became progressively devalued in relation to average earnings; and the distribution of income became more unequal. For example, the value of supplementary benefit in proportion to full time male earnings fell from 26 per cent to 19 per cent between 1979 and 1993.

More than this, Hutton used this analysis to suggest that as the market became the sole organizing principle of the country, Britain developed into a '40/30/30 society.' In short, only 40 per cent of the workforce enjoyed tenured, full-time employment; the next 30 per cent were insecurely self-employed, involuntarily working part-time or casually; 'while the bottom 30 per cent, the marginalised, are idle or working for poverty wages' (Hutton, 1995: 14). Thus Hutton, like Young, was adamant that work—being employed and how one is employed—is of crucial importance, not only for the sense of self that it creates for the individual, but also for creating cohesion in communities. For example, work offered a 'sense of place in a hierarchy of social relations, both within the organization and beyond it, and men and women are, after all social beings ...

those who work belong; those who do not are excluded' (Hutton, 1995: 99-100). Thus, exclusion had in turn led to the collapse of local communities where, he suggested, there was less stigma attached to criminality because:

> the informal sanctions and expressions of disapproval which offenders fear are no longer there; and they have little reason to have empathy with their victims. There are fewer inbuilt deterrents and greater incentives to criminal behaviour.
>
> (Hutton, 1995: 225)

All of this might seem far too theoretical and divorced from how people live their lives. So, let's consider here two very real examples of what is being described, both taken from Scotland. The first is from an essay contributed to Buonfino and Mulgan's (2006) *Porcupines in Winter* and the second is some journalistic reflections by Ian Jack. In *Porcupines in Winter*, John Matthews, a church minister and former managing director of the General Electrical Company of America, describes the changes that he observed in his parish in Ruchill in Glasgow. He remembered that one of his first duties when he took over the parish in 1992 was to conduct the annual Dedication Service of the 69th Ruchill Company of the Boys' Brigade, when former members of the brigade — all in their seventies — returned to Glasgow, and Matthews reflected on what he saw and what he was told.

The 70-year-olds spoke of Ruchill being a 'good working class area' in their day. Among the former members there were medical consultants, an airline pilot, a South African High Court judge, engineers, draughtsmen, managers and a range of tradesmen. Many of them by then lived some distance away but they were still so enthusiastic that they arranged their annual holiday each year to coincide with this reunion, travelling from South Africa, Australia, Canada and the south of England. This gives an idea of the calibre of the young men they had once been, their commitment to what had been for them a memorable part of their upbringing and the supportive homes they had come from (Matthews, 2006: 37).

Matthews compares all of this with what he found in Ruchill in 2006, with 'alcohol and drug abuse, dreadful housing, violence, vandalism, serial monogamy, lone parents, teenage pregnancy, and increasing numbers of step children' (2006: 37-38). He describes Ruchill as a 'forgotten community' and the people living there as 'powerless' and, memorably, as the 'left behind', given that they had nothing to offer the economy by way of skills, education or training. One such person who had been left behind was 16-year-old Debbie, whom he encountered on the streets 'gouching' — a slang term for someone on drugs who is standing on their feet half-asleep — and who had taken ten temazepam tablets. Like a good minister, Matthews told Debbie to be careful, but she replied: 'What do I care if I blow my life away? My life's just shite anyway'. She had been thrown out of her home by her mother and had then turned to prostitution to make ends meet. Matthews is left to conclude that 'for Debbie life was just excrement—and who was I to say otherwise?' (2006: 39).

Ian Jack also reflected on the differences between Scotland in the late 1950s and early 1960s and the present day, and he was particularly interested in the changing nature of the culture of Sunday. For example, he remembered that the Sundays of his youth as a secular young man were boring, depressing and gloomy: a time of 'a great external quietness meant to encourage reflection in our internal soul' (Jack, 2006: 15). 'Nobody knew then,' he continued, that with the collapse of Christianity and the introduction of the Sunday Trading Act 1994, Sundays would become characterised by 'arduous trips to Ikea and jams on the motorway' (Jack, 2006: 15). In short, the Church of Scotland had been replaced by the Church of the Market.

These two brief, personal portraits are used here simply to illuminate the broader arguments of both Young and Hutton. Specifically they suggest that what might be seen as personal circumstances—or the result of fate—are in fact connected and related to impersonal forces that fundamentally affect the fabric of society, and therefore how individuals live their lives. So the first example is concerned with youth, the de-industrialisation of a community and how one young girl's response was to turn to prostitution. It was Debbie's way of overcoming having been 'left behind' by the economy. The second example asks us to consider the changing nature of Sunday in a culture that has become increasingly secular and commercial.

At a structural level, Young's and Hutton's arguments connect these personal portraits to the policies that have shaped the British economy and consider how this has made an impact on our own daily lives. They also help us to understand how crime has risen in Britain over the last 40 years and, I would argue, how the social and economic structure has facilitated serial killing. In particular the move from an inclusive to an exclusive society, or one that is characterised by '40/30/30', with a minority of winners and a majority of losers (the 'left behind'), and where the growth of insecurity—both ontological and economic—and the rise of individualism have inevitably disjointed communities, there are simply fewer people prepared to look out for each other. Too busy trying to look out for themselves, people no longer see their neighbours' lives and the life of the community as part of their own lives, despite the fact that they might be living side by side, in each other's pockets and cheek by jowl.

The campaigning journalist Nick Davies caught something of all this in 1997, when he described one part of the Britain that he had encountered on a journey as 'hidden'. He explained:

Outwardly all the landmarks of normality would remain clearly in sight. There would be rows of red brick terraced houses with televisions in the front rooms and cars waiting outside by the kerbs; there would be crowds of people tracing the paths of their regular routines, buying and selling and building their futures—all the symptoms of an orderly community. But at some point, it was as if I crossed an invisible frontier and cut a path into a different country ... to put it more broadly it is the place where the poor gather. (Davies, 1997: vii)

In short, the poor are in society, but not of it. More than this, partly through a fear of the risk that they might pose (a recognition that difference has not necessarily made people feel more secure) some individuals or groups are seen as having inherently less worth than others. An individual's worth becomes based on his or her relation to the market, and as such whole swathes of the population have been excluded, while the rest in turn have had to return to a state where everybody has to look inwards and provide for themselves. The post-war settlement has long disappeared, and with it a sense of what Britain was once like and how it could be ordered.

Yet how does this work in relation to those who are murdered? And, more specifically, how can it be applied to the reality of British serial killing since 1960? Before developing an answer to these questions, some basic information is now provided about what we mean when we call someone a serial killer, and about serial killing more generally, before explaining the concept of 'homicidal protest' and beginning to try to apply it to British serial killers.

SERIAL MURDER—DEFINITIONS, TYPOLOGIES AND ONE OR TWO KILLERS

To be labelled as a 'serial killer' a murderer would normally have to have killed three or more victims in a period of greater than 30 days (see, for example, Holmes and de Burger, 1988). Thus the label implies that there is an element of time and a numeric threshold in terms of the number of victims that has to be reached before a killer can be described as a serial killer. Seeking to identify serial killers in this way allows us to differentiate, for example, between those people who murder a large number of people—such as Michael Ryan, who shot and killed 16 people at Hungerford in August 1987, or Thomas Hamilton who shot and killed 16 children and their school teacher at Dunblane in March 1996—and who thus qualify in terms of the numeric threshold, but not in relation to the element of time. Indeed, Hamilton or Ryan would be described in the literature as 'spree' or 'mass' killers. So, as far as this book is concerned, to be labelled as a serial killer there has to have been at least three victims, who have been murdered in a period of greater than 30 days.

This definition notwithstanding, it should be noted that defining serial killing is fraught with difficulties and even the simplistic time/numeric threshold that is being employed here masks a variety of criminological debates that are worthy of further consideration. Egger (1984), for example, suggests that there is a six point identification of the serial killer; that there should be two victims; and crucially that there should be no relation between the victim and the perpetrator. He also suggests that the murders should occur at different locations. As Grover and Soothill (1999) have argued, these stipulations are far too prescriptive and would in the British context exclude some perpetrators such as Dennis Nilsen and Frederick and Rosemary West, who all clearly had a prior relationship with many of their victims, and who murdered them in the same locations in London and Gloucester respectively. I have tended to follow the arguments used by Grover and Soothill, but even so it should be noted, for example, that the numeric threshold of three victims excludes some killers such as Graham Young who murdered two victims by poisoning them and attempted to poison several more. Thus, his exclusion from the list of British serial killers is simply a matter of luck, for it is clear that he intended to kill others. Indeed, elsewhere I have argued that it is possible that we might extend the definition to include 'potential serial killers'. This would include Young and others such as Paul Brumfitt,[2] Benjamin Green[3] or Glenn Wright, whose case is of interest for it again throws light onto the problems of definition, given that he killed in the same location, and had a relationship with his victims (Wilson, 2005). So too his case introduces other criminological themes, such as 'organization' and 'disorganization' and as such I now spend a little time discussing Wright, which also allows us to move some of the theory that has been outlined into practice. Specifically it allows us to determine whether the 'individualistic discourse' does indeed explain serial killing.

Glen Wright

In 1996 Glenn Wright, at the time aged 27, was remanded in custody at HM Prison Woodhill in Milton Keynes, for various offences of dishonesty (all details taken from Wilson, 2005: 87-97). When he was arrested, he slashed his wrists at the local police station and so prison staff thought that he might be vulnerable to attack. As such they placed him in what used to be called a 'Rule 43' unit, which segregated prisoners from the main prison population for their own protection. He was placed in a cell that he had to share with William Scott—who was also on

---

[2] Brumfitt killed two men in the 1970s—allegedly because they made gay advances towards him (personal communication)—served a sentence of 15 years, and then on release killed again, only this time a female prostitute. Technically he fits the definition of a serial killer, but the time gap between his first and last victim pushes our definition too far for his inclusion, although I use aspects of his story in *Chapter 3*.

[3] Green was a nurse who murdered two elderly patients in January 2004, by deliberately administering fatal overdoses of drugs. At his trial at Oxford Crown Court in 2006 it was alleged that he tried to kill at least 16 other patients. His case has several striking parallels with the case of Beverly Allitt whose story appears in *Chapter 6*.

remand, awaiting trial for the murder of his girlfriend. Scott was depressed and, in discussion with Wright, initially thought that the best way to end his life was to cut his wrists. However Wright soon convinced him that a better way to commit suicide would be to hang himself and that he would help him. He was as good as his word and had soon fashioned a noose from a bedspread. Wright then placed the noose around Scott's neck, eventually looping the end of it over the bathroom door and placing a chair outside for Scott to stand on. Scott kicked the chair away and then passed out. As he had agreed, Wright then pressed the emergency call button and a prison officer found Scott hanging from the bathroom door. Wright was later to argue that he had been lying on his bed at the time, facing the wall listening to his Walkman with his back to the bathroom door, had only turned around when he heard a thump and then had found Scott hanging.

Scott was taken to hospital, where he was eventually to recover and Wright was given counselling by the Prison Service to help him cope with the experiences that he had just gone through. Imagine their horror when only three months later Wright's new cellmate, Karelius Smith, attempted 'suicide' too and, unlike William Scott, succeeded.

On 1 February 1997 Smith was found in his cell unconscious and apparently lifeless, lying on his back on the floor with a piece of brown bed sheet tied around his neck. He was resuscitated, but died a week later. Wright said that whilst he was asleep, Smith—a very immature young man who was described as 'a little depressed and acting strangely'—had hanged himself. Yet staff who had spoken to him just an hour before he was found thought that he had been cheerful and had been discussing a possible transfer to another prison, Shepton Mallet. Smith left a suicide note explaining: 'I'm hanging myself because Wilson is spreading rumours that I'm queer. I can't handle it. I'm sorry to Glenn for finding me this way'.

Should this be a case of more counselling for Wright, or time to bring in the police on the common sense theory that lightening doesn't strike in the same place twice? And, even if they couldn't prove anything, perhaps the authorities might reasonably have concluded that it would be best to keep Wright in a single cell. Yet, more counselling was the Prison Service's response and the alarm bells did not start ringing until Kenneth Cross, Wright's next cellmate, thought that Wright was a 'bit odd' when they shared a cell at HMP Pentonville in January 1998. Kenneth Cross was well known to the Prison Service and almost the perfect example of someone who perhaps should have been treated in the community. In and out of jail for most of his life, he was a petty offender who committed his crimes to feed a raging drug addiction. The senior medical officer at Pentonville, Dr M A Yisa, described Cross as 'heavily dependent on opiates' and put him on suicide watch after he had self-harmed. He was also placed in the same cell as

Glenn Wright—ever eager to be helpful to the prison authorities. Since Cross survived Wright's attack we now also know something of the methods that the latter used when he killed.

First, Cross remembered that Wright gave him some tablets, which 'made me feel out of my head', then he watched helpless and horrified as Wright tore up their bedsheets and fashioned them into a noose. Wright then attached one end of the noose to the window, whilst all the time re-assuring Cross that he would raise the alarm, not to be worried and that faking a suicide would bring its rewards from the prison (a move to a prison closer to home, extra medication, or some other desired perk). Too confused and helpless from the tablets that Wright had given to him, Cross didn't—or couldn't—resist as Wright put the other end of the noose around his neck (as he had with William Scott), picked him up and placed him by the window. Then slowly, but with a certainty that comes with practice, Wright began squeezing the life out of Cross.

Kenneth Cross survived this attack, partly because Wright miscalculated the time that he needed to choke his victim—perhaps exacerbated by the effect of the tablets that he had given to him—and he simply raised the alarm too early.[4] If Wright had waited another few minutes, Cross would in all likelihood have died, like Karelius Smith. Kenneth Cross was lucky, as were other potential and former cellmates of Wright's, whose killing spree had come to an end and who is now, finally, segregated in a single cell back at HMP Woodhill, serving a life sentence for the murder of Karelius Smith.

Wright, Young, Brumfitt and Green do not qualify as serial killers by the definition that is being used in this book, but their exclusion does not mean that their cases are without interest, nor that the argument that is being outlined here more generally cannot be applied to them. Indeed, what better paradigm of 'exclusion' exists than being sent to prison, and we should question whether Wright would have been able to continue in his desire to kill if the Prison Service had been more vigilant in how they handled him after William Scott's attempted 'suicide'. In short, should this be a case of trying to uncover Wright's motivation in relation to his psyche and mental health needs, or instead one of investigating the adequacy of the social structure that contained and imprisoned him? After all, there are many people with severe mental health issues in prison—a closed world that is filled with dangerous and damaged people—but not all of them go on to murder their cell-mates. However, let us pursue for a little longer the 'individualistic discourse' and how it might be applied to Wright, by considering a classic serial killer typology.

---

[4] We do not know what these tablets were, as the blood sample that Cross provided when he was revived was not fully analysed by the Prison Service, nor do we know how Wright came to have so much medication in his possession.

Perhaps because definitions of serial killing are so problematic there have been only a few academic attempts to devise a typology of serial murders. The most comprehensive of these remains that devised by Holmes and De Burger (1988), which was based on interviews and analysis of more than 400 cases of serial murder. They identified four types of serial murderer—the visionary, the person with a mission, the hedonistic killer and the person motivated by power/control (see *Table 1.1*).

***Table 1.1:** Types of serial killer (male)*

Visionary	Killer is impelled to murder because he has heard voices or seen visions demanding that he kill a particular person, or category of people. The voice or vision may be for some a demon, but for others may be perceived as coming from God.
Mission	Killer has a conscious goal in his life to eliminate a certain identifiable group of people. He does not hear voices, or have visions. The mission is self-imposed.
Hedonistic	Killer kills simply for the thrill of it—because he enjoys it. The thrill becomes an end in itself.
Power/Control	Killer receives gratification from the complete control of the victim. This type of murderer experiences pleasure and excitement not from sexual acts carried out on the victim, but from his belief that he has the power to do whatever he wishes to another human being who is completely helpless to stop him.

Source: Adapted from Holmes and De Burger (1988).

However, there are other typologies. For example, Hickey (1991) suggests that there are *place/specific* serial killers who murder in particular physical locations, such as hospitals or nursing homes and that this is also helpful in our discussion of Glenn Wright. So too we should note that these typologies are not necessarily hard and fixed, nor mutually exclusive, and a serial killer might display aspects of more than one typology (see, for example, Cresswell and Hollin, 1994). Other commentators have attempted to understand the behaviour of serial killers from the perspective of their intrinsic and extrinsic motivations. In other words whether their motivation to kill lies outside of their personality (such as with 'hit men'), or deep within their psychological make-up. Holmes and Holmes (1994: 114-115) conclude that most serial killers are motivated by intrinsic considerations, but that it is useful to try and understand what a given killer 'has to gain from the commission of a particular crime', either materially or psychologically. They suggest that, through the interviews that they have conducted with serial killers, most murder for psychological reasons. They continue:

> In interviews, many [serial killers] have told us that the principal motivating factor in their killing was that they simply enjoyed killing. Others have stated that they were motivated by the intense feeling they got out of holding the fate of other persons in their hands. The more a person kills, the greater becomes his need to experience those feelings of gratification or power. The feeling becomes more than a compulsion, it becomes an addiction. (Holmes and Holmes, 1994: 115)

Of course all of this is firmly within the 'individualistic discourse' and is very much the basis of Holmes and De Burger's 'Power/Control' typology. Indeed there is a temptation to see all of this as a means by which to analyse and understand Glenn Wright. Look again, for example, at what Kenneth Cross tells us about how Wright tried to kill him and the intricacy of the process of the attempted murder. There are at least eight phases that we can uncover. First, Wright gives Cross medication, which serves to overcome the latter's resistance to what is about to happen and indicates a degree of planning and organization. We might also reasonably conclude that prior to this there had to have been some discussion of suicide which either Wright or Cross initiated, but which undoubtedly Wright encouraged. Secondly, as the medication was beginning to have its effect, Wright tore up some bed sheets and fashioned them into a noose. Presumably this was witnessed by Cross. Next Wright attached the noose to the window, whilst fourthly continuing to reassure Cross not to worry and that everything will be fine—in effect promising him that he will raise the alarm. Here it should also be noted that the medication that Wright had given to Cross had not resulted in the latter becoming unconscious, but simply that he was 'out of his head'. In short it had made him groggy and incapable of resisting. We might also speculate as to whether this was part of the psychological benefit that Wright sought—most obviously the power he was able to exercise over another person, but that this was all the more enjoyable by having Cross conscious; a living victim with whom he could converse and tease and observe as his plan unfolded. Fifthly, Wright attached the noose to Cross's neck, before, sixthly, picking him up (remember that Cross is 'out of his head') which is a physical manifestation of the power and control that Wright was able to exercise over Cross, before the seventh stage—attempting the murder itself.

Whilst all of this might be of interest, does it in fact help to explain why Wright killed? Does this type of theorising get us much further in understanding the reality of serial killing? I would suggest that it does not, for two reasons. First, despite Cross's testimony as to what took place, there are many gaps in our knowledge. For example we can only speculate as to whether there had been some prior discussion about suicide as an issue and who might have first raised this topic. Nor can we be clear about how the murder was actually attempted. For example, did Wright strangle Cross, or did Cross jump from the window that Wright had carried him to, which would be similar to what had taken place with William Scott? So too we do not know how long this seventh stage might have lasted. Was it a few minutes, or much longer? We can guess that it must have lasted for some time, especially as the power and control that Wright seems to have craved could be made all the more exciting by having that power and control continue for as long as possible. Here we might also suggest that Wright had learned from what had happened with William Scott and Karelius Smith. By the time that he came to be sharing a cell with Kenneth Cross, Wright would have refined what he had wanted to get out of these encounters and would, in all likelihood, have fantasised about certain aspects of the murder of Karelius Smith and the attempted murder of William Scott that he most enjoyed. Indeed it would be this fantasy that would facilitate, in the words of Holmes and Holmes which I quoted above, the 'compulsion' becoming an 'addiction'.

Finally, there was an eighth stage—that point at which Wright raised the alarm. After killing, a murderer must dispose of the bodies of his victims, and in relation to serial killing 'disposal' is seen as an important indicator as to whether a killer is 'organized' or 'disorganized' (see Holmes and DeBurger, 1988; Holmes and Holmes, 1994). Here we would also do well to remember that, for example, Dennis Nilsen (*Chapter 4*) was caught largely because he was unable to continue to dispose of the bodies of his victims either through burning them or cutting them up and flushing them down the toilet (see Masters, 1986).

There are two ways to dispose of bodies. First, the killer might simply abandon the body at the site where the murder took place, without attempting to conceal it, making the body's discovery all the more likely and easy. This is usually associated with disorganized offenders. Or the killer might remove the body from the scene of the murder and place it where it would be found, or where discovery would be difficult. This behaviour is normally associated with organized offenders. Other behaviours associated with organized offenders would include the planning of their offence, targeting strangers as their victims, controlling conversation with their victim, ensuring that the victim is submissive (through using restraints) and leaving as little evidence at the crime scene as possible. On the other hand disorganized offenders usually commit their offences spontaneously, employing sudden violence on the victim, and thus leaving behind at the crime scene a great deal of evidence.

Again all of this is of interest and some practical use, but my second reason for distrusting this 'individualistic discourse' is that it fails to accommodate the reality of Wright's incarceration and the circumstances that he found himself in whilst he was in prison. His opportunity to kill, in other words—no matter what his internal motivation—was only made possible by the structure in which he was incarcerated facilitating his access to weak, anxious or vulnerable individuals, and by a pervasive culture of cell sharing as a means of managing those who could not cope, or as a mechanism employed by the Prison Service to deal with the reality of overcrowding.[5] So too Wright himself became socialised into this closed world of rewards and inducements for his 'help' to the system, and in the end it is impossible to see how he could ever have killed had not the penal system been as awful, overcrowded and as pressurised as it is. It was the structure that he found himself in, and the culture of that structure that was important, rather than any individual motivation that he might have had to kill. And, what is true for individuals in prison is, I argue, also true for those who occupy society more generally.

SERIAL KILLING—THE BRITISH EXPERIENCE

1960 was a remarkable year in British history and not just for the *Lady Chatterley's Lover* trial. It was also the year that Michael Copeland, a soldier, committed his first murder whilst serving with the British Army in Germany and he would kill two other people in Derbyshire before coming to trial four years later in 1965 (although in a curious echo of Larkin's poem quoted at the beginning of this chapter, he had actually confessed to the murders in 1963). Copeland is the first of our British serial killers, and he seems to have murdered gay men, but what else do we know about the 19 British serial killers who have been caught since 1960 and their 326 victims?

For ease of reference, *Table 1.2* provides an overview of those who meet the definition of serial killer that is being employed and some general themes can be outlined quite quickly. First, the victims of British serial killers are clearly drawn

[5] I will use a similar argument when I consider the case of Beverly Allitt in *Chapter 6*.

from certain groups: the elderly, gay men, babies and infants, young people moving away from home for one reason or another, and prostitutes. Of course there are overlaps between these general categorisations, and so, for example, the description 'the elderly' masks the fact that many of the elderly in question were elderly women, rather than elderly men. This also underscores the persistence of patriarchy as a means of understanding one of the continuities of the period under discussion. So too 'young people' is a very broad description, although it is being employed here so as to capture those young people, as opposed to babies and infants, who have by and large left home and are attempting to make their own way in the world. Here too there is a gender imbalance, but whilst some serial killers, such as the Wests, concentrated their efforts on young women, others, like Dennis Nilsen, were more interested in young men.

Secondly, a theme outlined more fully in *Chapter 4,* gay men have been regular targets of serial killers, both in the days of the monoculture of the inclusive society, and in those of the diversity of the exclusive society—which suggests the persistence of homophobia throughout this period. (Indeed if we had included the case of the Italian Michael Lupo, who killed some four gay men in London in 1986 the numbers of gay victims would have been higher still.) It is worth noting here that whilst two of the serial killers are open about their sexuality, such as Peter Moore and Dennis Nilsen, we do not know if Michael Copeland was gay. So too Colin Ireland suggested that he chose to kill gay men only because they were vulnerable, and their vulnerability would allow him to achieve his objective of becoming famous through their serial murder (*The Times,* 21 December 1993).

Thirdly, it is important to note that the elderly are the group that has been attacked most regularly by British serial killers—a theme taken up more fully in *Chapter 2.* Here we should note that some 225 elderly people have been murdered by serial killers—a figure that constitutes just under 70 per cent of the total number of victims (326) since 1960. As I have argued elsewhere, this appalling statistic should make us question the place of the elderly in late modernity, although this has yet to happen despite the awful reality of the Shipman murders (Soothill and Wilson, 2005).

Finally, we should note absences. For example, there are no Asian, or Black British serial killers, and with the exceptions of Myra Hindley, Beverly Allitt and Rosemary West (two of whom killed in conjunction with male partners), the majority of British serial killers are male, rather than female.

It is also interesting to note when the serial killers that I have identified in *Table 1.2* were active. The graph that is reproduced in *Figure 1.1* identifies by year when the victims of British serial killers were murdered.[6]

---

[6] It was not always possible to identify the specific date of a death, and this accounts for the different totals used in this graph from *Table 1.2*.

Table 1.2: Known serial killers, 1960-2006[7]

Name	Year tried	Occupation	Victims[8]	Number
Michael Copeland	1965	Soldier	Young Person/2 gay men	3
Brady/Hindley	1966	Clerk/typist	Children/young person	3
Patrick Mackay	1975	Gardener	Elderly women/priest	3
Donald Neilson	1976	Builder	3 men/Young person (Female)	4
Hall/Kitto	1978	Butler/ unemployed	Acquaintances/employers	5
Peter Dinsdale	1981	Unemployed	Random	26
Peter Sutcliffe	1981	Lorry driver	Women	13
Dennis Nilsen	1983	Civil servant	Gay men	15
John Duffy	1988	Unemployed	Women/Young person	3
Kenneth Erskine	1988	Unemployed	Elderly	7
Beverly Allitt	1993	Nurse	Children	4
Colin Ireland	1993	Unemployed	Gay men	5
Robert Black	1994	Van driver	Children	3
Frederick/Rosemary West	1995	Builder/ housewife[9]	Young people/family members	10
Peter Moore	1996	Cinema owner	Gay men/random[10]	4
Harold Shipman	2000	Doctor	Elderly	215
Mark Martin[11]	2006	Unemployed	Women	3

Source: Adapted from Grover and Soothill (1997).

---

[7] At the time of writing there are ongoing proceedings with regard to a man who is accused of serial murder in Ipswich. I have not included this case within this table, although details of some of the victims appear in the *Conclusion*.

[8] The number here reflects the number of victims that the perpetrator was tried for at court. The exception is for Harold Shipman, who was tried at court for the murders of 15 of his elderly patients, but the Smith Inquiry has clearly established that he was responsible for the murders of 215 people and perhaps as many as 260. The lower estimate has been used.

[9] Grover and Soothill (1999) also describe Rosemary West as a 'part-time prostitute'.

[10] One of Moore's victims was married and his murder is perhaps best described as simply him having been in the wrong place at the wrong time.

[11] Martin killed two of his victims in the company of two other men—Dean Carr and John Ashley.

This also helps us to perceive peaks and troughs in their activities, and the use of a trendline clearly demonstrates that the numbers of victims increases over our time-frame—despite the relatively few numbers of victims between 1960-1972 and between 1999-2006. Statistically, 1986 emerges as one of the most interesting years, as it was during this year that the greatest numbers of serial killers were active over the period under discussion. It was during this year, for example, that Duffy and Mulcahy murdered their three victims, Kenneth Erskine murdered seven and Robert Black murdered ten-year-old Sarah Harper. So too we now know that Harold Shipman murdered eight people in 1986. Indeed if we had included Lupo's victims in this graph the number of serial killers active in Britain in this year would have been six, compared to an average over our time-frame of two per year.

Figure 1.1: The victims of serial killers 1960-2006

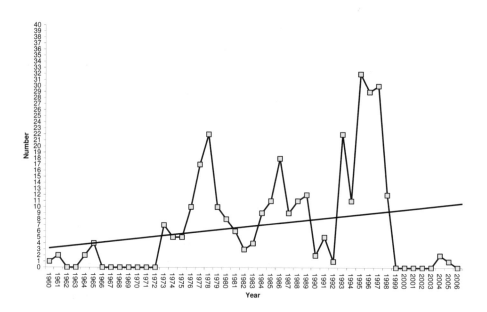

For a large scale version of this graph see p. 177.

It is also important to remember that the number of victims that I am attributing to serial killers during this period is an underestimate. This is the result of several factors. Firstly, as is obvious from the case of Harold Shipman, whilst a killer may be tried for a specific number of murders, there are suspicions about others that he or she may have also committed. Indeed, in Shipman's case it is thought that he might have been responsible for another 45 victims, and there are similar suspicions about other murders possibly committed by Dennis Nilsen, Peter Sutcliffe, Robert Black and the Wests.

Secondly, there are often spates of murders that can be attributed to one specific killer, but for any number of reasons that killer is never caught. For example, the murderer of Patricia Docker, Jemima McDonald and Helen Puttock in Glasgow in the late 1960s has never been caught, although the police have attributed their deaths to a serial killer nick-named 'Bible John'. Indeed, the Strathclyde police exhumed the body of a man in 1996 in the hope that a DNA match might prove conclusive, although it did not, and as recently as December 2004 further DNA samples were taken from suspects who are now in their early sixties. Nor have the murders of eight prostitutes in London between 1959-1965—attributed in the media to 'Jack the Stripper'—ever been solved (for a recent overview of the case see Seabrook, 2006).

Thirdly, there can be a spate of murders that are widely assumed to be the work of a serial killer, but when caught the killer is in fact only charged and convicted of one murder. For example, Raymond Morris was convicted of the murder of seven-year-old Christine Darby in 1968, and is widely suspected of having murdered two other young girls—Diane Tift and Margaret Reynolds. Nonetheless he and his child victims are excluded from our list given that he was convicted of only one murder, although it should be noted that Jenkins (1988) includes Morris in his list of British serial killers between 1940-1985. Finally, as I have drawn attention to with the case of Michael Lupo, I have excluded those serial killers who were caught, but had not been born or raised in Britain.

This brief outline of British serial killers and their victims is more fully explored in subsequent chapters, and is presented here simply to introduce the reader to the broad parameters of serial killing that forms the basis of the book. However, here I wish to compare the general characteristics of those who have been the victims of serial killers, with other people who were murdered during this period. In doing so I want to explore whether serial killing is in fact a separate phenomenon or merely related to the everyday reality of British murder. Moreover if it is, as I argue, a different phenomenon, what it is that we can learn about murder more generally in Britain, and how can this be applied to the argument that is being outlined?

MURDER IN BRITAIN 1981-2000

In the most recent comprehensive analysis of murder in Britain, Danny Dorling, Professor of Human Geography at the University of Sheffield, analysed the 13,140 people who had been murdered—on average 1.8 murders per day—between January 1981 and December 2000 (Dorling, 2005; see also Brookman and

Maguire, 2003; D'Cruze, *et al.*, 2006). This is of interest for our purposes because Dorling is trying to look 'behind' each murder, and in doing so he concentrates on who it was who had been victimised, and in what circumstances, rather than investigating the person who had committed the murder. In short, he too is less interested in the 'individualistic discourse', and rather more concerned with the structural reasons that might be the cause of why some people end up dead. In doing so he offers us a way of comparing the general phenomenon of murder in Britain with British serial killing.

So, what can we discover through making such a comparison? Most immediately there is a gender imbalance. Thus Dorling notes that men are murdered at roughly double the rate of women, and that a quarter of all murders during this period are of men between the ages of 17-32. So too the single age group with the highest murder rate is boys under the age of one. A male's chance of being murdered doubles between the ages of 10 and 14, doubles again between 14 and 15, 15 and 16, 16 and 19 and then 'does not halve until 46 and again by age 71 to be roughly the same then as it stood aged 15' (Dorling, 2005: 27). Thus, what Dorling shows is that not only is there is a gender imbalance to murder in Britain (more men are killed than women) but also that very young boys are most likely to be victimised, with the murder rate falling off after age 46, and again after age 71. Finally he tries to account for the fact that the murder rate for women is lower—a consequence, he argues of women gaining 'self-worth, power, work, education opportunity,' over the period that he is concerned with (Dorling, 2005: 37).

As can be seen immediately, this is all quite different from the general pattern that emerged in relation to those who were the targets of serial killers— although Dorling's figures include the victims of serial killers. (However, it should be noted that his analysis does not include those people murdered by Harold Shipman.) Most notably the gender and age imbalance is reversed, with serial killers targeting women and the elderly. However, because Dorling is interested in using murder as a 'social marker', his investigations about the circumstances in which murder takes place amplify the theme of the 'exclusive society' that has already been presented. Thus, for example, Dorling notes that murder occurs in a particular social context. He suggests that: 'the key component to what makes one place more dangerous to live in as compared to another is poverty. The poorer the place you live in the more likely you are to be murdered' (Dorling, 2005: 30) and that for one group of men—men aged 35 or below in 2000, or 'men born in 1964 or after'—their murder rate is increasing. In trying to understand why this is so, Dorling argues that: 'the lives of men born since 1964 have polarised, and the polarisation, inequality, curtailed opportunities and hopelessness have bred fear, violence and murder' (2005: 37). So, the murder rate, he suggests, tells us something about 'society and how it is changing', and he applies this insight into theorising why men born since 1964 are being victimised, by remembering that they would have left school at 16 in 1981.

The summer of 1981 was the first summer for over 40 years that a young man living in a poor area would find work or training very scarce, and it got worse in the years that followed. When the recession of the early 1980s hit, mass unemployment was concentrated on the young: they were simply not recruited (Dorling, 2005: 37).

In his final analysis he argues that the murder rate of this age group of men has to be viewed through their relationship to these wider social, economic and political issues:

> Behind the man with the knife[12] is the man who sold him the knife, the man who did not give him a job, the man who decided that his school did not need funding, the man who closed down the branch plant where he could have worked, the man who decided to reduce benefit levels so that a black economy grew, all the way back to the woman who only noticed 'those inner cities' some six years after the summer of 1981, and the people who voted to keep her in office. (Dorling, 2005: 40)

In passing it is also worth noting here that Oliver James (1995) uses a similar argument to explain the rise in violence in Britain since 1950. Whilst James's interest is in those who are the perpetrators of violence rather than the victims, he concludes that 'the winner-loser culture' which took hold in the late 1980s, and which particularly affected the poorest sections in British society, changed the way that excluded young men—the 'losers', 'interpreted the new inequalities'. For James, the 'spirit of the age' of the 1980s was 'a nakedly materialistic one which specifically emphasised inequalities that already existed but which had not, until this point, been presented as a matter of "winners" and "losers"' (1995: 131). As a result, the 'losers' reacted 'with physical violence' (James, 1995: 2).

Leaving James's argument to one side, and simply considering those who are the victims of physical violence, it seems fair to conclude that serial killing is in fact a different phenomenon from murder in Britain. Nonetheless, we should also acknowledge that there are clearly linkages between the argument that is being presented here more generally about the victims of serial killing, and with those who are 'routinely' the victims of murder. However, so as to extend our understanding of the phenomenon of serial killing at a structural level, and begin the process of unravelling how the changing nature of our social and economic structure has facilitated serial killing, I now consider the concept of 'homicidal protest'. In particular I question whether or not this concept can be applied

---

[12] Dorling notes that the most common way that someone is murdered in Britain is by having been cut with a knife or by a broken bottle (Dorling, 2005: 33).

within the British context, and if it is inappropriate how else we can theorise about British serial killing.

HOMICIDAL PROTEST?

As has been described earlier, Elliot Leyton (1986) has been at the forefront of attempts to move the analysis of serial killing away from the individualistic discourse, or what Grover and Soothill (1999: 4) describe as the 'medico-psychological tradition'. Whilst Leyton's focus is on serial killing *and* multiple murder, he is nonetheless arguing that psychological explanations are insufficient to explain the phenomenon of serial killing.

Specifically, he argues that it is necessary to find the roots of serial killing in the social structure that the serial killer inhabits. In doing so he identifies three broad, historical periods (see *Table 1.3*), and further suggests that the origins of serial killers and their victims are socially specific. Thus, in very general terms, what he is implying is that the socio-economic position of the serial killer has fallen, and—again in very general terms—that the socio-economic status of the victims of serial killers has risen. In attempting to explain this change, Leyton employs the concept of 'homicidal protest'. In short, serial killing in the 'Modern' era (post-1945) can be explained by understanding that frustrated members of the upper working and lower middle classes will tend to kill victims from the middle classes. However, Leyton does acknowledge that: 'Occasionally …they [serial killers] continue a metaphor from the earlier era and discipline unruly [sic] prostitutes and runaways,' but he goes on, 'much more commonly … they punish those above them in the system—preying on unambiguously middle-class figures such as university women' (Leyton, 1986: 297).

Is this analysis useful for understanding the phenomenon of British serial killing since 1960? In a thorough review of Leyton's analysis, Grover and Soothill (1999: 9) argue that:

> The British experience certainly does not confirm the latter aspect of the Leyton thesis. … the victims of modern British serial killers are *not* from the relatively powerful middle classes, but are from relatively powerless and vulnerable groups—children and young adults; gay men; women (particularly those vulnerable through their work in the sex industry or on account of the breakdown of familial relations); and pensioners. In fact, the general *absence* of persons from relatively powerful positions is especially noticeable.

Table 1.3: Historical epochs, serial killers and their victims

	Pre-Industrial	Industrial (late 19th C—1945)	Modern (post-1945)
Killer	Aristocratic	Middle classes (doctors, teachers etc)	Upper working class/ lower middle class (security guards, computer operators)
Victim	Peasantry	'Lower orders' (prostitutes, housemaids)	Middle class

Source: Leyton (1986), and also see Grover and Soothill (1999).

They go on to argue that in relation to serial killing 'in many respects the recent British experience seems to have more of the resonances of how Leyton describes the "industrial" era', and suggest that 'perhaps Britain has not yet reached the "modern" era which seems to encapsulate the United States' (Grover and Soothill, 1999: 10). Leyton argued that the industrial era (roughly from the late 19th century until 1945) was one:

> in which middle class functionaries—doctors, teachers, professors, civil servants, who belonged to the class created to serve the needs of the new triumphant bourgeoisie—preyed on members of the lower orders, especially prostitutes and housemaids.
>
> (Leyton, 1986: 276)

However, according to Grover and Soothill even if we were to accept that this happened in the industrial era, it does not seem to fit readily with what we know of recent British serial killers, and thus fails to offer much of an explanation of this phenomenon since 1960. Indeed more recently Soothill and Wilson (2005) have rejected Leyton's notion of homicidal protest when considering the case of Harold Shipman (and see *Chapter 2*). After all, in the industrial era, Leyton suggests that the serial killer's crimes were a symbolic extension of the need for industrial discipline. In other words, serial killers were taking to their most heinous conclusion the unprecedented control demanded by the cash-nexus of industrial capitalism. Serial killers removed those who lived outside the new moral order, which demanded the maximum extraction of value from the industrial proletariat. In short, 'in killing the failures and the unruly renegades from the system ... they acted as enforcers of the new moral order' (Leyton, 1986: 276).

All of this seems far removed from the elderly, vulnerable women who formed the main constituency of Shipman's victims, although Peters (2005: 226) suggests that Shipman may have chosen his victims because: 'the elderly or infirm would go first because they simply ceased to be as valuable as human beings and so there was no reason to keep them'. However, while the class relationship of the perpetrator and victims in the Shipman saga has echoes of the class relationships of the industrial era that Leyton highlights, the explanation seems to have little or no validity. As a result, rather than trying to claim that Britain remains in the industrial era, it may be more appropriate to develop the theorising that Grover and Soothill commenced, and which has been picked up by Soothill and Wilson (2005).

As such, the theoretical basis of this book in relation to serial killers and their victims is one that has modified, and extended Leyton's analysis beyond the simple class relations between victim and perpetrator, to consider other social relations. Thus, I argue that to understand the phenomenon of serial killing in Britain since 1960, we need to think of homicidal protest as a form of revenge, but one that is wreaked upon relatively powerless groups in society. In making this case we need to employ other theoretical tools too, such as patriarchy to understand why so many serial killers seem to murder women and children (see also Grover and Soothill, 1999). Thus we need to think of Britain as a capitalist and as a patriarchal society, where the wider pattern of social relations that emerged during our period increasingly cast some members of society as a socio-economic burden, and which further allowed for their exclusion, either through their age, or sexual orientation.

More broadly, the social and economic competition that drove the move from the inclusive to the exclusive society—or the 40/30/30 society—threw overboard in its wake those who were unable to compete (or, as James has described them, the 'losers'), and in doing so also often pathologised them in the process as lazy, or incompetent. Crucially, as Grover and Soothill (1999: 13) have persuasively argued, the 'state legitimises this treatment of those deemed to be marginal to the production process by affording them minimal social and economic protection.' In doing so it is the state that has created the circumstances in which serial killing takes place, no matter what the individual genetic, psychological make-up of the killer concerned; it is the state that bears the awful responsibility of the serial murders that have taken place in this country since 1960. For it is this very lack of state protection for the weak and the vulnerable, which dangerously marginalises them, that serial killers exploit. In this way the actions of serial killers, sadly but usefully, also identify social breakdowns.

Put simply, serial killers prey on the vulnerable. Within Britain the vulnerable have always been those who could not compete within the structural conditions of patriarchal capitalism, but this vulnerability has become deeper and more intense in the 'exclusive society' that has developed since 1979, when the economic system was 'left to its own devices' (Hutton, 1995: 82). The vulnerable are and have always been those people who are marginalised and who, for various reasons, do not feel able to 'answer back' to those whom this structure adorns with power—often the power of life and death. The vulnerable are those people who are not afforded suitable protection from the state. The chapters that follow show exactly how this power is exercised, and the various ways that the state's protection is denied.

Finally by way of introduction, I wish to draw attention here to the fact that whilst the basic thrust of the book relates to the thesis that has just been presented, the focus of each chapter is different, not just in terms of the victimised group that it describes, but also in the various practical ways that the state can fail to provide protection.

Thus *Chapter 2* describes the case of Harold Shipman, but it takes its focus by attempting to apply directly Leyton's thesis of homicidal protest, and employing the concept of the 'silence' of the elderly. *Chapter 3* is concerned with prostitutes and prostitution, but is also as much about the failure of the police to protect this group, and how policing failures allowed Peter Sutcliffe to escape detection for so long. (It should be noted that there was also a botched police investigation in the Shipman case.) *Chapter 4* also uses policing and 'cop culture' to provide a focus for the discussion of the victimisation of gay men, as well as discussing homophobia more generally. The focus of *Chapters 5* and *6* is provided by considering the reconstruction of childhood that has taken place over our time-frame, and thus looks specifically at the place of children in our society, and the 'discovery' of paedophilia. *Chapter 5* also looks specifically at the phenomenon of 'runaways' and *Chapter 6* at the case of Beverly Allitt. Finally, *Chapter 7* tries to bring all of these various strands together, and returns to the theme of homicidal protest. In doing so it also offers some tentative suggestions as to why there were particular peaks in serial killing in this country, and whether we have created the circumstances in which there will be more, or fewer serial killers in the decades to come.

CHAPTER 2

The Elderly

CHAPTER 2

The Elderly

> I think Shipman's selection of elderly people as his victim fulfils all the criteria necessary for him to get what he wants. They are the least troublesome group of patients, the most easily accessible, the least well supported, the ones whose dying is not likely to raise very much of questioning or surprise.
>
> (Paul Britton, criminal and forensic psychologist, quoted in Peters, 2005: 27)

Eva Lyons had lived in Todmorden all her life. It was where she was born, raised, married, had a child and it would also be where she died. Like most of her contemporaries, when Eva left school she started to work as a weaver in one of the cotton mills that dominated the town and which were once a source of its prosperity. At 28 she met her husband, Dick, a shuttle-maker at another factory; they soon produced a child—a girl they named Norma. By early 1975 Eva was ill with cancer, although a new drug regime that she had started at Halifax Royal Infirmary was helping her with her condition. Eva's hair had started to grow back and she was eating again. Even so, on the night of March 17 she was in some discomfort and so Dick called out the doctor. Their local GP soon arrived at the house and he told Dick that he was going to give Eva something to 'ease the pain'. He took a syringe from his bag and injected it into Eva's hand, all the time maintaining a regular conversation with Dick. Five minutes later Eva was dead and so she became the very first victim of Dr Harold Frederick Shipman (see, also Peters, 2005: 162-165).

This chapter is concerned with the group that has been most victimised by British serial killers—the elderly. Some 225 elderly people (mostly women) have been murdered by serial killers since 1960 and this constitutes just under 70 per cent of the total numbers of deaths that can be attributed to serial killers in our time-frame, as I have outlined in *Chapter 1*. Indeed, the most prolific British serial killer—Harold Shipman—specifically targeted the elderly, and unsurprisingly his story dominates this chapter. However, two other British serial killers— Patrick Mackay and Kenneth Erskine—also targeted older people and I use aspects of their stories to gain further insight into the Shipman case. Indeed, in one of those twists of fate that history seems to so often throw up, four days after Eva Lyons met her death, Mackay murdered his final victim, Father Anthony Crean, a 64-year-old Catholic priest who had befriended him.[1] We can only

---

[1] Interestingly Martin Fido (2001: 141) suggests that Mackay killed Crean because there were rumours that the priest might be gay and the thought that this might be so had 'enraged' Mackay. I discuss the victimisation of gay men in *Chapter 4*.

speculate whether Shipman followed this case in the news, but whilst Mackay's crimes were coming to an end, Shipman had only just started on a journey that would see him become this country's worst serial killer.

At the start of this chapter I used the observations of Paul Britton. For me they neatly outline what this chapter is concerned with, and also what it is not about. Britton is a forensic psychologist and thus he is eager to understand why killing elderly people allowed Shipman to 'get what he wants'. This seems to me to be an empty answer to a rather futile question, especially as Shipman never responded to any queries related to motivation whilst he was alive, and Britton's analysis should simply be seen as part of the individualistic and medical discourse that I have challenged in the *Introduction*. However, I do find Britton's characterisation that the elderly were not 'troublesome', or 'well supported' and that their deaths raised no 'surprise' or 'questioning' to be of interest. After all, what is it about old age that creates this vulnerability? Why should the death of an elderly person not warrant surprise, or indeed questioning? I will use this lack of questioning—this 'silence', as a theme throughout the chapter and also try to uncover who it is that has a 'voice' in our culture.

In trying to answer these questions, I accept that I am not only using a sample of people who were victimised and murdered, but also a sample who were killed by their doctor. This very fact indicates that I am clearly not using a sample of elderly people that is representative of elderly people as a whole. Indeed, as Gilleard and Higgs (2000: 1) have pointed out, old age cannot be understood as a 'common or totalising experience', nor one that is fixed and homogeneous. Rather, there are a variety of cultures of old age, some of which might compete with each other, which clearly reflects a growing disparity of wealth within the retired population, who are living for longer and some of whom are richer than ever before. This diversity within the older population and the transformation of 'old age' more generally over our time-frame are important points to bear in mind and have led some academics to argue for a 'critical gerontology' (see, for example, Phillipson, 1998). Even so, as recently as 2005, the *Guardian* was reporting that, according to the National Pensioners Convention campaign group, there were 2.2 million older people living below the poverty line in the UK, and that around 1.5 million of Britain's older citizens were either malnourished or at serious risk of it (*Guardian*, 8 June 2005).

However, what concerns me here is not so much to try to understand how vulnerability and dependency are created in our society and why that creation becomes particularly attached to the elderly, but rather to uncover how that vulnerability and dependency might be experienced. In doing so I am trying to progress the analysis that I started in *Chapter 1* by seeking to understand why so many elderly people have fallen victim to serial killers in Britain. This specific criminological focus means that whilst pension arrangements, employment practices and health care policies would seem to be crucial in producing the 'structured dependency' of the elderly, I am more interested in how this dependency facilitated murder. For without wishing to totalise the experiences of the elderly, the specific sample that I have chosen allows us to catch a glimpse of what it means to be excluded, marginalised and powerless, and where as a consequence one's death leads to silence, rather than to questioning or surprise. Finally, given that this sample of victims constitutes the largest category of those who have been murdered by serial killers, I spend some time attempting to see if it is possible to apply Leyton's (1986) concept of 'homicidal protest' (*Chapter 1*) to the group that has been most victimised in our country.

HAROLD FREDERICK SHIPMAN[2]

Harold Frederick Shipman remains a puzzle. Why did he do it? A further puzzle is that few people seem willing to confront this conundrum. In fact, Keith Soothill has bemoaned the fact that the discipline of sociology has been remarkably loath to engage with the phenomenon of serial killing generally, never mind Harold Shipman specifically (Soothill, 2001). However, that cannot be said of other disciplines. Forensic psychologists, forensic psychiatrists, criminologists and all manner of other people have confronted the issue of serial killing and serial killers. Nevertheless, most have remained comparatively mute about the serial killing of Harold Shipman, beyond some vague notions related to his desire to have 'the power of life and death', a desire to 'get what he wants', his 'arrogance' and 'difficulties in his childhood'.

The comparative silence is easy to understand. There are at least three possible reasons. Firstly, everyone had been awaiting an authoritative explanation from Dame Janet Smith's inquiry and, with that amount of expense, time and evidence, who could compete with the inquiry as a source? Academic speculations seem meagre in comparison and it would have been premature to have tried to second guess Dame Janet. Secondly, academics, like everyone else, may be more attracted to the media agenda than they are willing to recognise and are therefore more comfortable in seeing serial killers as 'evil'. Thirdly, perhaps the Shipman episode is seen by some as such a freak of nature that, like lightning, is thought not likely to strike in the same place twice. There is so much

---

2 In fact, even his name is a puzzle. The website dedicated to the inquiry conducted by Dame Janet Smith considers his middle name to be 'Fredrick', but most sources, including Google, the BBC and *The Lancet*, spell it as 'Frederick'. Entering the words 'Harold Frederick Shipman' on Google produces around 29,400 responses, while entering 'Harold Fredrick Shipman' produces 4,070 responses with the query 'Did you mean "Harold *Frederick* Shipman"?' I am reluctant to argue with Google and so this is the spelling that I have used.

to do in tackling routine crime that academics—especially criminologists—can waste too much energy in considering the grossly unusual. In fact, these apparently easy explanations are both contradictory and unwise to support.

First, the authoritative explanation from Dame Janet Smith's inquiry about why Shipman committed his crimes has not been forthcoming. Despite the massive amount of time and money spent on the inquiry, the cupboard seems remarkably bare on such a key issue. Indeed, even though the inquiry produced six reports between 2002 and 2005 Dame Janet, in her first report, *Death Disguised* (July 2002), which contains a chapter on Shipman's character and motivation, reminds her readers that:

> The inquiry's terms of reference require me to consider the extent of Shipman's unlawful activities. They do not expressly require me to consider the motives behind Shipman's crimes, or the psychological factors that underlay them. However, I decided that I ought to consider and report on those matters, as well as I am able.[3]

Thus, with a team of forensic psychiatrists to support her—comprising Professors John Gunn and Pamela Taylor, and Drs Clive Meux and Alec Buchanan, Dame Janet raised hopes and expectations at the outset that an authoritative explanation about Shipman's motivation might emerge. However, those reading her various reports will have had these expectations dashed almost immediately, as Shipman refused to have anything to do with the inquiry, or with Dame Janet's team of forensic psychiatrists. This meant that they could not interview him and had to rely on, at best, second-hand information concerning him—an issue that I have raised in the *Introduction*. As such, Dame Janet points out that the psychiatrists could not 'gain any real insight into Shipman's character', had been 'unable to reach any conclusions' and thus 'in the end I have been unable to attempt any detailed explanation of the psychological factors underlying Shipman's conduct' (Smith, 2002: 13.7).

A second reason for the comparative silence on Shipman is that the media slur on academics may be inappropriate. After all, the media itself has not tried particularly hard to investigate the Shipman saga robustly at all and it has often floundered on exactly the same ground as Dame Janet. For example, ITV's *To Kill and Kill Again*, which was broadcast on 1 March 2005, did not markedly help reveal any deeper understanding as to why Shipman killed, despite a whole plethora of 'experts' (mostly forensic psychologists) offering opinions. However, Carole Peters, the producer/director of *To Kill and Kill Again*, in a useful book of the same name, did attempt to go beyond the confines of the broadcast documentary, although ultimately all she could conclude was that Shipman became a serial killer because 'he enjoyed what he did' (Peters, 2005: 232).

---

[3] Unless otherwise indicated all extracts are taken from www.the-shipman-inquiry.org.

More perniciously, perhaps there is a conspiracy of silence to which we are all willing to contribute, because the possible implications of understanding the Shipman story may be too difficult to confront. It invades our comfort zone too much. However, conspiracies of silence are more often crimes of omission than commission and perhaps we have not yet really bothered to consider the implications of his killings. In this respect, though, the official Shipman inquiry has at least done some useful work in trying to ensure that it cannot happen again. The concern here, of course, is that without understanding why Shipman did it, we are in the position of trying to mend a leak without knowing the cause.

A further possibility for silence—that Shipman is a freak of nature who is unlikely to appear again—will be shared by everyone, for it helps to secure the defences of that same comfort zone. However, we also know it may not be true. Indeed, the setting up of an inquiry (and it should be remembered that initially it was going to be held in private), in part suggests that the official view is that it could happen again. Of course, an inquiry can also be used to dampen down speculation and contribute to a conspiracy of silence—'We can't say anything until the inquiry has reported'. So, by the time that the inquiry reports, perhaps there is an official hope that serious interest in the topic will have all but disappeared.

The 'freak event', however, is often the most important in the general scheme of things. A freak happening can be the source of the very test so beloved by Karl Popper in his approach to scientific method. Popper suggests that we should be looking for instances that attempt to falsify our theories, rather than seeking instances that simply confirm or verify them. Popper's opposition to the verification principle and his solution remain part of the contemporary scientific canon, so perhaps we could usefully use the Popperian approach in confronting the Shipman 'phenomenon'. However, before starting that journey, there are two preliminary tasks to confront. First, we need a short description of what can be termed 'the Shipman phenomenon' and secondly we need to consider whether this phenomenon was indeed a freak.

The Shipman phenomenon

Shipman was convicted at Preston Crown Court on 31 January 2000 of the murder of 15 of his patients, whilst he was working as a GP from a singleton practice in Market Street, Hyde, near Manchester and with one count of forging a will (for a general introduction to the background of the Shipman case see, Peters, 2005). Shipman was sentenced to life imprisonment, but ultimately took his own life whilst serving his sentence at HMP Wakefield, in January 2004.[4]

---

[4] In another puzzle, *Inside Time*—the prison newspaper produced by the charity New Bridge— claims that Shipman was in fact murdered, drawing attention to the unexplained bruises on his body and the inordinate time that staff took to find his body (*Inside Time*, November, 2004: 1, 18).

Following his training at the University of Leeds Medical School, Shipman acted as a pre-registration house officer at Pontefract General Infirmary and then moved to the Abraham Ormerod Medical Practice in Todmorden in 1974. Perhaps during his student days, but certainly over this period, he developed an addiction to pethidine for which he was ultimately charged and appeared before Halifax Magistrates' Court in 1976, where he pleaded guilty to three offences of obtaining ten ampoules of 100mg of pethidine by deception, three of unlawfully possessing pethidine and two of forging prescriptions. He asked for 74 further offences to be taken into consideration and was fined £600. Shipman thereafter moved to Newton Ayclife Health Centre, where he worked as a clinical medical officer, before moving to Hyde in 1978.

In Hyde Shipman originally worked at the Donneybrook Practice, before setting up his solo practice in Market Street in 1992. During his time in the town he rapidly gained a reputation as a particularly good, 'old fashioned' doctor, especially with elderly people, whom he was prepared to visit in their own homes. A measure of his esteem in the Hyde community can be gleaned from the fact that there was a 'Shipman's Patient Fund', which raised money to buy medical equipment for his practice and that when allegations about the murders that he had committed started to circulate, a group of incredulous patients formed a support group for their erstwhile GP (Peters, 2005: 12-15). At the time of his arrest over 3,000 patients were registered with his practice, a not inconsiderable number for a sole practitioner.

It would seem that Shipman was caught largely through a bungled attempt to forge the will of his last victim—Kathleen Grundy, whom he murdered on 24 June 1998—which raised the suspicions of Mrs Grundy's lawyer daughter, Angela Woodruff. So poorly was the will forged that it could be suggested that Shipman may have wanted to be caught, although equally this raises the issue that there may have been a financial motive for his killings. When he was arrested for the murder of Mrs Grundy it would seem that Shipman was killing at the rate of once every ten days and Dame Janet concludes that by that time Shipman was 'no longer in touch with reality' (Smith, 2002: 13.64). His first victim was Eva Lyons, who was killed on the day before her 71st birthday in March 1975. Over the next two decades until the murder of Kathleen Grundy it is believed that Shipman killed 215 people—mostly elderly women (171 women and 44 men) and Dame Janet has suspicions about the deaths of another 45 of his former patients, making a total of some 260 people whom he may have killed.

Before considering whether or not the Shipman case was a freak event, it is worth reflecting on his last offence—the murder of Mrs Grundy—and how this was exposed, and on other less celebrated locals who harboured suspicions about him. Indeed, these reflections also allow for further consideration of who it is who has a 'voice' and who it is that is 'silenced'. For example, John Shaw started *K Cabs* in 1988, having spotted the niche business of driving elderly clients in Hyde around the town. His business prospered, largely because these elderly ladies grew to trust him and over time most of his clients came to be on first name terms with their taxi driver. However, Shaw started to notice that not only were significant numbers of his 'ladies' suddenly dying, but that they were all also Shipman's patients. He started to compile a list and periodically voiced his concerns to those who would listen. Few did. Accusing a doctor of murder was not something that could be done lightly and so his list of sudden deaths and the dates that these had happened were ignored during a first and botched police investigation into Shipman. Shaw and his concerns were only taken seriously after the awful truth about Shipman began to emerge (see Peters, 2005: 59-61 and 74-76).

So too we might reflect that Shaw's 'ladies' were, to use another of Britton's descriptions, 'ordinary people who could be guaranteed to trust and respect their GP' (quoted in Peters, 2005: 27). Their very 'ordinariness' can be compared with Shipman's final victim. Kathleen Grundy, a former Mayor of Hyde (who had also been married to a Mayor of Hyde), was a local councillor who owned property in the town and also in the Lake District and had some well chosen investments. Indeed Mrs Grundy's daughter, Angela Woodruff, was a solicitor and it was her legal knowledge (and her familiarity with police, coroners and magistrates) which allowed her suspicions about the forgery of her mother's will to begin the process of unravelling Shipman's crimes. Even so Mrs Woodruff and her husband had to begin the investigation of Mrs Grundy's will themselves, before handing over their findings to the police (Peters, 2005: 8-10). Nonetheless it is tempting to conclude that it was a forged will that brought Shipman to justice and concerns over inheritance being voiced by professionals who understood how to make their anxieties known, rather than the suspicions of a taxi driver who recognised that there was a surprisingly high number of the doctor's patients who were dying suddenly for no apparent reason.[5]

A 'freak' event?

Was the Shipman case a 'freak event'? The stance of the inquiry seems to have been that they wanted to deal with those issues that could be definitively 'proven' one way or another—where evidence could be weighed up and a decision about that evidence delivered. Thus, for example, the first of Dame Janet's reports concentrated on the numbers of patients who had been murdered; the second on the conduct of the police investigation; the third on the conduct of coroners and death certificates; the fourth on the regulation of controlled drugs

---

[5] This conclusion is not intended to be disrespectful to either Mr or Mrs Woodruff, but rather is meant to encourage us to reflect on who has the power to complain and demand action and who is silenced.

in the community; the fifth made suggestions about how patients might be protected in the future; the sixth and last concerned Shipman's career as a junior doctor in Pontefract.

It is worth noting here that Shipman was not the first doctor to be accused of killing his patients and, for example, there is an interesting and seemingly parallel case involving Dr John Bodkin Adams. Bodkin Adams was a similarly popular GP working in Eastbourne and had been favoured over 100 times in the wills of his elderly patients. In 1957 he was tried for the murder of two of them—Edith Morrell and Gertrude Hullett—which was, at that time, the longest trial for murder in English criminal history (Simpson, 1980: 265). Bodkin Adams was acquitted unanimously of these charges of murder, which perhaps explains why he is not mentioned in the Smith inquiry, although he was later tried under the prevailing drugs legislation on a minor charge of 'loose prescribing' of hard drugs. This was a relatively technical offence, although here we should note that there are some clear echoes with Shipman. As a result of this conviction, Bodkin Adams was struck off the Medical Register, but his name was later restored and, in the words of Professor Keith Simpson, the first Professor of Forensic Medicine at London University, 'he was free to continue to treat rich elderly widows with such quantities of morphia and heroin as he considered appropriate' (Simpson, 1980: 266).

Despite Bodkin Adams' acquittal, Simpson (1980) includes the case as a chapter in his book, *Forty Years of Murder*. The chapter opens quite poignantly:

> Doctors are in a particularly good position to commit murder and escape detection. Their patients, sometimes their own fading wives, more often mere ageing nuisances, are in their sole hands. 'Dangerous drugs' and powerful poisons lie in their professional bags or in the surgery. No one is watching or questioning them and a change in symptoms, a sudden 'grave turn for the worse' or even death is for them to interpret. They can authorise the disposal of a dead body by passing the necessary death certificate to the Registrar of Deaths, who has no power to interfere unless there is some statutory shortcoming in the way the certificate is filled out, or death appears due to accident or violence of some kind, or the working is so vague or unintelligible that the Registrar has to seek the help of the Coroner. (Simpson, 1980: 253)

Simpson goes on to ask:

> Are there many doctor murderers? … No one can know, but if doctors do take the law into their own hands, the facts are only likely to emerge by chance, through whisperings of suspicion or, rarely, through carelessness in disposal of the dead body, as when Dr Buck Ruxton threw the remains of his wife and her maid Mary Rogerson in an open ravine at Moffatt in Dumfrieshire. (Simpson, 1980: .253)

His examples should remind us of some earlier spectacular cases—Dr Crippen lying stupidly about his wife's 'disappearance' and his historic dash by liner to America; Dr Neill Cream unwisely complaining to Sergeant McIntyre of Scotland Yard about the investigation into the deaths of his prostitute victims by strychnine. Less well known is Dr Lawson walking into a private school to poison his crippled brother-in-law with aconite in a piece of cake, being caught when the chemist supplying the poison read the account of the murder. Simpson mentions others: 'Dr Clements, Palmer the Staffordshire horse-racing doctor, Dr Pritchard, Dr Smethurst, Dr Waite, Dr Webster—all but the last used poisons and might well have escaped but for faulty planning or behaviour, or some mere chance' (Simpson, 1980: 254). While the details are sparse, the cases seem to show that doctors simply suffer from the same range of emotions as the rest of us and are just as likely to make a mess of the murder or their escape. Nevertheless, as Simpson suggests, 'there are 70,000 doctors in England and Wales alone, so a mere handful of professional murders in 50 years speaks generally very highly of their moral fibre, *or the ease with which they can conceal crime'* (1980: 254, emphasis added).

The Adams case is again helpful here. Adams was described as a portly bespectacled Irishman of 60, who had practised medicine in Eastbourne for many years. In brief, the crux of the case was whether 'this elderly seaside doctor [had] merely been handing out rather too heavy sedative doses to his more troublesome senile patients, or ....?' (Simpson, 1980: 263). While the whispers as to what was happening to Bodkin Adams's wealthy old ladies were widespread, the murder trial focused on the death of one rich widow, Mrs Edith Alice Morell. It is clear which version Simpson—acting on behalf of the Medical Defence Union (MDU) who undertook to organize Bodkin Adams's defence—supported:

> On the face of it the case looked hard to prove. There was no body (an obvious handicap in a case of alleged poisoning) as Mrs Morell had been cremated, at her own request. She had died six years before. She was eighty-one and half paralysed by a stroke, after which she had been given from six to twelve months to live, only to survive another two and a half years under the care of the doctor now charged with her murder. She had left an estate of £157,000, out of which the doctor received an elderly Rolls-Royce and a chest containing silver valued at £275 ... Hardly a rich legacy. (Simpson, 1980: 256)

The prosecution case seemed to collapse as a result of unreliability and conflicts in the medical and nursing evidence. Even Simpson conceded:

> one mystery remained. The defence had proved that the amount of morphine and heroin prescribed (and supplied by the chemist) greatly exceeded the amount administered to Mrs Morell: what had happened to the rest?' (Simpson, 1980: 256).

Owing to the legal and moral difficulties of speculating about an acquittal, the term 'potential serial killer' has not been used widely (although see Wilson,

2005) and the focus of the various reports on the case has been on the alleged murder that brought Bodkin Adams to court rather than the investigations surrounding the others. Nevertheless, the nature of the discourse about motives that Simpson introduces remains instructive—'would an elderly Rolls-Royce or a canteen of cutlery in an antique chest be likely to turn the head of a professional man in a good way of living?' (Simpson, 1980: 255). In other words, the motive must be pecuniary or, by implication, nothing.

Since that case in the late 1950s the concern about serial killers and theorising about them have grown enormously; no longer would the potential motivation for serial killing be considered to be limited to pecuniary gain. Of course, the possibility of pecuniary gain cannot be dismissed entirely and Peters, for example, quotes Paul Britton as suggesting that Shipman's forgery of Mrs Grundy's will may have been a means by which Shipman hoped that he could have gained funds to have moved to a different location (Peters, 2005: 227-228). Certainly the clientele of both Bodkin Adams and Shipman would seem to have much in common. So too their doctors' long experience is somewhat similar. However, there is at least one major difference—Bodkin Adams was acquitted in court, while there apparently is no doubt about the guilt of Shipman. Whether Bodkin Adams was a precursor or not, one certainly needs to understand how Harold Shipman fits into the pantheon of serial killers and through that understanding some explanation for his behaviour might emerge.

Explaining Shipman

Probably many disciplines can contribute to an explanation of serial killing. However, it is important to recognise that some disciplines may be more suited to explaining particular aspects of the phenomenon. So, for example, it seems unlikely that sociological insights alone will help much towards a complete understanding of the puzzle of Harold Shipman. Nevertheless, sociology can make a contribution towards understanding why a case like this remained hidden for so long.

Here we can perhaps usefully turn to the work of Eliot Freidson who has provided some of the classic insights into medical practice. Well over 30 years ago Freidson (1970) stressed that the central issue in the analysis of work is the control of performance. This is a special problem for professional work because professions, unlike other occupations, have successfully gained freedom from control by outsiders. Freidson, in fact, pointed to solo practice—such as Shipman's—as the most likely setting where professional abuse might occur, for in solo practice the burden of control rests almost entirely on individual motivation and capacity. Freidson's main point is that physicians generally create an informal structure of relatively segregated, small circles of practitioners, the extremes of which are so isolated from each other that the conditions necessary for mutual influence on behaviour are missing. As such, they create opportunities to gain access to vulnerable people and also the opportunities to do them harm.

Elsewhere Soothill (2001) has argued that in cases of this kind one can see political statements masquerading as science. In his Foreword to *Harold Shipman's Clinical Practice 1974-1998*, Professor Sir Liam Donaldson—the Chief Medical Officer of the Department of Health—maintained that 'everything points to the fact that a doctor with the sinister and macabre motivation of Harold Shipman is a once in a lifetime occurrence' (2001: iv). While common sense might suggest this, there is nothing in the report that helps towards this conclusion. The statement is an attempt to allay any fears of the public without providing the evidence. Nevertheless, the Chief Medical Officer's standpoint is that this is an aberrant case in the history of medicine.

The Chief Medical Officer's audit sought 'to describe factually the circumstances applying to the deaths of Shipman's patients, [but] it cannot explain how or why the events came to happen' (Donaldson, 2001: 106). It was said at the time that the 'why' question would probably remain hidden until Shipman agreed to co-operate more fully but, now that he has died, that avenue is closed. However, the assumption that he could explain if he had been willing to co-operate may be flawed. Even without accepting the full panoply of the Freudian approach with its insistence on the importance of the 'unconscious', one still may not be aware of the wider social forces that may drive someone in a particular direction. Certainly Durkheim pioneered this approach by pointing to a more societal explanation for what had been regarded as the individualistic act of suicide. Again, whether or not one accepts the Durkheimian approach to suicide, his overall signpost is clear—there are certain groups of people who seem more prone to suicide than others. In fact, with this type of behaviour, doctors—together with veterinary surgeons, pharmacists and dentists—are much more prone to suicide than most members of other professions are (http://www.mentalhealth.org.uk/htlm/content/brief001.cfm). While this may reflect their more ready access to the drugs that can facilitate death, it also suggests that doctors may more readily internalise aggression that can be transformed into suicide. But what of those, like Shipman, whose aggression seems to have been deposited elsewhere?

Social explanations often begin to pinpoint *which* social groups may be more vulnerable to a phenomenon than others, while psychological explanations may be more attuned to identify which persons *within* a social group are more likely to be vulnerable than others. In short, it seems likely that developing a complete explanation of serial killing will have to draw upon the skills of both traditions but, as they are analytically distinguishable, we can consider them separately.

I have suggested—along the lines initiated by Grover and Soothill (1999) that the dominant *individualistic* discourse has failed to meet the challenge of causation satisfactorily and there is a need to consider explanatory frameworks, which are more ambitious in their scope. Certainly Elliot Leyton (1986) can be considered as a leading protagonist who has argued that, in order to understand the phenomenon of serial killing, factors beyond the psychological tradition need to be analysed. Leyton's structural account focuses on socio-economic factors and, using evidence of American serial killing, he seems to provide a powerful argument. Grover and Soothill (1999), however, focusing on known British serial killers since the 1960s, suggested that Leyton's work cannot be wholly applied to the modern British experience. They argued that, while supporting the general approach of Leyton, they found his analysis both limited and limiting; they argued that the focus needed to be widened to include other social relations, such as patriarchy. In particular, they suggested that Leyton's central thesis of 'homicidal protest' (*Chapter* 1) did not seem particularly applicable to the British experience. All this was written before the full force of the Shipman crimes was established. However, I want to use the suggested developments of the Leyton approach as a platform for considering the Shipman case, but first let us consider the central plank of the Leyton analysis.

Shipman and 'homicidal protest'
The crux of Leyton's thesis relates to his notion of killing as a form of 'homicidal protest' by frustrated members of the upper working and lower middle classes who tend to kill *victims from the middle classes.* However, Leyton does acknowledge that: 'Occasionally …they [serial killers] continue a metaphor from the earlier era and discipline unruly [sic] prostitutes and runaways'. But, he goes on, 'much more commonly … they punish those above them in the system—preying on unambiguously middle-class figures such as university women' (Leyton, 1986: 297).

As noted in *Chapter* 1, but worth re-emphasising, Grover and Soothill (1999) argue that:

> The British experience certainly does not confirm the latter aspect of the Leyton thesis. … the victims of modern British serial killers are *not* from the relatively powerful middle classes, but are from relatively powerless and vulnerable groups—children and young adults; gay men; women (particularly those vulnerable through their work in the sex industry or on account of the breakdown of familial relations); and pensioners. In fact, the general *absence* of persons from relatively powerful positions is especially noticeable. (Grover and Soothill, 1999: 9)

In focusing on the Shipman phenomenon and trying to follow the Leyton thesis, the perpetrator—Shipman—could not be described as upper working or lower middle class and similarly his victims do not seem to be from the relatively powerful middle classes. In short, this is roughly the position that Grover and Soothill found themselves in when assessing Leyton's conception of homicidal protest in the British context. Should we dismiss it in the light of the British experience or, perhaps more constructively, can we begin to modify the Leyton approach to accommodate the British experience, of which the Shipman case is now a further ingredient?

And as already noted in *Chapter 1*, Grover and Soothill (1999: 10) argue that 'in many respects the recent British experience seems to have more of the resonances of how Leyton describes the "industrial" era', going on to suggest that 'perhaps Britain has not yet reached the "modern" era which seems to encapsulate the United States'. Leyton argued that the 'industrial' era (roughly from the late nineteenth century until 1945) was one 'in which middle class functionaries—doctors, teachers, professors, civil servants, who belonged to the class created to serve the needs of the new triumphant bourgeoisie—preyed on members of the lower orders, especially prostitutes and housemaids' (Leyton, 1986: 272). However, even if we were to accept that this happened in the industrial era, the explanation for their actions does not seem to readily fit what we know of the Shipman case. In the industrial era, Leyton suggests, their crimes were a symbolic extension of the need for industrial discipline. In other words, serial killers were taking to their most heinous conclusion the unprecedented control demanded by the cash-nexus of industrial capitalism. Serial killers removed those who lived outside the new moral order, which demanded the maximum extraction of value from the industrial proletariat. Thus, 'in killing the failures and the unruly renegades from the system ... they acted as enforcers of the new moral order' (Leyton, 1986: 276). All this seems far removed from the largely poor, elderly, vulnerable women who formed the main constituency of Shipman's victims, although Peters suggests that Shipman may have chosen his victims because 'the elderly or infirm would go first because they simply ceased to be as valuable as human beings and so there was no reason to keep them' (2005: 226). However, and again as intimated in *Chapter 1*, while the class relationship of the perpetrator and victims in the Shipman saga has echoes of the class relationships of the industrial era that Leyton highlights, the explanation for the behaviour has little or no validity. Thus, rather than trying to claim that Britain remains in the industrial era, it may be more appropriate to develop the theorising that Grover and Soothill commenced.

Widening the analysis?
Grover and Soothill (1999) have suggested that by broadening the focus of social relations beyond class relations to include other social relations—such as patriarchy, it is still possible that 'homicidal protest' has some conceptual value in the British context. In their article they suggest that 'widening the analysis in

this way provides scope for being able to classify a greater variety of serial killers' (Grover and Soothill, 1999: 10). In this respect Harold Shipman is certainly an unusual addition to the serial killer pantheon and in the spirit of a Popperian analysis whereby one looks to cases that might falsify the theory, then focusing on Shipman seems ideal.

In studying British serial killers since the 1960s Grover and Soothill maintained that there is evidence that among some British serial killers a degree of socio-economic frustration may have existed. However, they claimed that it would be both bold and inappropriate to identify socio-economic frustration as either a necessary or sufficient condition for serial killing. Equally, they claimed that as a result of Leyton's failure to consider social relations other than those of capitalism (class), Leyton cannot easily explain why the victims of British serial killers tend to be females, children, young people, gay men and pensioners. In short, they argue that we need to locate serial murder within power relations that go beyond those of class.

Feminist commentators have argued with fervour and conviction that it needs to be recognised that Britain is both a capitalist *and* a patriarchal society. Violence against women and children is thus seen as being reflective of patriarchal relations through which 'men maintain power over women and children' (Kelly and Radford, 1987: 238). Hence, recognising patriarchal relations, it becomes clearer as to why serial killers often murder women and children. It is an expression of power through which men are able to dominate and oppress women and children. In developing the analysis to explain the murder of gay men, the evidence stemming from British serial killers begins to be persuasive, but certainly not conclusive. But what of Shipman's focus primarily on elderly women living alone?

In the Grover and Soothill analysis of British serial killers since the 1960s there were just two—Patrick Mackay and Kenneth Erskine—who were identified as deliberately choosing pensioners as victims. However, these offenders seemed to choose pensioners as providing opportunities for theft rather than simply providing scope for revenge (and see further below). Nevertheless, as Grover and Soothill (1999: 13) claim, 'the vulnerability of these victims, among others, also demonstrates how serial killing shows the limitations of current societal organization'. This is theme to which I will return.

There is a dearth of information about the likely motivation of Harold Shipman. However, for it to be included within the broad framework of Leyton's ideas where revenge is the pivot, one would need to identify the constituents of revenge in Shipman's case. This seems hard to do, especially since his suicide.

In contrast, the analysis of Grover and Soothill (1999) perhaps begins to move us beyond the constraint of 'revenge'. They ask us to recognise that the victims of serial killers not only reflect wider social relations, but also that they may have been victimised because they were perceived as living outside the moral order of competitive capitalist society. The argument is that many of the victims of British serial killers have been those individuals who are increasingly seen as a socio-economic 'burden' on society. It is abundantly clear that some elderly people are increasingly marginalised and it should be remembered that, whilst acknowledging Shipman's advantages of being seen as a 'respected' GP, which certainly provided cover for his murders, it is noteworthy that he was able to continue killing his patients for over two decades precisely because they were isolated and often out of touch with family members. Indeed, the very fact that he gained the respect which allowed him to build up his practice, was largely because he was seen as 'old fashioned' by being willing to visit his patients in their homes.

This structural argument might not please everyone, but even if we were to probe the 'psyche' of Harold Shipman we would, in all likelihood, simply find a mass of contradictions that would not necessarily take us much further towards an explanation (and see the *Introduction*). We would not find the evil man so beloved of tabloid headlines. In fact, he was a man who had done some things adjudged as evil, but he was also a man who was seen as a 'good doctor' and who was respected by many of his patients who remain alive.

He has been described as 'arrogant' and whilst this may begin to provide the clue that at times he saw himself as above the law, an arrogant belief that some laws do not apply to oneself is clearly not confined to doctors. The notion of the 'good doctor' has some widespread echoes in relation to other doctors who have come before the courts; patients of Bodkin Adams, for example, were very willing to come forward to testify that he was a 'good doctor'. However, what this demonstrates is how doctors have power over life and death. While this is nothing new, the social context is changing.

Over Shipman's lifetime, there were both continuities and changes in British culture and society which provide the context for Shipman's crimes. In many respects the dominant economic change was the move from production to consumption, which left in its wake large numbers of poor people who were no longer 'useful'—their labour was not needed nor could they consume to the same extent as those who had money. In short, they were a burden and this is a theme that I return to in the *Conclusion*.

So too during Shipman's lifetime Britain was becoming a more secular society and thus the sanctity of life was less preserved by religious conviction. In contrast, doctors—both in appearance and in reality—are increasingly becoming the moral arbiters of life. Shipman was simply demonstrating this power in an outrageous way. Exactly *why* he wanted to demonstrate this power will now probably never be known. However, the message from the Shipman case remains the same as Grover and Soothill (1999) identified, although this more recent case reveals how the stereotype of the serial killer needs to be revised.

PATRICK MACKAY AND KENNETH ERSKINE

Whilst Shipman does not fit the stereotype of the serial killer, the same cannot be claimed for either Patrick Mackay or Kenneth Erskine, both of whom also targeted the elderly. Mackay in particular, had what might be called the 'classic' background of the serial killer from within the individualistic or medical tradition. His father was a violent alcoholic who had beaten Mackay as a child, who in turn seems to have found some solace in torturing animals and bullying other children.

He was a loner, attended school only intermittently and spent most of his time getting into trouble with the police for a range of increasingly serious offences. By the age of 15 Mackay had been described as a 'cold psychopathic killer' by a psychiatrist who had seen him during a spell in Moss Side, where he had been sent under section 60 Mental Health Act 1959. There was to be a further spell in the same secure hospital before he was released again in August 1972. Mackay was fascinated by Nazism and like his father became addicted to alcohol.[6]

On 14 February 1974 Mackay knocked on the door of Isabella Griffiths, the 84-year-old widow of a surgeon who lived by herself at 19 Cheyne Walk, Chelsea, London. She answered the door with the security chain still attached, but Mackay broke this immediately. Isabella backed into the hallway and it was there that Mackay strangled her. He dragged her body into the kitchen and then, wandering through the house, he claimed that he had a 'strong compulsion to kill her outright'. He returned to the body and stabbed it with a kitchen knife, whilst listening to Edward Heath on the radio talking about the Common Market referendum. Isabella's body lay undiscovered for 12 days and the crime remained unsolved for over a year, by which time Mackay had added significantly to his tally of victims.

In July 1974 Mackay was sentenced to four months at HMP Wormwood Scrubs and it was there, according to his biographers, that he 'planned the campaign of terror and violence that he was to wage when he was released' (Clark and Penycate, 1976: 85).

This campaign was to rob elderly women, something that Mackay had done off and on over the years when he had needed money. Clark and Penycate (1976: 90) claim that 'Mackay never forgot how vulnerable and defenceless old ladies

---

[6] For a general introduction to the Mackay case see Clark and Penycate, 1976.

were as potential victims of robbery ... in the winter of 1974-75 this became a planned and systematic reign of terror.' Over the next few months he attacked 80 year-old Jane Comfort, an actress who was appearing in Agatha Christie's play *The Mousetrap*, Lady Belcher, two other unnamed elderly women and then on 29 January 1975 he:

> descended on an old ladies' hostel, Murray House in Vandon Street, Westminster, within a stone's throw of New Scotland Yard. He snatched a handbag containing £5 from Mrs Evelyn Grahame. He made a mental note of the fact that many elderly ladies seemed to live in the hostel. Easy pickings. (Clark and Penycate, 1976: 91)

Mackay killed again on 10 March 1975, when he gained entry to the flat of 89-year-old Adele Price by asking for a glass of water. He then strangled Mrs Price and left her face-down on her bedroom carpet. Finally, on March 21 he travelled to Gravesend where he killed Father Crean. These two murders are of interest for a variety of reasons as they reveal differences in the ways that Shipman and Mackay killed. For example Shipman gained access to his victims through the trust and respect that they had for him as a doctor, whereas Mackay needed to use guile, trickery and brute force. Shipman liked to pose the bodies of his victims before he left them, for the 'good doctor' wanted to give the impression that his victims had just peacefully 'slipped away', whereas Mackay had no such interest. Whereas Shipman's victims were killed with a syringe of morphine, Mackay killed through strangulation, stabbing or, in the case of Father Crean, with an axe. In this last case, for example, Mackay had to barge through the door into the bathroom where the priest had taken refuge:

> He tumbled and half fell into the bath. He then started to annoy me even more and I kept striking at his nose with my arm and the side of my hand. I then pulled out my knife from my coat pocket and repeatedly plunged it into his neck. I then got a little more excitable and stuck it into the side of his head and then tried to plunge it into the top of his head. This bent the knife. I grabbed for the axe and with this repeatedly lashed out with it at his head. He sank into the bath. He had been in the sitting-up position with the knife but when I first hit him with the axe he sank down into the bath. I then got increasingly more annoyed and lashed at him with the axe. (Clark and Penycate, 1976: 105)

This graphic account of the murder provided by Mackay himself probably does capture the violence and gothic horror of this dreadful crime. It also leaves unanswered other questions. For example, why did Father Crean 'increasingly' 'annoy' Mackay? After all by this stage in the attack the priest was absolutely at the mercy of Mackay, having been repeatedly stabbed in the head. However, perhaps what is of more interest is that the deaths of both Mrs Price and especially Father Crean were sufficiently violent to arouse the suspicion of the authorities that a murder had taken place. There could be no silencing of these awful events, but rather they generated questioning and surprise. Who could have done such a thing? How could this be stopped from happening again? Who was a likely suspect? On the other hand Shipman's tactic of 'posing' his victims and especially of encouraging their families to have the bodies cremated—thus destroying vital forensic evidence—ensured that he was able to continue to kill for decades. After all a 'doctor' was above suspicion, whereas it was only a matter of time before the police would track down the boy who had been labelled a 'cold psychopathic killer' at 15. Here too we would do well to remember the characterisations of 'organized' and 'disorganized' serial killers introduced in *Chapter 1* and the relative ease of capturing the latter.

Kenneth Erskine—dubbed the 'Stockwell Strangler'—was another 'disorganized' serial killer who targeted elderly men and women to rob, sodomise and kill in the summer of 1986. His first victim was 78-year-old Nancy Elms, whom he sexually assaulted and then strangled in her flat in Wandsworth, London. In June similar fates befell 67-year-old Jane Cockett, 84-year-old Valentine Gleim and 94-year-old Zbigniew Strabawa. A month later Erskine strangled and sexually assaulted 82-year-old William Carmen, 74-year-old William Downes and his final victim 80 year-old Florence Tisdall. Writing in *The Times* on the day of Erskine's arrest, 28 July 1986, Marcel Berlins attempted a 'portrait of a serial killer' and used extensive quotes from a consultant psychologist called Edmund Hervey-Smith to discuss what might be the motivation for the murders. In an echo of what would later be written about Shipman, Dr Hervey-Smith suggested, 'it is possible, for instance, that his preoccupation with old people stems from something that has happened to him.' He continued:

> Perhaps his mother died after a lot of suffering and as a result he feels sorry for old people. If he is a schizophrenic he may genuinely believe that he is putting his victims out of their misery. (*The Times*, 28 July 1986)

Whatever Erskine's motivation, he had to be stopped from masturbating when he entered the court room during his trial, which probably reveals a great deal about his state of mind (Fido, 2001: 177).

AND AT THE END OF IT ALL?

That Shipman, Mackay and Erskine all targeted the elderly should make us question the provision of social and economic protection for this age group. In the case of Shipman, what was also lacking was provision for the control of professional performance. While other people may speculate about the psychological mechanisms that enabled, facilitated or propelled Shipman, Mackay and Erskine to commit their crimes, here I would suggest that we need also to embrace a more structural approach that brings us closer to understanding the *meaning* of serial killing at a societal level. In brief, the actions of these serial killers, sadly but usefully, identify social breakdowns. In this respect, the warning is dire. Serial killers prey on those groups who are rendered vulnerable by their inability to compete within the structural conditions of patriarchal capitalism, those people who, for various reasons, do not feel able to 'answer back' to the individuals whom this structure gives power—and who will sometimes use that power to kill. This conclusion is most obviously true of Shipman and we can perhaps suggest that Mackay and Erskine were caught relatively quickly because they did not have the same intellectual resources to escape detection, nor the same degree of social or cultural power possessed by a 'respected GP'.

However, these observations notwithstanding, Shipman's murders continued for as long as they did because ultimately there was inadequate social protection for the group on which he preyed. Not only this but, echoing a theme that I have employed throughout this chapter, I have also used the issue of 'silence' to capture the sense of who has a 'voice' in our culture and who does not. In short, who is able to make themselves 'heard', able to protest and complain? The activities of Mackay, Erskine and especially Shipman reveal all too graphically that the voices of the elderly in our culture are too rarely heard.

CHAPTER 3

Women Who are Involved in Prostitution

CHAPTER 3

Women Who are Involved in Prostitution

Q: How did all this start?
A: With Wilma McCann. I didn't mean to kill her at first but she was mocking me.
After that it just grew and grew until I became a beast.
(Peter Sutcliffe, statement to the police, February 1981 (Bilton, 2003: 692))

This chapter is concerned with women involved in prostitution—one specific group of women who have regularly been the targets not just of murderers but also of serial killers. So too I discuss some recent serial murders of young women involved in prostitution in Ipswich in my *Conclusion*. Women involved in prostitution were most notably the targets of Peter Sutcliffe—the 'Yorkshire Ripper'—although he killed and attacked other women too. I used a quote from his confession to the police in 1981 at the start of this chapter and his story dominates what follows. However, I do not here simply re-tell the story of the Yorkshire Ripper and how he was caught, but instead try and understand why he was able to escape detection for so long.

In total Peter Sutcliffe was interviewed eleven times by West Yorkshire detectives and nine times during their formal investigation of a series of attacks and murders of women in the north of England between 1975-1981. Thus the chapter takes as its focus police incompetence in handling this case—an incompetence that was to be the subject of an investigation by Lawrence Byford. Byford presented his report to the House of Commons in January 1982, but it was suppressed by successive governments until June 2006, when its contents were eventually released under the Freedom of Information Act 2000. I use the Byford Report (2002) extensively throughout this chapter, as well as attempting to understand the police investigation through the criminological lens of 'cop culture' and the Macpherson Inquiry into the murder of Stephen Lawrence in 1993.

Sutcliffe is suspected of having killed more than the 13 women he was charged with murdering and whilst his story dominates what follows, we should not ignore the fact that there have been other serial killers during our time-frame who have preyed on women involved in prostitution. For example David Seabrook (2006) has written about the murders of eight women who worked as prostitutes in London. Beginning with the murder of Elizabeth Figg in 1959 and ending with that of Bridget O'Hara in 1965, these murders have been attributed to a man dubbed 'Jack the Stripper' but the true culprit has never been caught. Ironically, the murders seem to have started just months after the introduction of the Street Offences Act 1959 which made it an offence for a woman to loiter or solicit in a street or public place for the purposes of prostitution. The maximum penalties were a fine of £10 for a first offence and a term of imprisonment for subsequent offences. However, despite what may have been intended and no matter how many women ended up in jail, the Act does not seem to have stopped either the supply, or the demand for women prepared to sell their bodies for sex.

Natalie Pearman

Natalie Pearman has been described as a 'walking portrait of an ordinary girl' (Davies, 1997: 131) and to be fair there was not much in her background that would have made her stand out. She had four brothers and sisters; a cat named Lucy; and she lived with her mother and step-father in a neat council house on the edge of the village of Mundesley, half an hour's drive north of Norwich. Natalie took ballet lessons, liked to draw and had wanted to join the RAF, but a part-time job that she took after turning 14 in the village's take-away burger bar proved to be her passport into a completely different world. Within a year she was in care and within two years—when she was 16—she had changed her name to Maria, dyed her hair blonde and was working the streets in 'The Block' in Norwich. Her patch was outside the Ferry Boat public house, where she charged £15 for a 'hand job', £20 for a 'blow job' and £30 for 'straight sex'. Her killer has never been caught, but they found her body dumped in a lay-by just outside the city's boundaries.[1]

What was it that propelled this ordinary girl with dreams of a career in the RAF to turn to prostitution? How did she come to fall out of the bottom of village life and find her way to the nearest big town, where she changed her name and her destiny? Was this simply the self-indulgence and self-destruction of youth, or were there broader forces at work?

Nick Davies has no doubts as to what happened to Natalie or the root cause. For him, the key is to remember that the Pearmans were 'poor … they were trapped at the bottom of the financial cliff. They had enough to get by, but no more' (Davies, 1997: 132). Natalie had no money for Brownies or to go on school trips and gradually as one crisis after another hit the family she had to stop ballet lessons too. Prostitution provided her with a wealth that she could barely have dreamed of and whilst the short life that it gave to her was a grotesque parody of the life that Natalie had wanted, she was not poor anymore. For Davies this was not a question of Natalie being forced to do something that she did not want to, but rather a conscious choice that she had made. For, when she looked at her life:

---

[1] Her story is further recounted in Davies, 1997: 131-9.

She saw that she was trapped and when she looked at her future, it was even worse — getting pregnant, getting married, getting a house and stewing slowly in front of a television for 40 years. What else was there? (Davies, 1997: 138)

We do not need to agree with Davies's conclusion that Natalie made a conscious choice to become a prostitute to accept that many young people drift from one place to another as they reach adolescence and in doing so they make themselves vulnerable in various ways — a theme picked up on in *Chapter 5* when I discuss the victims of Fred and Rosemary West. Some adolescents will turn to prostitution. Indeed, the Government has recently calculated that of the 80,000 people involved in prostitution in this country 70 per cent began when they were children or young teenagers (Home Office, 2004: 7). Nor do we have to see prostitution as the only alternative for women who do not want to spend years 'stewing slowly in front of a television'. However, what Davies does reveal through his very sympathetic and tragic portrayal of Natalie are the dangers faced by women who turn to prostitution and the ability of their attackers to escape justice. As many as 60 women involved in prostitution were murdered between 1994 and 2004, although there were only convictions in 16 cases — including the case of Paul Brumfitt which is discussed below (Home Office, 2004: 488).

Marcella Ann Davis

More recently, in 1999 Paul Brumfitt murdered Marcella Ann Davis, a young, single mother who earned her living as a prostitute in Wolverhampton. Brumfitt had previously served 15 years of a discretionary life sentence for murdering two men in 1979. Given the time lapse between these two murders and the killing of Marcella Ann Davis I have not included Brumfitt in my list of British serial killers. However, Marcella's story can be used to throw some light onto the deaths of many other young women who worked as prostitutes and who, like Natalie Pearman, ended up dead.

Marcella Ann Davis was just 19 when Brumfitt murdered her on 7 February 1999. She worked the red light area in Wolverhampton and had perhaps turned to prostitution to support her nine-month-old daughter, Dione. On the night of her murder she left her daughter with a friend, promising to be back by 11 p.m., and then took a taxi into Shakespeare Street. She phoned her friend some six times during the evening to check on her baby and the last call — presumably just before she was picked up by Brumfitt — was at 9.11 p.m. Brumfitt, who would also rape two other women involved in prostitution before being caught for Marcella's murder, took her back to his flat in Woodsetton. It was there that Marcella was killed, although we still do not know how she died. Brumfitt, who had hired a small yard in Cooper Street, dismembered and then burned Marcella's body after he had killed her in an attempt to cover his tracks.

Eventually she was identified by her dental records and a small bunch of keys found in some ashes that perfectly matched the front and back doors to her house (*Birmingham Post*, 22 July 2000).

For Marcella Ann Davis, read: Natalie Pearman, Elizabeth Figg, Bridget O'Hara, Wilma McCann and all the other women who appear in this chapter. For finally, as feminist commentators have argued with conviction, we need to remember that the Britain of our time frame is both a capitalist *and* a patriarchal society. Police incompetence gets us so far in understanding why the Yorkshire Ripper escaped detection for as long as he did, but he, his victims, the communities in which they lived and the police themselves, all inhabited a culture that valued one gender over another. Thus the violence against women (and children) generally, and women involved in prostitution specifically, can be seen as being reflective of patriarchal relations through which 'men maintain power over women and children' (Kelly and Radford, 1987: 238). Recognising these patriarchal relations allows us better to understand why serial killers often murder women and children. It is an expression of power through which men are able to dominate, oppress and in some circumstances kill.

THE VICTIMS OF THE YORKSHIRE RIPPER

Peter William Sutcliffe was born in 1946 and during 1969, when he was 23, he came to the attention of the police on two occasions in connection with incidents related to women involved in prostitution. Described by Lawrence Byford as 'an otherwise unremarkable young man' (1981: 6), Sutcliffe, in the company of his friend Trevor Birdsall (who drove the pair around in a Reliant Robin motor car), had become fascinated by women involved in prostitution soliciting in Leeds and Bradford. This fascination soon turned to violence and one night in August 1969, leaving Birdsall in the car, Sutcliffe attacked a woman from behind with a cosh (a sock with a stone in it) and then returned to the car to boast to his friend of what he had done. His victim gave a statement to the police, which allowed them to trace Birdsall's car. Birdsall then pointed them in the direction of Sutcliffe, who was questioned about the incident. He admitted assaulting the woman, but said that they had had a fight after he had been drinking and 'the incident was written off as typical of the local culture of birds and booze' (Bilton, 2003: 456). A month later, on 29 September 1969, Sutcliffe was arrested in the red light area of Bradford having been found in possession of a hammer.

Look again at these two incidents—both of which are dreadfully resonant with all that we now know of the *modus operandi* of Sutcliffe and which would feature in his next two assaults, six years later, of Anna Rogulskyj and Olive Smelt. He frequents red light areas, targets women involved in prostitution and he attacks his victims from behind by hitting them over the head—usually with a hammer (as time went on and he became more confident, he would also repeatedly stab his victims). Not only this, one of his victims is able to describe the circumstances of her attack sufficiently for the police to track Sutcliffe down, but this 'otherwise unremarkable young man' is merely cautioned, given that assaulting women is 'typical of the local culture of birds and booze'. In other words, Sutcliffe rather than his victim is believed in a culture where violence towards women—especially those involved in prostitution—is the norm.

We can only speculate what might have happened if these incidents had been dealt with differently, but they set in train a pattern of assaults, murders and police investigations that was to continue for six years between 1975 and January 1981, when Sutcliffe was eventually arrested.[2] For ease of reference I set out below the 20 assaults and murders known to have been committed by Sutcliffe in those years and include in this table the dates when he was interviewed by the police. I then describe in some detail the first two murders, of Wilma McCann and Emily Jackson, as well as the assault on Marcella Claxton and the murder of Josephine Whitaker.

Wilma McCann

Wilma McCann was the first woman whom Sutcliffe murdered. Wilma was from a family of eleven children, born and brought up in Inverness. After leaving school she worked at the Gleneagles Hotel near Perth and was pregnant with her first child, Sonje, before she was out of her teens. She then met Gerald McCann, an Irish joiner, married him on 7 October 1968 and they moved to Leeds, where they had three children of their own. The marriage failed in 1974 and Michael Bilton suggests that this was because Wilma 'couldn't settle, she hadn't the self-discipline to adapt to either marriage or motherhood. She liked her nights out. And she liked other men' (2003: 9). After Gerald left, Sonje—even though she was only nine years old—assumed many of the responsibilities of bringing up her siblings, as her mother went out on the town to earn her living. Indeed, on the morning that Wilma's body was found Sonje and her brother were discovered freezing cold at the local bus stop wearing their school coats over their pyjamas, hoping to meet their mother whom they thought might have caught an early bus home.

All of this was quickly evident to Dennis Hoban, head of Leeds CID, and as Bilton puts it, 'the fact that [Wilma] was a good-time girl would be a major complication' (2003: 5). Hoban needed to establish Wilma's movements on the night that she had been killed and this involved asking for witnesses to come forward. For various reasons some witnesses might not be willing to do so and

---

[2] There is of course the question of why Sutcliffe did not attack other women between 1969 and 1975, although, to quote Byford (1981: 6), 'It is highly improbable that the crimes in respect of which Sutcliffe has been charged and convicted are the only ones attributable to him'.

'to label a victim a prostitute in this situation was unhelpful. Experience showed that the public were somehow not surprised at what happened to call girls' (Bilton, 2003: 13) so photographs in the local papers concentrated on the four children that Wilma had left behind to evoke sympathy. Hoban, who was dubbed by the local newspapers 'the crime buster in the sheepskin coat', had at one stage 137 officers working on the McCann case, all of whom worked for a total of some 53,000 hours, calling at 5,000 houses and generating 538 witness statements (Bilton, 2003: 16). Even so, Sutcliffe was not apprehended and less than three months later the body of Emily Jackson was found.

Table 3.1 Assaults/murders of Peter Sutcliffe

Name	Date	Murder/Assault	Interview date
Rogulskyj	5 July 1975	Assault	
Smelt	15 August 1975	Assault	
McCann	30 October 1975	Murder	
Jackson	20 January 1976	Murder	
Claxton	9 May 1976	Assault	
Richardson	5/6 February 1977	Murder	
Atkinson	23 April 1977	Murder	
MacDonald	26 June 1977	Murder	
Long	10 July 1977	Assault	
Jordan	1 October 1977	Murder	2 November 1977; 8 November 1977
Moore	14 December 1977	Assault	
Pearson	21 January 1978	Murder	
Rytka	31 January 1978	Murder	
Millward	16/17 May 1978	Murder	13 August 1978; 23 November 1978
Whitaker	4/5 April 1979	Murder	29 July 1979
Leach	2 September 1979	Murder	23 October 1979; 13 January 1980; 30 January 1980; 7 February 1980
Walls	20/21 August 1980	Murder	
Bandara	24 September 1980	Assault	
Sykes	5 November 1980	Assault	
Hill	17 November 1980	Murder	

Source: Adapted from Byford (1981: 23).

Emily Jackson

Emily had been killed in a factory yard in Leeds. She had been hit over the head with a hammer, dragged to where her body was eventually found and then stabbed repeatedly with a Phillips screwdriver. Emily had died on her front, but Sutcliffe had turned her body over onto her back so that he could continue to stab her and in total there were 52 stab wounds found on her torso. Hoban linked these two murders immediately and tried to build up a picture of Emily's background so as to help him better identify her killer. Through her husband Sydney (who was originally a suspect), Hoban discovered that Emily seemingly had an 'insatiable sexual appetite' and that Sydney would often drive her to meet her clients. As Bilton puts it, all of this meant that when Hoban had to deal with the press he had to 'put the best possible gloss on the woman's private life' (2003: 26). Nonetheless, even with this gloss, the investigation didn't get very far and within a few months Marcella Claxton was savagely attacked in the city.

Marcella Claxton

Marcella was a 20 year-old woman from St Kitts who lived in the Chapeltown area of Leeds. She was an unemployed, single mother of two children and is described as having an IQ of 50. At the time of her attack she was three months pregnant and insisted to the police that she was not a prostitute. Sutcliffe had picked her up as she left a nightclub, but she had tried to hide from him. Thinking that he had left her alone, she emerged from her hiding place only to discover that Sutcliffe was still waiting and he then hit her on the back of her head with a hammer. She was knocked to the ground and Marcella pretended that she was unconscious. Sutcliffe masturbated over her and then he left. At this point Marcella half-crawled, half-dragged herself to a phone box and dialled 999. As she waited for the ambulance to arrive, Sutcliffe re-appeared—clearly trying to ensure that he had in fact killed her—but he was unable to find where Marcella had gone.

Marcella was eventually taken to Leeds General Infirmary where she had 52 stitches put in her head and lost the baby that she was carrying. Even so, she gave the police an excellent description of the white man who had attacked her, but the police refused to believe her. In fact they insisted that it was a black man who had assaulted her and not the white, bearded man that she described. Bilton suggests that 'the simple truth was that West Yorkshire police did not believe what Marcella Clacton was telling them' (2003: 92) and they even claimed that the description that she had given had been 'hopelessly inadequate' as a basis for rejecting her claim for criminal injuries compensation in 1978. Indeed, Marcella was only included in the list of Sutliffe's victims after Sutcliffe himself admitted to her attack after his arrest (Byford, 1981: 9).

Josephine Whitaker

Josephine Whitaker was born in 1959, the only daughter of Thelma and Trevor Whitaker. Two years later her parents separated and so Josephine lived with her mother at her grandparents' house in Halifax. Josephine was devoted to her grandparents and even after her mother re-married, she continued to visit them on a regular basis. On the night of 4 April 1979 Josephine was returning to her mother's house, having made one of her regular trips to her grandparents. On her return home she was attacked by Sutcliffe, who hit her twice on the back of the head. He then proceeded to stab her 21 times—nine on her front and 12 on her back. The post-mortem would later show that Sutcliffe had bitten Josephine's breast and that he had also stabbed her several times through the vagina. Sutcliffe himself described the attack in an interview with the police in the following way:

> I saw Josephine Whitaker walking up the street … and I caught up with her after a couple of minutes. I realised that she was not a prostitute but at that time I wasn't bothered I just wanted to kill a woman. When I caught up with her I started talking to her. I asked her if she had far to go. She said, 'It's quite a walk' … she started speaking to me about having just left her grandmother's and that she had considered staying there but had decided to walk home … We were approaching an open grassland area. She told me she normally took a short cut across the field. I said, 'You don't know who you can trust these days'. It sounds a bit evil now, there was I walking along with my hammer and a big Phillips screwdriver in my pocket ready to do the inevitable. We both started to walk diagonally across the grass field … I asked her what time it was on the clock tower which was to our right. She looked at the clock and told me what time it was. I forget the time she said … I lagged behind her pretending to look at the clock. I took my hammer out of my pocket and hit her on the back of the head twice. She fell down and made a loud groaning sound. To my horror I saw a figure moving along the main road from my right. I took hold of her by the ankles and dragged her face down away from the road further into the field. She was still moaning as I did this … I saw at least two figures walking along the path across the field [and] I forgot to mention that we passed a man walking a dog. We were within five feet of him. As these people were walking on the path she was still moaning loudly. I took my screwdriver. I remember I first pulled some of her clothing off. I was working like lightening and it [was] all a blur. I turned her over and stabbed her numerous times in the chest and stomach with the screwdriver. I was in a frenzy. (Bilton, 2003: 6883-685)

The murder of Josephine Whitaker should have been a turning point in the police investigation. As this testimony of Sutcliffe makes clear, there were a number of potential witnesses for the police to interview (one of whom walked past within five feet of Josephine and Sutcliffe) and new leads in relation to the bite marks, footprints left at the crime scene and witnesses who had seen a man with an unshaven appearance and a 'Jason King'[3] moustache, park his car in the vicinity. As his interview suggests, Sutcliffe himself was anxious about these potential witnesses, whom he clearly thought would hear Josephine moaning which was why he dragged her further into the field. More than this Josephine was an 'innocent woman', or as Byford (1981: 15) described her 'a respectable local girl,' rather than a woman who worked in prostitution. This had an impact on the investigation in two ways. Firstly, there was an exceptional public response to the Whitaker murder and within a few days there had been over 1,000 calls to the police from concerned members of the public who had information to share. Secondly, there was a change of attitude amongst the police themselves. For, as one female detective working on the case told Bilton, 'before that [murder] I just thought, well, he seems to be hanging around prostitutes, I'm OK, but after that one, I thought no one was safe' (2003: 324).

However, yet again there was little movement in the investigation and in June—some two months after Josephine had been murdered—a tape was sent to the police by a man claiming to be 'Jack the Ripper', which undoubtedly seems to have thrown the police off their tracks. Several letters purportedly from 'Jack the Ripper' had previously been sent to the police and then, for various reasons, detectives set great store by the tape being genuine. However, we now know that the tape had in fact been sent by 23-year-old John Humble, who in March 2006 admitted to four counts of perverting the course of justice by sending three letters and the tape to the police, and who as a result was sentenced to eight years imprisonment. In court Humble was described as a 'hopeless alcoholic', who had led a 'spectacularly inadequate life' (*Guardian*, 22 March 2006).

This tape and what it may have done to the police investigation notwithstanding, it is instructive to look at the descriptions of the women that are used by the police and how these descriptions might have influenced the way that their murders were investigated. Wilma, for example, is described as having no 'self-discipline', liking her nights out and liking her men; Emily's 'insatiable sexual appetite' is highlighted, as are her marital arrangements; and poor Marcella—who heroically survived a vicious attack and gave the police a perfectly good description of Sutcliffe—is simply not believed by detectives, who continually tried to insist that she was attacked by a black man, rather than the white man that she remembered. There seems little doubt that her gender and her ethnicity meant that the police were less than sympathetic to Marcella. So too detectives seem to have presumed that because of these women's backgrounds in prostitution (although this is denied by Marcella), male violence was an occupational hazard that they had to face. As a result they believed that a gloss had to be put on the victims' private lives, so as to appeal to a public whom they

---

[3] *Jason King* was a TV spin-off from another TV series called *Department S*. Peter Wyngarde played the flamboyant, eponymous detective. The series ran from September 1971 to April 1972.

thought would not be surprised by what happened to women involved in prostitution, or sympathetic to their plight. These were 'bad woman'—single mothers, who lacked self-discipline, with insatiable sexual appetites and who thus could be held morally responsible for what happened to them. In short it was their own fault that they were murdered.

On the other hand Josephine Whitaker was 'a respectable local girl' and whilst the use of the word 'respectable' is clear and obvious in comparison with those words that are used to describe Wilma, Emily and Marcella, it is also interesting to note the word 'local'. 'Local' implies belonging to the community: being part of 'us', rather than belonging to an alien 'other'—like women involved in prostitution, who might be in the community, but not of it. As such, their deaths—like prostitution itself—were something to 'turn a blind eye' to: deaths to ignore and to forget. Josephine was therefore different and Byford certainly believed that her respectability prompted the huge public response to her murder. Here too we should also note that whilst we discover the numbers of police officers, man-hours, houses that were visited or witness statements that were generated in Wilma's case, it is the number of telephone calls from members of the public that are revealed when Josephine's murder is discussed. What does this tell us? Most obviously that there were fewer calls from the public in response to Wilma's death—despite all this police manpower being devoted to uncovering her killer.

Not that any of this mattered to Sutcliffe. For, as he told his police interviewers, whilst he recognised that Josephine was not involved in prostitution, by that stage he 'just wanted to kill a woman'. As such her life was ended in exactly the same manner as Wilma's and Emily's, by this 'unremarkable young man', in a local culture of 'birds and booze', where assaulting a woman was an everyday event. Sutcliffe made no moral judgement when he chose to kill Josephine Whitaker; she was simply vulnerable because of her gender. He could victimise her in exactly the same way that he had victimised Wilma, Emily and Marcella.

What had changed was that whereas previously he had only gained access to his victims because of their involvement in prostitution, he was now confident enough as a killer to feel that he could gain access to other women too. In short, he had worked out how to incapacitate his victims and then how to kill them, and he must have by that stage have begun to think that, no matter which women he killed or attacked, he was not going to be caught. Indeed it is interesting to note that none of his remaining victims were women involved in prostitution. For example, his next victims were: Barbara Leach, a humanities and economics student at the University of Bradford, in September 1979; Marguerite Wells, a civil servant in Leeds, whom Sutcliffe murdered in August 1980; Uphadya Bandara, a doctor from Singapore, who was attacked in

September 1980; Teresa Sykes, who was also attacked; and finally Jacqueline Hill—Sutcliffe's last murder victim, whom he killed in November 1980, only days after attacking Teresa. Jacqueline was a social worker and a Sunday School teacher, and on the night that she was killed was returning from a seminar organized by the Probation Service.

Here it might be argued that all of this is unfair to the police, who were merely reflecting the broader patriarchal culture in which they worked; a culture that both used, but did not value women generally and certainly did not value women involved in prostitution. Indeed in some ways this is why we are told about the number of officers, police 'manhours' and witness statements that were involved. This is in effect special pleading: trying to convince us that it was the public who were reluctant to become involved because of what Sutcliffe's victims did, and that it was not police incompetence or lack of effort which had failed to find the killer.

However, to pursue this further we need to examine more closely the police investigation itself and in particular consider the number of times that Sutcliffe was interviewed and ask how he was able to escape detection for so long. For, whilst much of the debate about the police investigation of Sutcliffe has in the past centred on the administration of the investigation—whether a computer would have helped, the use of the Major Incident Room, how records were stored and cross-referenced (or not), whether one local force shared enough information with other forces interested in the case and so forth, no attempt has been made to view the police handling of the Sutcliffe case through the lens of 'cop culture'. In doing so we are also helped by remembering that, over a decade later, when the police had all the advantages of numerous technological developments and were much more experienced in sharing information, the policing failures in relation to the investigation of the murder of the black teenager Stephen Lawrence in April 1993 were related to the police's 'institutional racism', rather than to administrative failures or lack of access to a computer (Macpherson, 1999).

INTERVIEWS, INTERVIEWS, INTERVIEWS

Within the ongoing police investigation between 1975 and 1981 Sutcliffe was interviewed nine times and eleven times in total.[4] For ease of reference I attach the dates of these interviews and the names of the interviewing officers in *Table 3.2*, which should be cross-referenced with the first table in this chapter (*Table 3.1*).

---

[4] Sutcliffe was also interviewed on 15 October 1975 for the theft of tyres and on 25 June 1980 for drink/driving.

Table 3.2: Police interviews with Peter Sutcliffe

Number, date and reason	Interviewers and decision
1. 2 November 1977/£5 note	DC Howard — further inquiries
2. 8 November 1977/follow up	DCs L Smith and Rayne — filed; knew of **1**
3. 13 August 1978/cross area sightings	DC P Smith — further inquiries; knew of **2** and **3**
4. 23 November 1978/follow up	DCs P Smith and Bradshaw — further inquiries; knew of **1, 2** and **3**
5. 29 July 1979/triple area sightings	DCs Laptew and Greenwood — filed; did not know of **1, 2, 3,** or **4**
6. 23 October 1979/follow up	DCs Vickerman and Eland — filed; knew of **1, 2, 3** and **4**
7. 13 January 1980/£5 note	DS Boot and DC Bell — further inquiries; knew of **1** and **2**
8. 30 January 1980/follow up	DCs McAlister and McCrone — further inquiries; knew of **1, 2, 3, 4, 6** and **7**
9. 7 February 1980/follow up	DCs Jackson and Harrison — filed; knew of **1, 2, 3, 4, 6, 7** and **8**

Source: Adapted from Byford, (1981: 23 and 69).

Using the time parameters of this table, Sutcliffe was interviewed on average once every four-and-a-half months during the investigation. He was interviewed twice each year in 1977, 1978, 1979 and three times during 1980. On one occasion — during 1977 — he was interviewed twice within the space of six days and in 1980 twice within eight days. On no occasion was he arrested as a result of these interviews, or taken to a police station for further questioning and indeed none of these interviews would ultimately form the basis for his eventual arrest.[5]

Within this table I have identified the three main reasons for these interviews, based on the leads that police were using to catch Sutcliffe. Thus, for example, he was initially interviewed about a £5 note that was discovered in a secret compartment of the handbag of Jean Jordan who was murdered on 1 October 1977. It was presumed, correctly, that this was the payment from the killer for sexual services. This was a significant find and it was also clear that Jean's killer had returned a week or so later to the undiscovered body to see if he could retrieve the note. What was so significant about the note was that it was

---

[5] Even Sutcliffe's arrest on 2 January 1981 was as much a matter of luck as judgement. Interestingly, he turned his attention once more to women involved in prostitution — this time in Sheffield. He was arrested with a prostitute in his car and police became suspicious when they realised that the car had false number plates. Before being taken back to the police station Sutcliffe was able to hide the hammer that he would have killed with and this was not recovered until the following day (for an account of Sutcliffe's arrest see Bilton, 2003, pp. 462-71).

one of a brand new batch of £5 notes and the police were able to determine from the Bank of England that this batch had been delivered to branches of The Midland Bank in Manningham, Shipley and Bingley. Some 34 local firms, employing 6,000 people, used these branches to pay their staff's wages, including a local firm of engineers called T & WH Clark (Holdings), who employed Sutcliffe.

The other police interviews of Sutcliffe related to 'cross area sightings', or 'triple area sightings', which some police dubbed the 'punter's index'. In other words, Sutcliffe's car (which he changed regularly) had been spotted cruising the red light areas of Leeds and Bradford and later the red light areas of Manchester, Leeds and Bradford. So, for example, between 19 June and 7 July 1978 Sutcliffe's red Ford Corsair had been seen on seven occasions—six times in the red light area of Bradford and once in the red light area of Leeds. Between 26 June and 22 November 1978 his black Sunbeam Rapier had been seen passing through Bradford's red light area 36 times, Leeds's red light area twice and then on 22 February 1979 he was spotted on Moss Side, in Manchester. By that time he had been spotted on a further three occasions in Leeds and Bradford, thus making Sutcliffe a 'triple area sighting' and a potential, if not a prime suspect.

Of note, the 'cross area sightings' and 'triple area sightings' were developed because so many cars were being logged in each individual red light area. In other words, there were so many men using women involved in prostitution that the police simply couldn't cope with the numbers of cars that they were spotting. In one night in Manchester, for example, 4,000 cars were sighted and logged. One female police sergeant described how:

> It really hit me how many men were involved with prostitutes ... after a fortnight there were so many actions coming through I remember thinking: 'Surely there cannot be that many men who need to go to a prostitute?' I couldn't believe the numbers of men doing it. (Quoted in Bilton, 2003: 307)

All of this helps us to contextualise the reaction to Sutcliffe's first assault on a woman in 1969, which was dismissed as 'typical of a local culture of birds and booze'.

DC Howard conducted Sutcliffe's first police interview within the ongoing investigation on 2 November 1977, at Sutcliffe's home in Bradford, which he shared with his wife Sonia. Sutcliffe was unable to produce any of the £5 notes that he had received in his September 29 wage packet—a few days before Jean Jordan had been murdered on October 1. Further he suggested to DC Howard that he had been at home with Sonia on the night of October 1, and on October 9 (when the killer had returned to Jean's as yet undiscovered body) he had been at a house-warming party. Sonia corroborated this version of events, but failed to mention that her husband had driven relatives home after the house-warming and was gone for some time. Surprisingly, DC Howard noted in his report that Sutcliffe did not own a car (all details are taken from Byford, 1981: 67-80).

A follow-up interview was conducted six days later by DCs Smith and Rayne when Sutcliffe's alibi for October 9 was strengthened by his mother who confirmed that they had all been at a house-warming party. The officers also discovered that Sutcliffe owned a red Ford Corsair but—despite being ordered to do so they did not examine the car, Sutcliffe's garage or his house. Byford is especially critical of all this and suggests that this interview was superficial, not at all probing and that the officers seemed to accept every answer at face value. He suggests that had the officers dug a little deeper, they would have broken Sutcliffe's alibi for 9 October and had they examined his car they would have discovered that it had on it 'similar tyres to those which were left at the Richardson[6] scene' (Byford, 1981: 72). Byford concludes that the interviewing officers' attitudes were 'not as positive as [they] should have been'; that they 'failed to comply with their instructions'; and, that the interview was a 'lost opportunity' (Byford, 1981: 72).

Sutcliffe was interviewed again some eight months later, after the 'punter's index' identified his Ford Corsair in the red light areas of Bradford and Leeds. However, by the time he came to be interviewed he had changed his car to a Sunbeam Rapier, which too had been sighted in the red light area of Bradford, although DC P Smith, the interviewing officer, was unaware of this fact. When DC Smith arrived at the Sutcliffe home on 13 August 1978—some four months after Vera Millward had been murdered in Manchester, he found Sutcliffe busy decorating the kitchen. Sutcliffe was unable to account for his movements on the night that Vera had been murdered, but Sonia suggested to DC Smith that her husband 'would have come home from work and stayed with her all evening' (Byford, 1981: 73). When she left the room to make some tea, DC Smith asked Sutcliffe if he used prostitutes, but this was strenuously denied. So too Sutcliffe seems to have satisfied DC Smith that his car had been sighted merely because the red light area was on the route to his place of work. Once again neither Sutcliffe's home, garage nor car was searched and Byford concludes that 'not unreasonably Constable Smith accepted that the Sutcliffes were a normal young couple who were anxious to improve their home and putting most of their effort into doing so' (1981: 73).

A follow-up interview was belatedly conducted, but it was 'treated as a matter of simple routine to the extent that DC Bradshaw who accompanied DC

---

[6] Irene Richardson was murdered by Sutcliffe on 5 February 1977 on a playing field in Leeds. She had been struck over the head with a hammer and then her body had been exposed and slashed with a knife. Tyres marks were left at the scene of the crime and a 'tracking inquiry' was mounted to identify the car that had been used. Fifty-one different vehicle models were identified, with 53,000 registered owners in the West Yorkshire area—including Sutcliffe and his Ford Corsair. Whilst 20,000 owners were interviewed, Sutcliffe was never seen.

Smith on his visit to Sutcliffe's home did not even get out of the police vehicle' (Byford, 1981: 74).

Sutcliffe was next interviewed as part of the 'triple area sightings' on 29 July 1979, given that his Sunbeam Rapier had been seen in the red light areas of Bradford, Leeds and Manchester. He was interviewed by DCs Laptew and Greenwood, who were unaware that he had previously been interviewed. This interview lasted over two hours and DCs Laptew and Greenwood were not satisfied with many of the answers that Sutcliffe had given. For example, they felt that his alibi was loose for the sightings of his car in Bradford and Leeds; they were unhappy that he had denied the positive sighting of his car in Manchester; they were aware that he resembled some of the photofits that had been provided by survivors of his attacks; and that he wore the same size of shoes as the footprints found at the sight of Josephine Whitaker's murder.

The officers did not arrest Sutcliffe, but rather submitted a comprehensive report about their misgivings to Inspector Slocombe. However, the inspector reported that he could not remember receiving this report and Byford, with great restraint, concludes:

> Despite the most probing investigation it has not been possible to trace what happened to Constable Laptew's report after he submitted it ... I cannot help concluding that one or other of the senior officers involved in these events is now loathe to accept responsibility for what in effect was a serious error of judgement.
> (Byford, 1981: 77)

In effect Laptew's report was simply filed, thus requiring 'no further action'.

The remaining four interviews with Sutcliffe within the ongoing police investigation were, in effect, follow-up interviews of the 'cross area sightings', or of the £5 note interviews. Indeed, whilst several of the detectives involved remained suspicious of Sutcliffe—thus ensuring that he was never ruled out of the inquiry—these follow-up interviews were often perfunctory, with the last two being held at his place of work. Overall Byford concludes that Sutcliffe should have been arrested as a result of these interviews and quotes Ian Fleming's 'Goldfinger': 'Once is happenstance. Twice is coincidence. The third time is enemy action.' He continues, 'if this concept had been applied to the record of Sutcliffe's association with the Ripper inquiry there were clearly grounds for him to be placed in the 'suspect' category' (Byford, 1981: 83). He suggests that those interviewing Sutcliffe had failed to take a positive line and pursue his lies, and that this was as a result of their being inadequately briefed due to being 'bogged down in routine paperwork' which meant that they had little time to read files properly.

However, all of this seems a little charitable to those involved with the Sutcliffe investigation. Quite apart from the fact that Laptew's report was simply 'filed' requiring no further action, we should also take into account that in September 1978 two detectives on the case were forced to resign and 13 others were subjected to internal disciplinary procedures, as a result of not completing the tasks assigned to them and making false statements that they had (Byford, 1981: 72). Why should this be so? Bilton suggests that we should remember that:

> even before the Ripper attacks, the attitude of the police in the 1970s towards violence against prostitutes was hugely ambivalent … police officers felt that it was hard enough keeping the peace and controlling crime at the best of times, without women putting themselves in harm's way by going with men with money and making themselves vulnerable. (Bilton, 2003: 201)

He does not develop this insight further, nor seek to understand how 'vulnerability' is created by the wider cultural climate of 'booze and birds' and the failures of the police to provide appropriate professional policing to women involved in prostitution. Instead he simply accepts that police ambivalence towards women in prostitution exists and that their vulnerability is their own responsibility. How widespread was this ambivalence? Here we need to consider the issue of 'cop culture'.

'COP CULTURE'

Robert Reiner has been at the forefront of academic attempts in this country to try to understand if there is a distinct, identifiable set of beliefs and assumptions that determines how the police will behave operationally in the streets or whilst conducting investigations. He suggests that 'an understanding of how police officers see the social world and their role in it—"cop culture"—is crucial to an analysis of what they do and their broader political function' (Reiner, 1992: 107). In other words, cop culture shapes police practice. Some academics, such as Waddington (1999), deny this 'conceptual bridge' of saying and doing and are more 'appreciative' of cop culture (which is usually seen as a 'bad thing'). However others have reminded us that, especially given the great discretionary powers that the police have over individuals or in shaping investigations, it is not unreasonable to presume that what police officers say and how they socialise will mould their responses to what they find in the streets or how they attempt to solve problems (see, for example, Wilson, Ashton and Sharp (2001)).

Based on extensive interviews with various police officers of different ranks and in different police force areas, Reiner suggests that the main characteristics of cop culture are:

- mission-action-cynicism-pessimism;
- suspicion;

- isolation/solidarity;
- conservatism;
- machismo;
- prejudice; and
- pragmatism.

Given the importance of these characteristics to an understanding of cop culture and the impact that they might have had on how the Yorkshire Ripper investigation was conducted (see also *Chapter 4*), I will spend a little time outlining Reiner's argument.

Reiner suggests that the central characteristic of cop culture is a sense of 'mission'. In other words that being a police officer is not simply just another job, but one that has a worthwhile purpose of protecting the weak from the predatory. The police are an indispensable 'thin blue line' protecting society and this inevitably means that they have on occasions to take action. Indeed, some police officers might want to take rather more action than is often necessary and will pursue exciting and thrill-seeking activities, rather than repetitive, mundane or boring police tasks, such as filling in paperwork. Over time, Reiner suggests, police officers will become more cynical and pessimistic—they have 'seen it all before', with each new development in society seen in almost apocalyptic terms, with the potential to destroy the moral world that has shaped the sense of mission that the police have developed.

So too officers are trained to be suspicious, but the worry here is that this suspicion can lead to stereotyping potential offenders, which in turn means that this stereotyping becomes a self-fulfilling prophecy. For example, a disproportionate number of young black men get stopped and searched in the streets, leading to more young black men being arrested, which in turn 'confirms' the stereotype that more young black men are offenders than young white men. Indeed, given that police officers are often socially isolated there is little likelihood that they will encounter young black men who play the piano, read books or who might wish to become police officers themselves. Similarly the need to rely on one's colleagues in a 'tight spot' means that a great deal of internal solidarity exists, which does little to erode their sense of isolation from other members of society that police officers might encounter.

Of note, Reiner also suggests that police officers tend to be conservative both politically and morally and thus culturally would distrust those groups—such as gay men and prostitutes—which might be seen as challenging conventional morality. However, this does not mean that cop culture is puritanical. Rather, it is dominated by what Reiner describes as 'old fashioned machismo', where there are high levels of stress, drinking and divorce. Based on his own research from Bristol in the early 1970s, Reiner also suggests that the police were hostile to and suspicious of black people, an issue that was again to come to the fore with the Macpherson Inquiry into the murder of the black teenager Stephen Lawrence in April 1993.

The last aspect of cop culture that Reiner draws attention to is pragmatism. By this he means the simple desire that a police officer has to get through the day as easily as possible. A police officer does not want fuss—especially paperwork—and would rather stress the practical, 'no-nonsense' aspects of the job. Reiner describes this as 'conceptual conservatism' (1992: 128), given that this pragmatism often masks an atheoretical culture that dislikes research, innovation and change.

Before considering how these aspects of cop culture might have impacted on the Yorkshire Ripper investigation, it is also worth briefly mentioning some of the conclusions of Sir William Macpherson, who investigated how the police handled their investigation into the murder of Stephen Lawrence. These conclusions are of relevance for they reveal—many years after the Byford Inquiry—how the police might have reacted to the changes recommended by Byford and, more crucially, how several aspects of cop culture affected the policing of murder. Macpherson concluded that the police investigation was 'marred by a combination of professional incompetence, institutional racism and a failure of leadership by senior officers, (1999: para 46.1). Chief amongst his conclusions was that the police were 'institutionally racist' and that institutional racism consisted of:

> The collective failure of an organization to provide an appropriate and professional service to people because of their colour, culture, or ethnic origin. It can be detected in processes, attitudes and behaviour which amount to discrimination through unwitting prejudice, ignorance, thoughtlessness and racist stereotyping which disadvantage minority ethnic people. (Macpherson, 1999: para 46.25)

In this phrase 'processes, attitudes and behaviour' we can begin to see how there is a 'conceptual bridge' between 'saying' or thinking and discrimination in the 'doing' of police work with some groups, based on their 'colour, culture, or ethnic origin'. This is one of the most important contributions to recent analyses of policing and allied with what we know about cop culture, would also seem to allow us to re-interpret aspects of the police investigation into the Yorkshire Ripper.

CREATING VULNERABILITY THROUGH POLICING

Although Peter Sutcliffe was interviewed nine times during the ongoing Yorkshire Ripper police investigation, he was never seen as a suspect as a result of these interviews and was never arrested. Some of the interviews were at best perfunctory and Byford has drawn attention to the failure of several officers to carry them out in a way that was 'positive' and also their consistent failure to search—as had been requested by senior officers—Sutcliffe's house, garage or car. Indeed, the first officer who interviewed Sutcliffe incorrectly thought that he did not have a car at all and one officer, DC Bradshaw, did not even bother to get out of his police car and accompany his partner for a follow-up interview concerning Sutcliffe's identification in the 'cross area sightings'.

In all of this we might see the pragmatism that Reiner has identified; a desire to get through the day as easily as possible, with the minimum of fuss and paperwork. These interviews were not by any stretch of the imagination about 'action', but were rather routine, mundane and repetitive. Here too we should also remember that some officers saw their interviewing and administrative responsibilities so negatively that they fraudulently claimed that they had completed them when they had not and that two detectives were forced to resign as a consequence.

The failure to act upon the Laptew report is also worth considering, especially as Byford is at his most critical when trying to understand why this was simply filed requiring no further action. Look again at his conclusion. He suggests that: 'one or other of the senior officers involved in these events is now loathe to accept responsibility for what in effect was a serious error of judgement' (Byford, 1981: 77). In all of this there are echoes of Macpherson's 'failure of leadership of senior officers' in the Lawrence investigation, but there is more going on here too. For example, we need to note that Byford came to this conclusion after the 'most probing investigation' and here we can again detect another aspect of cop culture—solidarity in the face of adversity; of one police officer looking after another in a 'tight spot'. Even HM Inspector of Constabulary cannot get to the bottom of how Laptew's report came to be ignored and who might have been responsible. One is tempted to conclude that if Byford is unable to pierce this solidarity, then there is little likelihood that anyone else would be more successful.

Perhaps the most obvious examples of cop culture within the interviewing process relate to the opinions and attitudes that various officers formed about Sutcliffe and his wife, and how these can be used to throw further light onto what Bilton has described as police 'ambivalence' towards violence against women involved in prostitution. Thus, for example, the conservatism that Reiner identifies as a defining characteristic of cop culture, can be glimpsed in Byford's acceptance of DC Smith's conclusion that the Sutcliffes were a 'normal young couple who were anxious to improve their house and were putting most of their effort into doing so' (1981: 73), after DC Smith had discovered Sutcliffe at home decorating the kitchen. The description 'normal' is crucial here, for it suggests that in the Sutcliffes DC Smith saw something of himself and of his own moral order and values. The Sutcliffes were like him and people that he knew and as a result he could not conceive that he was in the presence of a serial killer. So, he finds a way to get Sonia Sutcliffe out of the room—to make tea (a woman's responsibility)—and then, man-to-man, asks Sutcliffe if he has ever 'used' prostitutes. This is of course denied and the denial accepted, despite the fact that Sutlciffe's car had been repeatedly seen cruising red light areas in two (and later three) cities.

It is also worth noting that the antonym of 'normal' is 'abnormal', unusual, or out of the ordinary. If we think about this in relation to gender then it is interesting to speculate what was it that was seen by these officers as normal behaviour for men and for women. Was it normal for men to use women involved in prostitution? Was it abnormal for women to become involved in prostitution? We have already gained some insight into this latter question by noting how Josephine Whitaker was described after her murder as a 'respectable local girl' and how this description can be compared with those of other victims that Sutcliffe murdered. In relation to the first question we might again use another of Reiner's cop culture characteristics—machismo—to think once more about how Sutcliffe's very first assault was dismissed as typical of a 'local culture of birds and booze'.

All of this seems important. For, if these interviews had been conducted in a more professional—Byford uses the word 'positive'—manner, then there is little doubt that Sutcliffe would have been viewed as a suspect and his alibis uncovered as lies. The interviews reveal how vulnerability can be created by the police failing to provide an 'appropriate and professional service to people'—on this occasion to women involved in prostitution. Thus these women's 'vulnerability' was not their own, personal responsibility—putting themselves in harm's way as Bilton puts it—but rather the responsibility of the police who collectively failed to police appropriately; collectively failed to deliver a service to one group within the community; and collectively failed to give to these women the protection of the state. And in the same way that stereotyping young black men as being involved in crime can become a self-fulfilling prophecy, so too accepting that violence and prostitution go hand in glove means that when violence is used against women who are involved in prostitution no one especially the police— finds that unusual or unexpected.

We can only speculate how Sutcliffe interpreted these nine police interviews—it was not something that was discussed after he was arrested. However, it would seem fair to conclude that, just like Harold Shipman, by escaping capture for as long as he did that he was able to perfect the way that he killed and gain the confidence that he needed to kill and kill again. It is not too fanciful to suggest that if Sutcliffe had been arrested after the first or second interviews related to the £5 note inquiry several of his victims would still be alive today and several others would not have been attacked. Shipman's victims died because there was and is inadequate social protection for the elderly, whereas Sutcliffe's victims died because they had inadequate police protection.

Over the course of our time-frame and especially towards the end of it, there have been various attempts to change attitudes towards women involved in prostitution (and see the *Conclusion* for a description of some recent serial murders of young women involved in prostitution in Ipswich). In particular of late in our social policy there has been a move to see women—especially young women (and increasingly also young men)—who are involved in prostitution as victims and to offer them protection, support and a way out of prostitution (see, for example, Home Office, 2004), rather than simply to prosecute them. Increasingly there has been a recognition that our social policy needs to alleviate the circumstances which make young people vulnerable to exploitation and coercion into prostitution and that many of those people who end up working on the streets suffer from the same catalogue of issues—physical and sexual abuse within their families, homelessness, poor school attendance and problematic drug use.

But there are continuities over the time-frame too and for some women prostitution remains a 'survival strategy' (Home Office, 2004: 14) whereby simple economic necessity and the seemingly insatiable demand for sexual services guarantee that there is money to be made (and see also *Chapter 5*). However, perhaps the greatest continuity of all remains our ambivalence towards women involved in prostitution and thus a corresponding lack of interest when they are victimised. After all Natalie Pearman's killer is still at large, but does anyone seriously doubt that her place has long since been taken by other young women working outside The Ferry Boat?

CHAPTER 4

Gay Men

CHAPTER 4

Gay Men

Colin wanted to rid the world of those sick perverts. He was sickened by what they get up to behind closed doors and decided that it was his mission to wipe them out. He did what he did and makes no apologies for it. It is the sado-masochists, the really sick ones, he cannot stand.

(Step-father of Colin Ireland speaking after his conviction, quoted in Gekoski (1998: 245))

David Morley was known to his friends as 'Cinders'. Originally from the West Midlands he had moved down to London to find work in the 1980s and in doing so managed to secure for himself a series of bar jobs. He was good at what he did and eventually by 2004 had reached a managerial position within the brewery where he worked. On the night of 31 October 2004 David was sitting on a bench with his friend Alastair Whitehead, near the Royal Festival Hall on the South Bank in London. The area is close to several gay entertainment venues, such as Heaven nightclub, which is located under Charing Cross station.

As they sat, the pair were approached by three young men and a 15-year-old girl who liked to be known by her graffiti tag—'Zobbs'. As Zobbs moved towards David she said, 'We're doing a documentary on happy slapping.[1] Pose for the camera.' This request seems to have been the signal for the four to launch a sustained attack on David and Alastair, with David in particular bearing the full force of the assault and who, as a result sustained 44 impact injuries and a ruptured spleen. Alastair watched as Zobbs landed the final kicks to his friend's head—'She kicked him like you would kick a football or rugby ball, just swinging her right foot back and kicking him really hard on the head. She did that two or three times, maybe more' (all quotes taken from various reports in *The Guardian,* 2 November 2004; 6 November 2004; and 15 December 2005).

David was to die from his injuries and whilst we do not know for certain if the motive for the attack on him that night related to his sexuality—the four had assaulted six other people within the hour before they encountered David and Alastair—we do know that David's sexuality had brought him into contact with violence five years previously in 1999, when he had been working as a barman at The Admiral Duncan public house in Old Compton Street, Soho in London. It was there at about half past six on April 30—with drinkers spilling out from the pub onto the pavement to catch the last of the sun and with most of them looking forward to the impending bank holiday weekend—that David Copeland planted

---

[1] 'Happy slapping' is a journalistic or media tag given to inter-personal attacks which are filmed on the perpetrator's camera phone and which are then viewed later or, indeed, placed on the internet.

a bomb that killed three people and injured over 60 others. Copeland, a member of the British National Party (BNP), had only weeks previously planted bombs in Brixton, south London and Brick Lane, north London in the hope of starting a race war and when that had failed he turned his murderous attention on gay men and women. He was later to claim that he did all of this because he was obsessed with 'being famous' (see *The Guardian*, 1 July 2000), but in any event David Morley survived this attack and then helped to distribute a poster that appeared up and down Old Compton Street and throughout Soho in the wake of the bombing. On it was a simple message—'They Can't Kill Us All'—although eventually Zobbs and her friends did manage to kill David.

David Copeland is not in our list of British serial killers and nor is David Morley one their 326 victims. However, each of their stories is emblematic of the violence that has been perpetrated against gay people in this country over our time-frame, whether within the 'inclusive society' of the early 1960s, when homosexuality was still illegal, or during the 'exclusive society' period, when civil partnerships between gay men and women are common, and when gay people have generally become more visible, influential and powerful. Yet homophobia—'the last acceptable prejudice'—persists and this chapter is concerned with how this homophobia has facilitated the deaths of large numbers of gay men at the hands of four British serial killers (two of whom are themselves gay).

The chapter takes as its focus the victims of Dennis Nilsen, Peter Moore, Colin Ireland and the very first British serial killer in our time-frame—Michael Copeland. Like the previous chapter, it also considers 'cop culture' and how this might have contributed towards the vulnerability of gay men. As such it uses primary research conducted in 2003-2004 which sought to evaluate a policing initiative in Birmingham called 'The Pink Shield Project'. I start by defining homophobia and in particular attempt to use the idea of the growing 'visibility' of the gay community, to see how this might—or might not—have created the circumstances in which gay people are less likely to become the victims of homophobic violence.

HOMOPHOBIA—'THE LAST ACCEPTABLE PREJUDICE'

Byrne Fone (2000: 3) defines homophobia in quite simple terms. For him it is 'antipathy towards them [homosexuals]—and condemnation, loathing, fear and proscription of homosexual behaviour,' and he goes on to describe homophobia as being 'perhaps the last acceptable prejudice.' The term 'homophobia' was first used in the 1960s and popularised by George Weinberg in the 1970s (Weinberg,

1972). It is based on the perception that homosexuals and homosexuality disrupt the gender and sexual order supposedly established by 'natural law'; therefore homosexuality can be seen as subverting the social, ethical, political, legal and moral order of any society. Fone also notes that homophobia can equally be found within the gay community, which he suggests might be a result of gay people internalising the lessons of a homophobic society—an insight that might be helpful to remember when considering the cases of Peter Moore and, especially, Dennis Nilsen (Fone, 2000: 6).

Whilst not disagreeing with this basic definition, Gail Mason (2002) notes that we should guard against individualising and privatising homophobia, and argues that individual acts of violence against gay men and women cannot be 'separated from the heterosexualist culture within which they are situated' (2002: 6). Indeed, basing her observations on primary research with lesbians in Australia, Mason suggests that the 'normality' of heterosexuality and the 'abnormality' of homosexuality emerged in the nineteenth-century as more and more people became visible, then 'diagnosed and labelled' (2002: 23). She further argues that as more and more gay people refuse to conceal their homosexuality and thus become more visible, homophobic violence is facilitated by this growing visibility and as a consequence gay people have to manage violence through 'spaces, situations and individuals'. As such she argues that gay people produce 'safety maps'—an ever changing personalised, yet shared 'matrix of attributes and relations that individuals employ to make their way in public and private space' (Mason, 2002: 83). In short managing visibility is for Mason the key to managing homophobic violence.

COLIN IRELAND AND MICHAEL COPELAND

Mason's observations about visibility and how gay people use safety maps to manage homophobic violence are of interest in thinking about the experiences of the gay men who are described in this chapter. However, I also employ the opposite of visibility—invisibility—as a way of understanding the numbers of gay men who have fallen victim to serial killers during our time-frame. After all, as the quote from Colin Ireland's step-father at the start of this chapter reveals, Ireland was just as interested (albeit 'sickened') by what happened 'behind closed doors'—which obviously was not visible—and he thus had had to learn and then adopt the symbols of a largely hidden sub-culture of sado-masochism so as to be able to gain access to his victims. (So too David Copeland had to 'go behind the doors' of The Admiral Duncan to plant his bomb, despite the fact that this pub may have been part of the safety map of many gay men living in London.)

Thus Ireland's violence was as much about invisibility as it was about visibility and it is of note that he had eventually to give himself up to the police. Here it is tempting to see the act of giving himself up as another exaggerated form of invisibility, for the police's inability to catch him is suggestive of the invisibility of the victims of homophobic violence more generally. In fact Ireland believed that the police were indifferent to the murders that he had committed because of the sexuality of his victims and, as he said to them on the telephone after he had killed four men, 'Doesn't the death of a homosexual man mean anything?' (quoted in Gekoski, 1998: 237-238).

Colin Ireland

City of Angels—a detective *film-noir* spoof set in 1940s Los Angeles, USA won the Tony award for best musical in 1990. The show's success on Broadway meant that it was not long before it transferred to London's West End and when it did Peter Walker, a 45-year-old choreographer, got a job on the musical as assistant director. Peter was gay and made no secret of the fact that he was interested in sado-masochism (S&M). He preferred a submissive role. He was also a regular in The Coleherne pub, situated on the Brompton Road in West London.

On the night of 8 March 1993 Peter was in The Coleherne, as was Colin Ireland, although they did not know each other. Peter seems to have accidentally spilled some drink over Ireland and then—given his interests and the fact that Ireland was posing as a 'top'[2]—begged to be chastised. Ireland and Peter returned to the latter's flat where he was tied up and gagged using knotted condoms. Ireland then proceeded to beat Peter with his fists, a dog lead and a belt, before finally producing a plastic bag which he placed over Peter's head to suffocate him. After he was dead, Ireland burnt Peter's pubic hair—he was curious, he later told the police as to how it would smell—and then proceeded to look through Peter's things. In doing so he discovered that Peter was HIV positive and, as his defence barrister was later to explain in court, this incensed Ireland. So he placed condoms in Peter's mouth so as to further humiliate him after death, another up his nostrils and then positioned two teddy bears on the bed in a sexual position (all details taken from Gekoski, 1998: 230-3).

Ireland—who seems to have been an avid reader of true crime novels and FBI manuals, and who may have been influenced by Robert Ressler's (1992) book *Whoever Fights Monsters,* carefully ensured that he did not leave any forensic evidence in Peter's flat that might have connected him to the murder. Indeed, it may be that Ireland had carefully selected his victims so that he could 'become' a serial killer and in doing so gain fame or notoriety (see, for example, the account in *The Times*, 21 December 1993). So too in Ireland's murders there is an echo of

---

[2] A 'top' is the dominant partner in an S&M relationship.

Leyton's 'homicidal protest' (*Chapter 1*)—a theme taken up later, given that he was killing victims who might be seen as members of the middle classes.

However, whatever Ireland's motivation, he was to kill again two months later. This time, again using The Coleherne as his base, he targeted 37-year-old librarian Christopher Dunn, who like Peter was interested in S&M. The pair returned to Christopher's flat in Wealdstone, where Ireland tied him up and then beat him, before suffocating him by stuffing pieces of cloth into his mouth.

Christopher's body was discovered two days later and four days after that Ireland was again in The Coleherne picking up another victim. This time it was 35-year-old Bradley Perry, the son of a US congressman, who was living in Kensington. Once more Ireland went to his victim's home and in Bradley's case found an opportunity to tie him up and attach a noose to his neck—even though Bradley had explained that he was not interested in S&M. Ireland then strangled Bradley and placed a doll on top of his dead body.

Just three days later Ireland struck once more, this time murdering 33-year-old Andrew Collier, a warden at a sheltered housing complex, who took Ireland back to his flat in Dalston. Once again Ireland strangled his victim with a noose and after the murder, as he had done on every occasion, Ireland took the opportunity to look through his victim's flat for what he could steal. In doing so he discovered that Andrew was (like Peter Walker) HIV positive, so Ireland burned parts of Andrew's body and then strangled his cat. As he later claimed to his biographer, he did not want Andrew to have any dignity in death, so Ireland then proceeded to place the cat's mouth round Andrew's penis—which he had encased in a condom and put the cat's tail, which was also in a condom, in Andrew's mouth (all details taken from Gekoski, 1998: 236-7).

The police had now connected the murders of Andrew and Peter. On 12 June 1993 Ireland himself contacted Kensington Police Station to tell them that he had killed four men and then telephoned Battersea Police Station where he asked: 'Are you still interested in the death of Peter Walker? Why have you stopped the investigation? Doesn't the death of a homosexual man mean anything? I will do another. I have always dreamed of doing the perfect murder' (quoted in Gekoski, 1998: 237-238). He was as good as his word.

His final victim was Emanuel Spiteri, a 41-year-old Maltese chef who was living in Catford, south London. By this time the police had attempted to reach out to the gay community and seek their help in finding the murderer. For example, they issued an e-fit (Electronic Facial Identification Technique) of a man who was seen with Emanuel catching a train from Charing Cross on the night that he was murdered, in the hope that this might jog people's memories. However, there is some evidence that the gay community was less than eager to help and we have to remember that in the same month that Ireland had started to kill gay men, some of whom were interested in S&M, the House of Lords had ruled that consent was not a defence in sado-masochistic activities and thus upheld the convictions of 16 men in the so-called 'Spanner Case'[3]. Given this decision why would anyone who might have been interested in S&M put themselves in a position when they might have been prosecuted? Indeed, it was some weeks later that Ireland gave himself up to police and eventually he confessed to all five murders.

We know relatively little about Colin Ireland's crimes, or about his victims and there was little of the near hysteria that marked the press reports in the cases of Peter Sutcliffe, the Wests and to a lesser extent Dennis Nilsen. In short there is an invisibility about his activities and what happened to his victims. His biographer thinks that this had to do with two factors. First, because Ireland pleaded guilty to murder there was no lengthy trial to report and so few details about him emerged to capture the public's imagination. Secondly, 'one suspects that the murders of a handful of gay men were unlikely to cause the sort of public outrage and fascination as the murders of young women or children' (Gekoski, 1998: 217). Gekoski does not consider the possibility that the lack of hysteria surrounding Ireland's case might also have had something to do with the fact that many people might actually have supported what he had done and agreed with him that, as his step-father explained (in the quote that begins this chapter) it was 'the sado-masochists, the really sick ones, he cannot stand,' and that there was as a consequence tacit support for his 'mission' to 'wipe them out'.

Michael Copeland

Even so we know more about Ireland than about Michael Copeland and his victims, who are now all but invisible except when they are fleetingly captured in back copies of *The Times*. From this source we know that Copeland was a former soldier who murdered a 16-year-old boy called Günther Helmbrecht in Verden, Germany in November 1960; William Arthur Elliott, a 60- year-old estate clerk in June 1960; and finally George Stobbs, a 48-year-old industrial research scientist in March 1961. The last two lived in Derbyshire.

---

[3] This related to an investigation by Greater Manchester Police which began in late 1987 after they had anonymously received a videotape of a group of men beating each other. Seemingly the police believed that someone must have died—such was the severity of the beatings and so they started to question some 200 men who they thought might have been involved. Eventually the police charged 16 men with wounding and causing actual bodily harm in September 1989 under the Offences Against the Person Act 1861. The men's defence that they all had an interest in S&M and that they had all consented to these acts was not accepted and as a result several of the defendants were sentenced in December 1990 to various periods of imprisonment. The men appealed and finally in the House of Lords in 1993—on a majority decision of 3-2—the convictions were allowed to stand. With the support of Liberty three defendants took the case to the European Court of Human Rights, but in February 1997 that court upheld the right of the Government to prosecute in its role of protecting public health and morals (see Thomas, 2000: 10).

Copeland seems to have picked up both William and George in a pub in Chesterfield that was used by gay men (perhaps The Nag's Head). We should remember that at this time homosexuality was still illegal and it would not be decriminalised so far as consenting adults were concerned until the Sexual Offences Act 1967 became law, and even then homosexual activities were only legal if they were undertaken in 'private'. (For 'private' we might again substitute 'invisible'). Copeland then drove with his victims in their cars out into the country, where he would eventually kill them by kicking or stamping on their heads, as Zobbs had done to David Morley. As he later explained to Chief Inspector Bradshaw at Chesterfield Police Station:

> I killed Elliott and Stobbs and the German boy. I killed them because it was something that I hated. That is why I killed [them]. I hated things like that. I killed [them] because I hated what [they] stood for. (*The Times,* 17 March 1965)

As he said of George Stobbs, 'I killed him because he belonged to something I hated most' (*The Times*, 17 March 1965). Even so, at his trial in 1965, his defence barrister stated that Copeland claimed, 'I hate such stuff, but I do not hate them more than most men. I have no obsession about them. My attitude is quite normal towards girls' (*The Times*, 26 March 1965).

All of this seems very resonant of the comments made after Ireland's trial by his step-father. Whilst Ireland's step-father emphasised his condemnation through repetition in the words 'sick' and 'sickened', he also claimed that 'it was the really sick ones that he cannot stand', which seems to echo perfectly the 'hatred' that Copeland described. Copeland 'hated things like that'; it was something that 'I hated the most'; and, 'I hated what they stood for', although it is of note that he could not bring himself actually to name the 'thing' that he hated, or describe what George or William in fact 'stood for'. These 'things' were left to the imagination; they were literally left behind the 'closed doors' that Ireland and Copeland had decided to open.

So too look again at the phrase used by Copeland that he did not hate them 'more than most men'. Surely this was an attempt to reflect a more general homophobia at a time when homosexuality was still illegal? Indeed, does this not also echo Ireland's step-father when he observed that Ireland 'did what he did and makes no apologies for it', at a time when homosexuality was no longer illegal, but when the highest court in the land was ruling that some sexual behaviours—even when in private and between consenting adults—were in fact against the law? In effect the House of Lords were also 'sickened' by what could go on behind closed doors, even though this was a private space, where gay men could manage their sexuality by being invisible. Nor did the private spaces offered by The Coleherne in London, or the pub in Chesterfield where Copeland picked up George and William, allow these gay men to escape victimisation.

Their safety maps provided no security. Instead Ireland and Copeland simply learned enough about these spaces to enter them and use that knowledge to gain access to their victims.

It is tempting to consider whether in fact Ireland and Copeland were themselves gay. Both denied this and in any respect their sexuality is of little concern, especially as this type of questioning takes us back into the territory inhabited by the medico-psychological tradition of analysing serial killers. Surely what is of greater interest is how homosexuality becomes marginalised through being viewed as 'sick' and how gay men (and women) come to be 'hated' as a consequence of being labelled as such.

This latter observation should also help us when assessing whether or not Ireland and Copeland were engaging in a form of 'homicidal protest', as described by Leyton (1986). After all, if we can use job titles to determine social status, their victims were a research scientist, an estate clerk, a librarian, a businessman, an assistant theatre director and a warden at a sheltered housing complex. Leaving to one side that they also murdered a chef and a 16--year-old, the occupations of their victims do seem to be of higher status than the semi-skilled jobs occupied by Ireland, or the career in the army that was at one stage being pursued by Copeland. However, when Copeland argued that he killed his victims because of what 'they stood for', this did not seem to be a reference to their economic power or to their job status. Rather it seemed to be a reference to their sexuality. So too what sickened Ireland was not what had happened in the boardroom of the business of Bradley Perry, or at the theatre where Peter Walker worked, or in the library that employed Christopher Dunn, but rather what they all did 'behind closed doors'. The 'homicidal protest' that was being made was not economic, but sexual and the context in which this protest took root was the homophobia of Britain more generally—a context that becomes all the more clear when we consider the victims of Dennis Nilsen and Peter Moore.

THE 'FAIRY LIQUIDATORS'

Dennis Nilsen and Peter Moore were both gay men who mainly targeted other gay men to kill. As with Ireland and Copeland, I am less interested in their motivation for killing and how this may be connected to their sexuality—although in prison they have been dubbed the 'fairy liquidators' by other prisoners [personal communication]. Instead I am more concerned with those people whom they victimised. There are a variety of elements common to the circumstances in which Moore, Nilsen, Ireland and Copeland came to kill their victims. For example, pubs (and alcohol) feature regularly, as does S&M in the case of Moore, whose case is less familiar than that of Dennis Nilsen. So too we can see homophobia, visibility, invisibility—to the extent that several of Nilsen's victims are in fact unnamed—and police incompetence.

Dennis Nilsen

Indeed, it should be remembered that Nilsen was caught largely because his fellow tenants could no longer flush their toilets—he was disposing of body parts down the drains and as a consequence it was the Dyno-Rod engineer who was in reality responsible for his arrest. According to Nilsen's biographer, the detectives who eventually arrested him were shocked by 'the fact that it was possible to kill undetected for four years in a London suburb' (Masters, 1985: 15). This is a curious reference given that the arrest of Peter Sutcliffe must have been relatively fresh in the memories of detectives, although it perhaps also reveals a difference between those who were victimised by Ireland and by Nilsen. After all, whilst Ireland killed relatively successful gay men, Nilsen concentrated his efforts on those who were, in the words of Brian Masters, 'without aim or purpose'. He explained:

> They [Nilsen's victims] all had the most slender connections with their origins. Some were in trouble with the police, some were drug addicts or 'punks', some (but not all) were homosexuals, many were homeless and jobless and many drifted through the crowds of London without aim or purpose, their disappearance being such a regular event that their few acquaintances were neither surprised nor alarmed.
>
> (Masters, 1985: 115)

The theme of young people becoming vulnerable by moving from one place to another is taken up more fully in *Chapter 5*, but it is also used here to explain why Nilsen in particular was able to kill some 15 young men between 1978 and 1983. The victims of Nilsen dominate this section, although I particularly concentrate on the first and especially the last of the young men that he killed and one or two others, such as Paul Nobbs and Douglas Stewart, who 'got away'.

The 'unknown Irishman'

Nilsen's first victim has no name and so, for example, appears in Fido's (2001: 205) *A History of British Serial Killing* simply as an 'unknown Irishman'. All that we do know is his nationality; that he had short, brown curly hair; and that he happened to be in The Cricklewood Arms—at the time a rough, Irish pub on the Cricklewood Broadway in London on the night of 30 December 1978, drinking Guinness by himself, when he was spotted by Nilsen. As the pub was about to close, the Irish youth must have decided to return with Nilsen to 195 Melrose Avenue (Nilsen later moved to Cranley Gardens), where the pair drank some more, until they were, according to Masters, 'insensible' (1985: 109). Nilsen got into bed with the youth, although no sexual activity took place and then in the small hours of the morning Nilsen first strangled him and then, when he thought that the youth might still be alive, drowned him in a bucket of water. Nilsen hid the youth's body under the floorboards of his flat until 11 August 1979, when he brought the body back up and burned it on a bonfire in the back garden, pounding the ashes to powder and then raking them into the ground (Masters, 1985: 113). Thus, as Masters concludes,

> The Irish youth disappeared without trace, his existence obliterated for no clear reason by a man who did not know him. He has never been identified and probably never can be. (Masters, 1985: 113).

McConnell and Bence (1983: 67), two *Daily Mirror* journalists who produced a true crime account of the Nilsen murders, suggest that 7,177 people were missing in the United Kingdom in 1980 and that in subsequent years New Scotland Yard's 'active' missing persons index hovered around the 5,000 mark. As they put it:

> The capital is still the magnet which attracts derelicts. They seek to survive without identity, lost among the large anonymous section of the population where they can, consciously or not, live on the fat of others without being identified, pilloried or punished. (McConnell and Bence, 1983: 67)

We do not need to accept the rather self-serving moralising of McConnell and Bence's characterisation of some of those people who are attracted to London as 'derelicts' bent on surviving on the 'fat of others', although the anonymity afforded by the capital probably was and remains attractive to some. So too we might question why there are so many people who do not want to be 'identified'—or made visible—and why they are afraid of being pilloried or punished. Of course we have no way of knowing if in fact the unknown Irishman was a derelict, or if he was escaping being pilloried or punished, as there simply isn't any information to go on. Indeed, we only know that he was actually murdered because Nilsen himself admitted to this crime. However, we know a great deal more about his final victim.

Stephen Sinclair

Stephen Sinclair was born at the beginning of our time-frame in the inclusive society of 1962, to an unmarried mother in Perth and was as a result almost immediately taken into the care of the local authority, the Perthshire County Council. He did not at first have the surname 'Sinclair' and on his birth certificate he was simply identified as 'Stephen Neil No Name', given that his mother was not married.[4] Stephen was fostered by Neil and Elizabeth Sinclair when he was 14 months old and then legally adopted by them a few months later. The

---

[4] We now know that his surname was in fact Guild—see Masters (1985: 128).

Sinclairs lived in a bungalow in Belbeggie, some six miles north of Perth. By this stage in their marriage the Sinclairs had had three daughters and yearned for a son, although as McConnell and Bence uncharitably put it, '[they] did not know that by nature Stephen was a misfit' (McConnell and Bence, 1983: 63). By this they mean that Stephen was an epileptic and for a long time had no control over his bladder or bowels.

As a result of his epilepsy Stephen was placed in the Royal Dundee Liff Hospital, which catered for some 600 mentally ill people and he remained there until he was 12, when he was sent back home to the Sinclairs. By that time they had had another two daughters, making five in total. Stephen proved difficult to handle, setting fires in the house and committing a variety of petty crimes. His early teenage years were marked by spells in remand centres, special schools and borstals, and he gradually drifted into a world of unskilled work. His first job was picking berries, but he was sacked from that on his very first day for unruly behaviour (all details taken from McConnell and Bence, 1983: 60-72).

As a young adult Stephen attempted suicide, self-harmed, spent time in custody, regularly used drugs of various kinds and threatened his sisters. Eventually, having tried all that they could, the Sinclairs renounced Stephen and stated that they wished to return their adopted son to the care of the council. In effect they were attempting to de-adopt Stephen; to return him to Stephen Neil No Name. After a great deal of legal debate the council fostered Stephen out again, but this fostering proved to be no more stable than his time with the Sinclairs. Soon he drifted towards the Norrie Miller Riverside Park in Perth, which has been described as 'an open Mecca to drug pushers, from pot or marijuana to smack or junk' (McConnell and Bence, 1983: 66). In effect Stephen was a vagrant, who went through punk and skinhead phases, associating with drug addicts, drunks and male prostitutes. One of the Sinclair girls spotted Stephen in a street in Perth in 1982 and after that he seems to have continued to drift—this time towards London.

Stephen didn't have much to offer by way of talent, education or skills. He seems to have survived as a male prostitute and found accommodation in hostels run by the Salvation Army, or the Scottish charity, The Mungo Trust. He also registered with various social security offices and job centres, such as the one in Kentish Town where Nilsen worked as a civil servant. By January 1983 Stephen had found accommodation in a hostel in Kentish Town, but he was almost immediately in trouble there for stealing from a fellow resident. As a result he was arrested and brought before magistrates at Highbury Corner, where he was remanded on his own recognisances for a week. It was during this week that he met Nilsen—although the pair had probably met before at the job centre. Stephen was never seen alive again, but because Nilsen didn't have time to dispose of his body, the police were able to identify Stephen through fingerprint records and the various body parts—including his skull—that Nilsen had started to butcher. Stephen was just 20 years old.[5]

Nilsen described his victims to his biographer as his 'tragic products' (Masters, 1985: 149) and by this he seems to imply that there was a tragedy in their lives prior to meeting him. This is of course a very self-serving conclusion and we might instead see the tragedy in their lives as their meeting with Nilsen, rather than the circumstances of their childhood and upbringing. Nonetheless there is no doubt that with those of Nilsen's victims that we know something about—and there are at least seven about whom we know nothing—there is a recurring and depressing regularity about the circumstances of the men that he murdered. Graham Allan, for example, originally from Newarthill in Glasgow, was an alcoholic and drug addict; John Howlett (described by Nilsen as 'John the Guardsman') was from High Wycombe and worked the travelling fairs until he had enough money to disappear from the police. Martyn Duffey, originally from Merseyside and constantly in trouble with the police, first left for London at the age of 15 and eventually returned there two years later, addicted to valium but determined to enrol on a catering course; and Malcolm Barlow from Rotherham was an epileptic like Stephen, who first encountered Nilsen when he was having a fit. Nilsen called an ambulance and when Malcolm returned from Willesden General Hospital to offer his thanks, Nilsen killed him. Other 'tragic' young men simply disappeared under Nilsen's floorboards, later to be burned or butchered prior to being flushed down the loo. Nilsen also killed a Canadian tourist, Kenneth Ockendon, who was not at all typical of his victims and he attempted to kill others, such as Paul Nobbs, who was a student and certainly not tragic in the way that Nilsen would have liked to have portrayed him.

Paul Nobbs

Paul was a 21 year-old student at London University where he was studying Polish. He came from Bushey in Hertfordshire and regularly cruised for partners in The Golden Lion in Dean Street in Soho, London. McConnell and Bence (1983: 92-93) offer the following description of the clientele of The Golden Lion in 1980:

> Gays of all shapes, sizes, colours, young and muscle bound, biceps rippling under lurid tattoos, well-dressed businessmen trying not to look ashamed and embarrassed at being spotted there, the old and seedy past their time, but still with their sexual fantasies. Racial and class barriers are non-existent, yet other stronger ones are erected against outsiders.

---

[5] There is a long and quite detailed account of how Nilsen killed Stephen at the conclusion of Master's *Killing for Company* (1985: 299-302). Here I have simply used details from the confession that Nilsen gave to the police, although those who are interested might like to learn how Nilsen dealt with Stephen's body after death and compare this behaviour with that of Colin Ireland after he had murdered his victims.

It was in The Golden Lion in November 1981 that Paul met Nilsen and initially he chatted with the latter as he, Nobbs, had wanted to escape the attentions of another man. Thus in one sense Nilsen 'rescued' Paul (as he had done with Malcolm Barlow) and they left the pub to go off to Foyles to buy books. After shopping they returned to Nilsen's flat in Cranley Gardens, where Paul twice called his mother on the telephone. They both drank quite heavily, which meant that there was no sexual activity, but went to bed together. Paul woke about two in the morning with a dreadful headache and very bloodshot eyes. Nilsen said something to the effect of, 'God, you look bloody awful,' but was largely very sympathetic and the pair went back to bed. It was only the following day, when Paul went to University College Hospital and asked for a check on his health, that the duty doctor pointed out that someone had tried to strangle him.

All of this is of interest for two reasons. First, as would be argued at Nilsen's trial where Paul gave evidence on behalf of the prosecution, Nilsen's failure to carry through with the murder seems to have been calculated. After all, Paul had telephoned his mother twice from Nilsen's flat. In other words, unlike those whom he normally targeted Paul would be missed if he had disappeared and there would be some very good evidence that the last person who had seen him alive was Nilsen.

Secondly and again something that would come out at the trial, Paul did not report this incident to the police. As Masters explains: 'He had not wanted to report the attack to the police because they would be unlikely to pay much attention to him when they realised he was homosexual' (1985: 209). The issue of police indifference to attacks on gay men is considered below after examination of the facts relating to another of the young men who escaped an attack by Nilsen, but who did report the matter to the police.

Douglas Stewart

Almost a year before the attack on Paul Nobbs, Nilsen was again in The Golden Lion drinking and looking for a partner. This time he encountered 25 year-old Douglas Stewart. Douglas was from Wick in the Highlands of Scotland and had come to London having trained as a chef at the Gleneagles Hotel in Auctherarder, Perthshire. In London he worked at the Holland Park Hotel in Ladbroke Terrace and had found himself a girlfriend called Dawn, who worked at the same hotel as a chambermaid. Douglas said that he liked drinking in The Golden Lion because he met other Scottish people there—people like Nilsen, who had also trained as a chef in the Army. They both drank a great deal and when the pub closed Nilsen invited Douglas back to his flat—at the time in Melrose Avenue, prior to his move to Cranley Gardens. At the flat Nilsen gave Douglas another lager and a large glass of vodka and very soon he had fallen asleep in an armchair. He woke up and, realising that it was now very late, accepted Nilsen's offer to stay until the morning. Nilsen also suggested that they sleep together, but Douglas declined this offer.

Some time later, Douglas woke again. He was aching from sleeping in the armchair and wanted to stretch, but immediately realised that he couldn't because his ankles were tied to the leg of the chair. He then sensed that his tie was being loosened and knotted around his throat. Nilsen was throttling him. Somehow Douglas managed to aim a blow at Nilsen's face and was then able to struggle out of the chair. There was an exchange of words, with Nilsen suggesting that Douglas should just take his money and get out, and Douglas accusing Nilsen of trying to murder him. Of note, Nilsen pointed out to Douglas that if he went to the police, 'They'll never believe you. They're bound to take my word for it. Like I told you in the pub, I'm a respectable civil servant' [6] (quoted in McConnell and Bence, 1983: 101). Nilsen then managed to get a knife, but Douglas was able to calm the situation down, so that Nilsen put the knife away. He then offered Douglas another drink, which was declined and even though it was only 3.30 a.m., Douglas left Nilsen's flat and walked down Melrose Avenue. He walked the length of two or three houses, then broke into a run. He soon found a telephone box and dialled 999.

When the police car arrived Douglas reported that Nilsen had tried to kill him and showed the two police officers the red marks on his throat. One of the officers stayed with Douglas whilst the other went and knocked on Nilsen's door. As Douglas was later to recall, 'Nilsen denied everything I had told the police. He gave them the impression that we were going out together and it was just a lovers' quarrel in a homosexual romance' (quoted in McConnell and Bence, 1983: 103). Douglas maintained that as soon as the word 'homosexual' was mentioned, the police lost all interest and that, despite leaving his brother's address so that they could contact him, he never heard from them again. It was only after Nilsen's arrest that the police eventually got in touch with Douglas, via his mother, who was then living in Milton Keynes, and traced him to a house in Thurso in the north of Scotland. As Douglas later stated:

> The police made a bad mistake. They let him off when he attacked me. Now we don't know how many more he killed at Melrose Avenue after he took me back there. Or Cranley Gardens after that. (quoted in McConnell and Bence, 1983: 104)

In fact we now know that Nilsen murdered another ten young men and assaulted three more after the attack on Stewart (see Fido, 201: 205-206).

---

[6] Nilsen was also a former police constable, having been in the Metropolitan Police between December 1972 and December 1973.

The role of the police

What should we make of the failure of Paul Nobbs to report Nilsen's attack on him and the failure of the police to pursue the attack on Douglas Stewart after it *was* reported to them? Are not these failures both related? After all, in many respects Paul's reluctance to report the matter to the police because he believed that they were 'unlikely to pay much attention to him when they realised that he was a homosexual' is confirmed by the behaviour of the police when dealing with Douglas after he had reported an attack. Nilsen—the former policeman, soldier and civil servant—was able to deflect the police by presenting what had happened as a 'lover's quarrel in a homosexual romance' and as soon as the word 'homosexual' was used the police lost all interest. Indeed, perhaps Douglas was prompted to report the attack precisely because he was not gay. Incensed at what had happened to him, his first thought was to dial 999 and—as a heterosexual who therefore presumed that he would be taken seriously, he expected the police to arrest the person responsible. The fact that they did not—for whatever reason—was a 'bad mistake', especially as it left the way open for the deaths of several other people. Indeed the failure of the police to act can also be seen as a factor in the invisibility of gay men and specifically the violence that takes place in their lives. If the police had arrested Nilsen they would have had to make public what had taken place 'behind closed doors' and in doing so would have exposed a world that they would seem to have wanted to remain hidden. So too, in making this private world public, the police would have been, in effect, delivering the protection of the state by offering an equality of service and protection to gay men equivalent to that expected by heterosexuals if they are attacked and assaulted.

In an appendix, Masters (1986) considers whether the police had 'blundered' in not arresting Nilsen sooner, as several newspapers, such as the *Sun* and *Sunday People,* had suggested before his trial. Masters considers three potential 'blunders', including the case of Douglas Stewart. He argues that the police had tried to contact Douglas, but were unable to trace him, or his brother—whose address Douglas had given them. In effect Masters gives the police the benefit of the doubt, although various parts of his account were denied by Douglas and also by his brother, who maintains that the police never contacted him at all at that address. McConnell and Bence are not as forgiving as Masters and simply ask:

> Why could a mass murderer commit such a gory succession of crimes over a period of almost three years and then only be discovered by accident when a plumber, summoned by a handful of people who could not flush their lavatories, found human remains in a blocked drain? True, so many victims were not reported missing but should the police have acted sooner? On Stewart's testimony the answer must surely be, 'Yes'. (McConnell and Bence, 1983: 105-106)

One way of gaining some perspective on this matter might be to consider an evaluation of a police initiative aimed at providing an equality of service to gay men and women in Birmingham from the end of our time-frame in the exclusive society. However, before considering The Pink Shield Project (below) we should also examine the murders of Henry Roberts, Edward Carthy, Keith Randles and Tony Davies, all of whom were murdered by Peter Moore in late 1995.

Peter Moore

Moore—the other of the 'fairy liquidators'—lived at Darlington House, in Kinmel Bay, North Wales. Of note, Darlington House was the most prominent house in the area and as such served as a community resource, as well as a residence for Moore and his elderly parents.[7] For example, it was also used as a library and a polling station. Moore was a local entrepreneur who owned a chain of cinemas and as a result was often in the regional broadcast and print media talking about his businesses. It would be fair to say that he was quite visible in the local community of North Wales, although he kept hidden the facts that he was gay and interested in S&M. Indeed, as his neighbour Joan Marland would later comment, 'we didn't talk about being gay—we never gave it a thought.' This observation would seem to be representative of the culture which Moore inhabited, although —like Nilsen, Ireland and Copeland—he knew of various hidden places within the community where he could express his sexuality without fear of exposure. After the death of his mother in 1994 (his father had died in 1979) Darlington House itself often became a place where gay men interested in S&M would meet.

Henry Roberts

Moore's first victim was Henry Roberts—a bachelor in his mid-fifties, who lived alone in an isolated farmhouse close to the A5 and who had an interest in Nazi memorabilia. Moore murdered him only two days after appearing on the local BBC news talking about opening another new cinema and only two weeks after having been fined for having an offensive weapon—a truncheon—in the van that he used to drive to and from his various cinemas.

Henry was killed in what Detective Superintendent Peter Ackerley of the North Wales Police described as ' a frenzied attack' and sustained 47 stab wounds to his front, back and buttocks. Henry's trousers had been pulled down during the attack. It was quite clear that Roberts was a gay man and there was some evidence of sexual activity prior to his death. This information was not released to the public, although David Sutcliffe—a BBC cameraman who is himself gay and was covering the story for the news—noticed a pathologist's

---

7   All details about Moore and his victims are taken from the Channel 4 documentary *Dressed to Kill* (2001, dir. Stuart Clarke).

report mentioning all of this when he was filming at the police headquarters. Sutcliffe was later to claim that an appeal to the gay community might have yielded Moore's name, had the police chosen to make public what had gone on 'behind closed doors' at Henry's farmhouse. Instead, Henry's sexuality was to remain invisible, in a community which did not readily talk about 'being gay'.

Edward Carthy and others
Two weeks later Moore murdered Edward Carthy—a gay man whom he had picked up in a bar in Liverpool. Again Moore stabbed his victim to death, before burying his body in a forest close to the A5. When interviewed by the police about Edward Carthy's death, Moore said that Carthy had asked him before he died:

> **Moore** ...was I one of these and I think he said, 'Nilsen type of fellows', apparently referring to one of the murderers who used to kill men.
> **DC**: Yeh, yeh. And what did you say?
> **Moore**: Yes.

Edward's body was only found when Moore himself directed the police to where it lay hidden after his arrest.

His final two victims were Keith Randles and Tony Davies. Keith was a father and grandfather who worked as a night watchman on a building site where he lived in a caravan close to the A5. Again he was stabbed to death and had extensive injuries. The final victim—Tony Davies—also had children and was murdered by Moore on 17 December 1995 on Pensarn beach, which lies between Rhyl and Colwyn Bay. Unknown to most local people Pensarn beach was a gay cruising area and on this occasion, faced with the third murder in as many months (they still did not know about Edward Carthy's death), the North Wales Police finally decided to appeal to the gay community for information that might assist them in their enquiries. As a result they had over 50 calls and one led them directly to Darlington House and Peter Moore. It is tempting to conclude that by making visible what had been invisible in relation to some aspects of these men's lives the police were able to apprehend a serial killer.

THE PINK SHIELD PROJECT

Throughout this chapter I have used the concepts of homophobia, visibility, invisibility, 'safety maps' and police performance to try to understand why gay men have so often become the targets of serial killers. In relation to this Douglas Stewart, for example, has claimed that the police made a 'bad mistake' in not taking more seriously his complaint about Nilsen's assault upon him, although there is also some evidence to support the claims of the Metropolitan Police

Service that they did attempt to follow up on his allegations, but were unable to locate him.

So too David Sutcliffe believed that the North Wales Police should have been more open about the sexuality of Henry Roberts and the fact that there was some evidence to suggest that he had been sexually assaulted before his murder. The implication here is that the police do not take seriously violence against gay men and women. Is this fair? Are gay men and women given the same protection of the state by being offered the same quality of service from the police as heterosexuals are offered? To try to make sense of these isolated complaints and see more generally how the police aim to support and assist the gay community at the end of our time-frame, I now make extensive use of materials gathered from an evaluation carried out in 2004 of The Pink Shield Project in Birmingham as one way of answering these questions.

The Pink Shield Project was an initiative of the Birmingham Police Forum for the Gay Community—an independent group of lesbian and gay community representatives, police representatives and other interested individuals. The project was launched in early 2002 and was primarily (though not exclusively) concerned with crime and policing issues related to the gay community in Birmingham and the West Midlands. As a result some 750 people filled in self-completion questionnaires while interviews and focus groups were also conducted. The product of this research was *A Matter of Trust: Recommendations of the Pink Shield Project*, which was published in November 2002.[8]

A Matter of Trust made nine recommendations, covering issues related to health promotion, improving the representation of minority ethnic communities and co-ordinating research and information. However, many of the recommendations related specifically to issues of crime and community safety. For example, recommendation 4 was concerned with tackling domestic violence; Recommendation 5 dealt with tackling homophobic bullying in schools; and Recommendation 8 with tackling homophobic bullying and discrimination at work. Significantly, Recommendation 3 was concerned with encouraging the reporting of homophobic incidents and crime as it was felt that this would allow 'the police [to] be better equipped to tackle and reduce homophobic crime' (all quotes from *A Matter of Trust* are taken from Wilson and McCalla, 2004).

The issue of under-reporting of homophobic harassment or violence was one of the principal findings of the research, with (comparing figures from the *British Crime Survey* 2001) 'only 20 per cent of those in this survey reported homophobic incidents—in comparison with 45 per cent of the general population reporting crime.' Over a quarter of those who were surveyed said that they did not report incidents to the police because they feared police reaction to their sexuality,

---

[8] For a general introduction to the Pink Shield Project, see Wilson and McCalla, 2004.

which would seem to reflect why these recommendations were called *A Matter of Trust*. In short, because there has been a history of mistrust between the gay community and the police, many in the gay community chose not to make visible the violence against them for fear of how they would be managed by the police.

Of note, the types of crimes being experienced by the respondents to the survey included a range of homophobic harassment and violence. For example, one in two respondents had experienced harassment or violence in the preceding five years, ranging from verbal abuse, to being beaten up (i.e. being punched or kicked), with five per cent reporting being attacked with a weapon.

Unsurprisingly, given these responses, the principal recommendations of *A Matter of Trust* related to the appointment of two specialist, full-time staff in both the West Midlands Police (WMP) and Birmingham City Council (BCC) to 'provide the capability to drive all further work forward', given the 'scale of the work needed, the paucity of existing statutory support and appropriate infrastructure and a need for clear co-ordination'. Thus what was required were (p.16):

- A full-time LGBT[9] Liaison Officer within West Midlands Police.
  The post would help formulate policies and learn best practice in other
  force areas, and share that practice within the West Midlands for the
  benefit of the whole community. All police officers working in and around
  the Gay Village area on a day-to-day patrol would continue to reassure the
  community which uses the village. However, the LGBT officer will carry a
  portfolio greater than a patrolling officer could hope to achieve given other
  duties and pressures of response. It would be prudent, therefore, to base
  the officer within the force HQ structure but also to provide a 9 a.m.-5 p.m.
  desk and phone, perhaps in the Gay Village.

- A full-time LGBT Officer within Birmingham City Council
  This post would complement that of the West Midlands Police LGBT
  Liaison Officer and build on the work already being taken on board by the
  Equalities Division in association with Stonewall. This officer would work
  closely with the planning of the LGBT agenda, [and] work with the
  Birmingham LGBT Forum, the national consortium of gay, bisexual
  voluntary and community organizations and Stonewall to achieve a higher
  and more positive role for Birmingham's LGBT community and
  Birmingham City Council staff.

It is important to see The Pink Shield Project, *A Matter of Trust* and these recommendations within an overall, national, statutory, legislative framework

---

[9] Lesbian, Gay, Bisexual and Transgendered.

that required local implementation at the end of our time-frame. Specifically, the Crime and Disorder Act 1998 required the police and local authorities to establish local Crime and Disorder Reduction Partnerships to conduct an audit of crime and disorder in their area and thereafter to develop a three yearly strategy to address the main priorities identified. Through The Crime and Disorder Strategies (Prescribed Descriptions) Order, 1998 No. 2452, para (3)(2)(m)(vi) these Crime and Disorder Reduction Partnerships have a statutory requirement to consult with the LGBT community.[10]

As McManus and Rivers (2001: 1)—in a guide specially written for community safety partnerships on responding to the needs of the gay community and published by NACRO—describe it, the Crime and Disorder Act 1998 gave local authorities and the police a duty to consider the impact of crime and disorder on everything they do. Equally it gave the same authorities every justification they needed to work specifically with and develop services for the gay community. Furthermore they warned, 'The partnership—in particular the local authority—could be open to action for failing in their duties under Section 17 of the Crime and Disorder Act', by which they mean 'legal action for negligence or failure of duty to care' (McManus and Rivers, 2001: 16).

Birmingham's Crime and Disorder Reduction Strategy 2002-2005, and its predecessor covering the period 1999-2002, developed by Birmingham Community Safety Partnership,[11] were produced to comply with the Crime and Disorder Act 1998. One theme within the strategy was 'Supporting Victims and Public Reassurance' and one of the 'Activity Strands' within this theme related to homophobic crime. The key aim of this strand was to 'improve confidence in reporting and response structures for tackling homophobic harassment and attacks' and one of the four key tasks was to 'complete the work of the Pink Shield Project and provide a report to include development proposals' (Birmingham's Crime and Reduction Disorder Reduction Strategy, 2002-2005: 15).

Both the WMP and BCC adopted similar approaches to dealing with this issue. Thus, for example, the WMP adopted a 'holistic approach' and BCC 'mainstreamed' gay issues. What this meant in practice was that the first two recommendations of *A Matter of Trust* were rejected and therefore no full time liaison officers were appointed. As part of the evaluation various interviews were conducted throughout the fieldwork about this approach so as to test whether it could deliver an appropriate level of service to the gay community in

---

[10] It should be noted that the Home Office document uses the description 'homosexuals' rather than 'LGBT community'.

[11] Birmingham Community Safety Partnership consists of Birmingham City Council, West Midlands Police, Birmingham Health Services, Birmingham Voluntary Service Council, West Midlands Fire Service and the National Probation Service for the West Midlands.

the West Midlands. Here all that is reported upon is the approach of the police, given the focus of this chapter, and no attempt is made to consider the position of BCC.

Of note, most of the police interviewees who were spoken to as part of the evaluation did not want to be identified. One who did was Detective Chief Inspector Steve Basterfield, who at the time was a crime manager with the WMP and who described the approach adopted towards the gay community as 'a holistic approach' and a 'whole picture view of crime'. He expanded on this by describing how the WMP approached the issue of providing a service to the gay community in Birmingham:

> The problem is that the force takes a whole picture view of crime and is loathe to single out a particular element of the community. Effectively what you've got are 21 OCUs [Operational Command Units]; within that you've got 21 Crime Managers who are responsible for all crime no matter who the victims are, or the type of crime. Within that you've got 21 Community Safety Bureaux. Within those you've got 21 Vulnerable Persons Officers. You haven't got one person, but you've actually got 21 who have responsibility for victims throughout the force area—so in Birmingham there are nine Vulnerable Persons Officers and nine Crime Managers for dealing with crime that affects the gay community.

When pushed about whether he thought that as a result the gay community was getting a good service from the police, DCI Basterfield suggested:

> I think that it is patchy … I would love to be able to say that if a member of the gay community walked into a police station with a gay related problem—homophobic attack or whatever, that they would get the best of service. I wouldn't be as stupid as to say that.

This theme of 'patchy' service to the gay community was taken up by other police interviewees, who also described the WMP's approach as 'diluted' and 'frustrating' and alleged that all of this was related to a performance management culture. For example, one interviewee commented:

> We are talking about performance management. We are driven by key performance indicators that are given to us by the Home Office and those are very prescriptive … what we have been discussing doesn't fit into a performance management culture.

Another argued:

> There are 21 OCUs and each has a Vulnerable Persons Officer who looks at issues in respect of hate crimes. But they have other areas of management too, so what you get is diluted. It is not their sole purpose to look at gay issues.

A third commented:

It's supposed to be everybody's responsibility to be aware of what the issues are … but that doesn't necessarily go down well when you are trying to increase confidence in a minority area of work where there has been a lack of trust. A key point of contact would increase confidence.

In trying to pursue this question of whether or not the 'holistic approach' of the WMP had resulted in a 'patchy service' and was a 'diluted' form of service to the gay community, three issues were further considered which had cropped up in interview, or through a close reading of the minutes of the Birmingham Police Forum for the Gay Community (BPFGC). First was the introduction of anti-homophobic bullying packs in schools; second was specific training for officers who might have to deal with the gay community in the West Midlands; and finally was the increase or otherwise of the reporting of homophobic crime.

In relation to the first issue an interview was conducted with the Education Development Manager of the WMP whose responsibility it was to introduce the packs. It is perhaps fair to summarise the situation which emerged with regard to anti-homophobic bullying in schools by quoting from one of the police interviewees:

Sometime next year [2004], after Christmas we can identify an area or a school where we can perhaps pilot it [i.e. the *Living It Project*—an anti-homophobic bullying pack developed by Greater Manchester Police].

This lack of precision—'sometime', 'perhaps', 'an area', 'or a school'—reflected the reality of the situation as it stood in 2004. The pack, which has been successfully launched in Manchester, had still not been piloted and the Education Development Manager was unable to explain when this might happen, or which school might be chosen. This manager commented:

We do have packages that tackle bullying, but we don't actually have a package that deals with homophobic bullying … I have little knowledge of the Living It Project. This is something that I basically received from a colleague a couple of weeks ago.

Officers who were spoken to did indeed want to be trained to deal better with issues that affected the gay community and on reading the minutes of the BPFGC it became clear that the National Crime and Operations Faculty at Bramshill had been asked to develop a National Hate Crime Training Package. As such contact was made with Alistair Lawson, who had been identified in the minutes, but he indicated that, due to the need to write new National Codes of Practice and Guidance, 'this has meant the temporary shelving of our existing projects,' including the National Hate Crime Training Package [personal communication, 10 November 2003]. Unsurprisingly, one of our interviewees described the training that he had received as coming 'through the role I perform … there is an issue there in training terms.' Just how great that issue remains can again be evidenced through the minutes of the BPFGC. For example, at the meeting held on 5 February 2004, a long-standing issue relating to the third-party reporting of a racial incident led to an admission by a WMP spokesman that some WMP personnel working on the central switchboard, did 'not know what a hate crime was or that there can be third-party reporting'. When this was pursued at the meeting the WMP spokesman continued: 'Hands up—we're guilty. We didn't have the systems in place and this is still a training issue for us.'

Given that this latter issue was about reporting—albeit, in this specific incidence about a racial incident—it perhaps also helped to reveal why reporting and specifically the various attempts to launch and maintain self-reporting packs to and for the gay community had difficulties. For example, information about the self-report forms provided by Sgt Neil Anderton in the February meeting of the BPFGC revealed that no self-report forms had been submitted at all since November 2003. In interview with various WMP personnel this failure to self-report was seen as being linked to the lack of a full-time member of staff within WMP and thus to the gay community lacking confidence in what the WMP were hoping to achieve. Indeed every operational WMP interviewee favoured the appointment of a full-time member of staff—although one, DCI Basterfield, saw this as a temporary appointment—specifically because they saw it as contributing to increasing the confidence of the gay community in coming forward and reporting crime. As one interviewee put it:

> If you have a direct point of contact, if their sole task is to look at that aspect of work, then I would say that it would have—it would make a big difference to reporting homophobic crime.

The failure to make this appointment was frequently described as 'frustrating'.

These issues of reporting homophobic crime and engendering the confidence of the gay community to do so—which were at the heart of *A Matter of Trust*—cropped up repeatedly in interviews conducted with members of the gay community and in e-mail communication through a website that was developed for the evaluation. For example, various people commented:

> I can't say whether I would report a homophobic crime in the current situation for a few reasons. I would have to out myself to Police Officers which could be very uncomfortable. If it did go as far as court I would have to out myself to lots more people. If the incident was serious I would go through all of that, but if it was minor, in the current climate it would be just too much.

It doesn't surprise me that nothing got actioned from *A Matter of Trust* ... I think that all of this has got something to do with coming out. It is hard to come out—or at least it was for me and so for me it would be easier to come out to one person than to 100. Birmingham had a self-report form, but I know that there was a feeling that nothing was going to happen if these forms were filled in and so they kind of wasted away. You do get the feeling that the police simply aren't gay friendly.

I can never imagine all of the police becoming gay friendly, or suddenly becoming sensitive to gay issues. I think that's why I could see people being prepared to talk to a specially appointed officer rather than any officer who just happened to be passing.

The provision of a full time officer within the Police and Birmingham City Council [are] vital necessities.

These comments are of interest as they repeatedly return to the issue of 'coming out', of being made 'visible', and the importance therefore of having a designated, full-time officer, which would lessen the difficulties of outing, in other words of being made visible to a large number of people. This is of course a different issue from, but related to the question of the trust between the gay community and the police, and it presented a challenge to the ideas of 'mainstreaming', or a 'holistic approach'. Specifically it was suggested that the issue of coming out is one that uniquely needs to be addressed within the equalities agenda and which requires a different solution from other equalities agendas such as gender or race.

TOWARDS A CONCLUSION

I have spent some time discussing The Pink Shield Project because it provides us with a glimpse of what it is like to be gay and the subject of homophobic violence. Specifically it allows us to look behind the culture of policing and see more clearly the quality of service that is provided to the gay community. In doing so—some ten years after Peter Moore was active and almost a quarter of a century on from the time that Dennis Nilsen was murdering gay men—it would seem fair to conclude that little has changed in relation to how the gay community is formally protected by the police. At best, on the evidence of The Pink Shield Project, the gay community are offered a 'patchy service'.

So Paul Nobbs, the London University student who escaped after an attack by Nilsen in 1981, but who was reluctant to report this matter to the police because he felt that they would not pay much attention to him when they realised that he was gay, would have found much in common with the gay men and women of Birmingham in 2004. So too, Douglas Stewart, who thought that the police had made a 'bad mistake' in not pursuing his complaint against Nilsen more robustly in 1980 would similarly have found much in common with them.

After all, there had been no 'self-report' forms completed during the period of the evaluation, which speaks volumes about the gay community's willingness to report violence. As it was put by one detective, someone reporting a homophobic attack might not get 'the best of service—I wouldn't be as stupid as to say that.'

Of course the background to all of this is homophobia and whether from the 'inclusive' society of our earlier period—when homosexuality was still illegal—or from the 'exclusive' society at the end of our time-frame—when gay men and women have become more visible and can, for example, engage in civil partnerships—antipathy towards the gay community seems as virulent as ever. In some cases, as with David Copeland, this antipathy can tip over into hatred, loathing and murder. Others, like Colin Ireland, use this antipathy to exploit the vulnerability of gay men for their own purposes. That some gay men themselves kill other gay men should not deflect our attention away from the fact that homophobia has created the circumstances in which gay men have become one of the prime targets of serial killers in this country. No wonder many gay men choose to remain invisible.

CHAPTER 5

Runaways and Throwaways

CHAPTER 5

Runaways and Throwaways

It is what happens when darkness meets light, when experience meets innocence, when the false meets the true, when utter godlessness meets purity of spirit, when this—. (Martin Amis, 2001: 172)

The words above were written in honour of Lucy Partington by her cousin, the novelist Martin Amis. Lucy became one of the 326 victims of serial killers over our time-frame, after she was abducted and then murdered by Fred West in (or near) Gloucester in December 1973. We know very little about how Lucy, a 21 year-old student met her end. What we do know is that on the night of December 27 she had been visiting a disabled friend in Cheltenham called Helen Render and that they had talked together about putting in an application to the Courtauld Institute in London, where Lucy thought that she might like to continue to study after completing her undergraduate degree at Exeter University. Lucy was, according to the compelling biography of her written by her cousin, serious, artistic, musical, religious and resolute. She had left Helen's house with a completed application in her hand and then walked the short distance to the bus stop to return home. She never posted the application or boarded her bus and it would be another 21 years before the Partington family finally discovered her fate.

Lucy's remains were found in 1994 in the cellar of 25 Cromwell Street, Gloucester—the home of Frederick (Fred) and Rosemary (Rose) West and their family. She had been decapitated and dismembered and her remains had been crammed into a shaft between leaking sewage pipes, along with a knife, a rope, some masking tape and two hair grips. The bodies of other victims lay close by. When he was eventually questioned about her murder West scandalously claimed that he had been in a relationship with 'Juicy Lucy'. He stated that she had wanted to move in with him after becoming pregnant and that when he had refused she had threatened to tell his wife. So, he had strangled her and buried her in the cellar (Bennett and Gardner, 2005: 166). This is of course self-serving nonsense, although her cousin was moved to 'rebut' the suggestion that there had ever been any relationship between Lucy and West. Instead, she was simply in the wrong place at the wrong time and their meeting was 'what happens when darkness meets light …'

In *Experience,* Amis (2001: 172) continues these opposites—darkness/light; experience/innocence; falseness/truth; godlessness/purity, with two passages of writing:

Hi May it is your Dad Writeing to you. Or lette me have your telephone number … or Write to me as soon as you can, please may I have to sort out watt Mr Ogden did to me, my new solicitors are Brillaint I Read What you sead about me in News of the that was loylty you read what Scott canavan sead he had — [.]

Things are as big as you make them —
I can fill a whole body,
A whole day of life
With worry
About a few words
On one scrap of paper;
Yet, the same evening,
looking up,
can frame my fingers
to fit the sky
in my cupped hands.

The first passage is from a letter that Fred West wrote from prison after his arrest to his daughter May.[1] In it he refers to his solicitor—Howard Ogden— whom he had just sacked from fear that Ogden was going to sell his story (as indeed, it seems he was trying to do) and he mentions other bits and pieces of news related to how his case had been covered in the press. West was also to write 111 pages of autobiography prior to his suicide and Canter (2003: 60) notes that it contains no mention whatsoever of his crimes, or of the deaths of his victims. Instead, he suggests that it creates a rambling, Mills & Boon-style account of West's life as a hardworking, loving father who was regularly being put upon by others and he proposes that this account had been deliberately manufactured by West so as to deceive and to present only those things that he wanted to be revealed. So whilst the language, spelling, missing words and lack of punctuation in the memoir (which are echoed in his letter to his daughter) reveal a man with an IQ of 84, Canter is nonetheless moved to describe West as having 'inherent savvy'. More than this, Canter suggests that he had been able to get away with his crimes for as long as he had, not because he was:

A clever killer who developed a well-articulated, deviant philosophy, using his intellect to tie investigators in knots. He survived for so long because of the world he created for himself. (Canter, 2003: 57)

It was into this world that Lucy stumbled and West's subsequent and ridiculous claim that she had become pregnant by him was nonetheless very much in keeping with what he would allege about other women in his autobiography, where he suggested that he had fathered 42 children. Indeed,

---

[1] May would eventually start spelling her name as 'Mae'.

Canter finds this constant reference to fathering babies 'most curious' (2003: 76). Whilst this is of interest from within the medico-psychological tradition, we do not need to accept Canter's conclusions that West had evaded detection for as long as he did simply on the basis of his 'inherent saavy' and by his creating a world—most obviously 25 Cromwell Street—that he could control and where he could commit murder.[2]

Rather, we need to investigate who it was whom West was able to control and murder and why a number of his victims willingly became part of the world of a 'bumbling yokel, devoted to a happy family life' (Canter, 2003: 79). After all, at least on the surface the Wests had a stable home where they had lived for many years and, as Howard Souness (1995: 333) has observed, they also had 'a mortgage which they worked hard to pay off and a large family. They were the people next door, who waved a cheery "hello" to neighbours as they walked down the street.' Many people were taken in by this façade and perhaps it should come as no surprise that the young women who do seem to have been persuaded by West's fantasies about himself and his life were not at all like Lucy, who could frame her fingers to fit the sky into her cupped hands, but were runaways, or 'throwaways', with very little to look forward to, or indeed back at.

This chapter takes as its focus the nine victims of Fred and Rose West whose bodies were found in the cellar and garden of 25 Cromwell Street, Gloucester. As such it does not investigate in any depth three other murders committed by West, including the murder of his first wife Rena, their eldest child Charmaine, or Ann McFall, a young Scottish woman who worked as a nanny and became West's lover. Rena and Ann's remains were found in a field in Much Marcle, where West had grown up in the 1950s and Charmaine's at 25 Midland Road in Gloucester where the Wests had once lived. Here too it should be noted that West is suspected of having committed many more murders and David Canter, for example, believes that he may have killed another 20 young women (2003: 57). The nine Cromwell Street victims, with the exception of Lucy Partington, but including the Wests' own daughter Heather, are used to investigate the phenomenon of young people moving away from home for one reason or another and how this makes them vulnerable to those with ulterior motives.

The focus on the Wests in this chapter is deliberate, for there is little doubt that 25 Cromwell Street was a house that attracted runaways. It became well known as a 'place where you could crash. Where the landlord was cool. No questions,' and which West himself described as a 'bloody communial [sic] centre' (Burn, 1998: 187). Indeed one of the earliest West biographers described 25 Cromwell Street as 'almost open house to every waif and stray looking for

---

[2] However, I do not discount the importance of 'place' that the Wests created and in this respect I have been interested in the work of Erik Larson (2003) writing about the nineteenth-century serial killer H. H. Holmes in Chicago, USA.

shelter … these visitors were not the sort who would be inclined to go to the authorities. In many cases they were in trouble with the police themselves, or runaways from institutions which they feared and loathed' (Souness, 1995: 342-343). Gordon Burn notes that the house attracted 'floaters and drifters. Floating and drifting. [The Wests] were like a magnet for these kind of people' (1998: 234). Some evidence for all of this was revealed during the police investigation in 1994 when over 150 people were traced who had spent some time at 25 Cromwell Street (Burn, 1998: 202). Indeed Detective Superintendent John Bennett described the house as a place where 'runaways from local children's homes, or absconders' gathered and which had a 'reputation that made it attractive to rebellious teenagers' (Bennett and Gardner, 2005: 66).

We do not need to accept Bennett's characterisation that the teenagers who found their way to the Wests, or indeed to Gloucester, were 'rebellious'. The motivations for young people leaving, or being forced out of their homes are many and varied and can be linked to, for example, family instability, violence, conflict, neglect, rejection, problems at school, or sexual and physical abuse (the Children's Society, 1999: 3), which reveal rather more structural reasons for 'floating and drifting'. Indeed, fewer than half of the Wests' victims were actually reported as missing to the police, which suggests something of the domestic circumstances from which they came (Souness, 1995: 345).

Here too it is also worth remembering that we have already encountered this phenomenon in other chapters. Look again, for example, at the case of Natalie Pearman—the 'walking portrait of an ordinary girl' in *Chapter 3*, who was dead by the age of 16 and whose body was found dumped in a lay-by outside Norwich. Or at the case of Stephen Sinclair—'Stephen Neil No Name' in *Chapter 4*, who was Dennis Nilsen's final 'tragic product'. However, so as to add some depth to these nine victims I also use materials gleaned from the Children's Society's research into young runaways. In this way I hope to contextualise the experiences of the young women murdered by the Wests and link their deaths to more contemporary issues related to young people and their circumstances.

RUNAWAYS AND THROWAWAYS

The Children's Society has conducted extensive research with young people aged 16 or under who leave home for one reason or another. As such they draw distinctions between those young people who make a decision to leave—or 'run away' from home and those who felt that they were forced to leave home—the 'throwaways'. Indeed, some young people do not see themselves as having run away from home at all and would prefer to describe themselves as 'staying away' from home. There are also important distinctions to be made between running away and young people being reported missing to the police by their carers, as not all young runaways are reported missing. (So too many young people reported as missing have not in fact run away.) However, research in the late 1980s based on missing person reports estimated that there were some 100,000 incidents of young people under the age of 18 being reported as missing in Britain annually, which gives some idea of the scale of the problem (Newman, 1989: 1).

The Children's Society has been at the forefront of attempts to understand the phenomenon of runaways. As such, their primary research—conducted first in 1999 and more recently in 2005 (the Children's Society, 1999; Rees and Lee, 2005) with 10,772 young people in 70 mainstream schools, 11 pupil referral units and 13 special schools paints a depressing picture about the numbers of young people who leave, or are forced out of their homes and the circumstances that they find themselves in as a consequence. They suggest, for example that in 2005 there were at least 66,000 first-time runaways who stayed away from home for at least a night in England and Wales and that the majority of young runaways are in the 13 to 15-year-old age group (all statistics in this section are taken from Rees and Lee, 2005). Indeed, they calculate that some 7.5 per cent of the total proportion of young people in England aged 14 or 15 run away for at least a night. Some ten per cent of their sample who had run away were under eleven years old. Girls rather than boys were more likely to run away, as were those children with moderate learning difficulties, or who characterised themselves as gay or lesbian. Indeed this latter characteristic would seem to confirm a pattern identified in *Chapter 4*. Most runaways were white, or young people of mixed origin.

In looking beyond these basic categorisations the Children's Society tried to determine if there was a link between the structure of the family within which young people lived as teenagers and the likelihood of them running away. They discovered that young people living in lone parent families were around twice as likely to run away as those living with both parents and young people living in stepfamilies were almost three times as likely. In every case, young people who ran away were more likely to have a negative view of their relationship with their parent or carer—a finding which suggests a general unhappiness at home, or at school. For example, a third of young runaways said that they had had problems attending school and those young people who had been excluded from school were three times more likely to run away than young people who did not have issues at school.

Poverty was also a factor and the Children's Society's research was specifically designed to identify young people living in low income families through asking questions about the number of adults in the household with a paid job and whether the young person was entitled to free school meals. Of the young people who indicated that they were entitled to free school meals, 13.4 per cent had run away overnight, compared to just under ten per cent of those who said that they were not entitled. So too 15.6 per cent of those young people who ran away lived in families with no adults in paid employment, compared with just under ten per cent of those young people in families where there was at least one adult in paid employment.

Most young people reported problems at home as being the primary reason for their running away. In particular they described conflict with parents and other family members, physical, sexual and emotional abuse, and neglect. Throughout the research the voices of young people being 'slapped', 'beaten up', 'hurt' and 'hit' are heard time and again. Quite simply it is clear from the Children's Society's research that many of the young people who ran away did not find home a safe environment. As a consequence many suffered from depression and some talked about self-harm and suicide.

Perhaps of greatest relevance to this chapter is what these young people's experiences were like after they had run away, or been forced to leave their home. Whilst the majority of those surveyed ran away for only one night, some ten per cent of the sample had stayed away for more than a month. During that time most were likely to sleep with friends, but one in six of those surveyed in the sample—largely boys—slept rough, or with someone whom they had just met. There were a variety of 'survival strategies' identified in the research by those young people who stayed away from home for a week or more. For example, many admitted to begging or stealing. As might be expected, a small number of the sample—one in 12—also admitted to having been hurt or harmed whilst they were away from home, especially if they were sleeping rough. Nonetheless very few sought help from any voluntary or statutory agency, and a staggering two-thirds of the sample stated that their parents or carers did not report them as missing to the police, which perhaps also reflects that they were not wanted in their homes in the first place.

So here is a picture of a vulnerable group of young people, moving away from home, sometimes having to sleep rough and begging or stealing to survive. Moreover this is a group who do not ask for help from anyone in authority who might be able to offer it and who as a consequence often report being harmed or hurt. But who are these young people? What are their lives when they lack stability and direction, to become dominated by stop-gapping and making-do? As might be imagined it is very difficult to get too many biographical details, although Alexander Masters' (2005) recent account of the life of Stuart Shorter provides one extraordinary insight into the sexual abuse that first drove Stuart to run away and the subsequent impact that this had on his life. So too Nick Davies (1997: 3-26) tells the story of Jamie and Luke in Nottingham—'two small boys in the middle of an English city in the 1990s,' which provides us with a compelling picture of the individual lives behind the Children's Society's research.

Jamie, Luke and Lisa

Jamie and Luke were eleven and 13 years old when Davies first encountered them touting for business outside a toilet in Nottingham. Over a cup of tea and some food Jamie described his life as best he could. He told Davies that he was one of nine children and that he had had three 'dads' and that it was 'the third one, that's the one that got rid of me and my brother and sister, got me put in care' (Davies, 1997: 5). Whilst he was in care he was beaten up and then sexually abused by another boy. That boy was reported to staff, but others took his place and forced Jamie into prostitution. Luke was two years older and from Mansfield. He remembers a fairly normal upbringing, until his father died. Luke was six when that happened. Within a year he, his sister and brother had been taken into care—his mother unable to cope. By nine he was sexually active and experimenting with drugs, and he too soon turned to the streets to sell his body. As Davies (1997: 10) puts it, 'they described lives that had become one long sequence of misery and pain.'

Jamie and Luke were not the only children whom Davies encountered in Nottingham out on the streets. With Jamie and Luke as his guides—'symbols of ruined childhoods, guards at the door of darkness' (Davies, 1997: 34), he was given a tour of the city and an introduction to what happens when children run away or are forced from their homes. Of note, Jamie and Luke led him to Lisa, whose story seems to echo what we will encounter when we consider most of the young women who met their end in 25 Cromwell Street.

Lisa had been put in care when she was ten—after her parents had gone their separate ways. She was regularly bullied and as a consequence she was always running away. She ran to London, Scotland, Birmingham and Manchester, but she was always found and brought back to Nottingham by social workers. Eventually she stopped running and simply hid from the authorities in Nottingham until one day she was found by an older prostitute who encouraged her to sell herself. That was when she was eleven and by 14 she suggested to Davies that she had had sex with 3,000 different men and was earning about £800 per week.

Lisa also told Davies about one client that she'd 'never forget':

This man had picked her up and said that he wanted to go back to the flat that she rented for business. So she had taken him there and she'd just got undressed and laid down on the bed when he turned around and put a knife to her throat. He had kept her there for nine hours, mucking about with her, pleasing himself. He had used the knife on her, on her thighs, teasing her and tormenting her and occasionally splitting the skin to show her he meant business and then he had broken off a chair leg and started shoving that into her. She had thought that he'd never stop, but eventually he had given up and got dressed and driven away in his car, leaving her all on her own … it was just before her thirteenth birthday. (Davies, 1997: 23)

These three children—three symbols of 'ruined childhoods'—were only the tip of the iceberg that Davies encountered in Nottingham and their stories provide a glimpse of the lives that children lead when, through various circumstances they leave, or are forced out of their homes. So too their stories amplify the Children's Society's conclusions, albeit that Davies was describing circumstances in Britain some three years before the society first undertook its research in 1999. Nonetheless the pattern of broken homes, running away, being forced from home, being placed in care and the survival strategies that had to be developed as a consequence by Jamie, Luke and Lisa would not seem to be too far removed from what was uncovered by the Children's Society. That Jamie, Luke and Lisa turned to prostitution might be at the extreme end of the experiences uncovered later, but there is little doubt that children and young people are extremely vulnerable when they do not have a home that is safe, or when parents or carers—for whatever reason—do not or cannot provide love and support.

25 CROMWELL STREET

The first victim of Fred and Rose West after they had moved into 25 Cromwell Street in August 1972 (which they had bought with the help of a Polish landlord called Frank Zygmunt) survived the ordeal. She was very lucky. Her story and the circumstances in which she came to be hired as a 'nanny', then what happened to her thereafter tells us a great deal about the lifestyles of many of the other young girls who would not survive and also something of the *modus operandi* that the Wests used as serial killers.

Caroline Raine

Caroline Raine was born in 1955 and came from a large family who lived in the Forest of Dean, some 12 miles from Gloucester. Carol's mother, Betty, was a pub cleaner who was married to a merchant seaman called Albert Raine (all details taken from Burn, 1998: 3-70). Albert was gay and Caroline's actual father—as well as the father of her brother Phillip (whom she hated) and one other child, who died in infancy, was an Irish roadman called Michael Mahoney. By 1960 Betty had divorced Albert, then married a miner called Alf Harris and moved Caroline and her brother to Alf's home in Cinderford. The marriage seems to have been 'a transaction of sorts' (Burn, 1998: 10) as Betty needed a home and Alf needed someone to look after him and his four children. This domestic situation was further complicated when Betty got pregnant with Alf's baby—they had a daughter called Suzanne and Betty was later to have twins. As can be imagined, there was a great deal of domestic rivalry, noise and tension in a home of eight brothers, sisters, half-brothers and half-sisters; Caroline, for example, did not like her eldest half-brother Raymond. So too, she was sexually abused by an elderly neighbour at the age of eight and again when she was ten. Later she would describe herself as a 'wild child' and she had numerous sexual liaisons before trying to live away from home for a while in Portsmouth. (Here we might characterise her move as 'staying away from home', rather than running away, or being thrown away). This time away did not work out so Caroline returned to Cinderford and then started to see a boy called Tony Coates.

Caroline had to hitch-hike into Gloucester to see Tony, which also suggests something of her financial circumstances at the time, as even bus fares seem to have been beyond her means. In August 1972 whilst hitch-hiking home she accepted a lift from the Wests. In the course of the journey they asked her to become a 'nanny' for their three children—Anna-Marie (8), Heather (2) and May (4 months). As many would later testify, Fred West was always good at putting a spin on things and undoubtedly he made this offer sound like an attractive opportunity for a young girl just coming up to her seventeenth birthday to get away from an overcrowded home and establish some independence for herself. Burn even suggests that Caroline must have thought that 25 Cromwell Street would give her 'some good feelings'. He continued:

> There was a sense of solidness and space. It was not prefabricated or fast built. It was old. You sensed the depth of its foundations and the weight of its thick walls.
>
> (Burn, 1998: 26)

This is an interesting passage for it probably suggests something of the attraction that 25 Cromwell Street must have had for many of the young people whom the Wests encountered. Their home—and here we should also remember that many of their victims had been in care and foster homes rather than in a 'real' home—was not 'prefabricated', but 'old'; there was space, rather than living on top of one another; and quiet, rather than noise. The walls were also 'thick' and the foundations deep, all of which must have suggested respectability and belonging within the community. Naturally it was a house where the occupants would need a 'nanny', rather than, for example, a child-minder. Of course the shabbiness of the interior and the lack of furniture (or locks on the toilet or bathroom doors) would have been a disappointment, but without understanding the potential attractions of the place—and the opportunity of being a nanny—we cannot grasp why Caroline would have entered willingly into the employment of the Wests, or why other young women would later do the same.

In the end Caroline only stayed at 25 Cromwell Street for six weeks, as she became tired of Fred West's continual sexual innuendos, his bullying of Rose (who at the time was only two years older than Caroline) and his boasts that he had performed 'operations' and 'abortions' on women. So too she was horrified when he revealed that eight-year-old Anna-Marie was not a virgin, with the implication (which we now know to be true) that he was having an incestuous relationship with his daughter. Caroline cannot remember how she escaped from 25 Cromwell Street, but she does remember reporting the abuse of Anna-Marie, although nothing came of this.

Despite being shaken up by her experiences, Caroline went back to hitch-hiking into Gloucester to see Tony. The Wests were waiting for her. On 6 December 1972 their car pulled up and Rose got out, saying, 'Oh, we really miss you. The children really miss you.' (quote taken from Burn, 1998: 58). In short they were being charming and Caroline once again accepted their offer of a lift. Rose got into the back of the car with Caroline and then Fred started making sexual suggestions. Rose began to sexually assault Caroline and after he had found an opportunity to stop the car, Fred knocked Caroline out. They took her back to 25 Cromwell Street, bound and gagged her, then subjected her to an appalling sexual assault which lasted all night, before West finally raped her. After the rape finished West started to cry and asked Caroline not to tell Rose what had happened. Caroline agreed on the basis that she would not be killed and a deal was reached—in return for not being killed, Caroline would keep quiet about the rape and would return to her job as the children's nanny. She stayed the night and even helped with the housework the following morning. Then, with the children safely sent off to school, the Wests decided that they had to go to the laundry. This allowed Caroline an opportunity to escape and when she had done so she reported what had happened to the police.

As might be imagined, Caroline was traumatised by what had taken place and her anxieties about appearing in court were not helped by the police officer who interviewed her and who suggested, 'You like your sex, don't you? Don't tell me you weren't loving it?' (quote taken from Burn, 1998: 70). Eventually the Wests appeared at Gloucester Magistrates' Court on 12 January 1973—the charge of rape having been dropped. They both pleaded guilty to indecent assault and causing actual bodily harm, and were fined a total of £100. They were also advised to seek psychiatric help.

After the trial Caroline tried to get on with her life and even became Miss Forest of Dean in 1977, which led to some 'glamour modelling'. The awful events in 25 Cromwell Street started to fade into the past, at least until 1994. So too the Wests returned to their lives and three months after their trial they murdered Lynda Gough. Indeed between April 1973 and April 1975 they would murder a total of five girls—Lynda Gough, Lucy Partington, Carol Cooper, Juanita Mott and Shirley Hubbard.

Whilst we do not need to investigate the impact of the trial on the Wests from the medico-psychological tradition, it is hard to underestimate its force given their relatively light sentences. Above all, from a practical point of view, it must have made them realise that once they had started an assault they could not thereafter let their victim go. Indeed imagining that Caroline would want to return to their home as the children's nanny after her ordeal clearly reveals some very warped judgement and the Wests must have seen in retrospect that allowing her to escape led only to the police, a trial, convictions and exposure.

So too, whilst I have deliberately avoided giving too many details about the actual assault that they subjected Caroline to, look again at Lisa's story. She too experienced a horrific sexual assault and feared for her life; so too she was kept against her will for a significant period of time. There is a dreadful similarity to these awful events, even if they are separated by over 20 years. Above all they reveal something of the persistence of the misogyny of men towards women over our time-frame and the vulnerability of young women—young girls in Lisa's case—when they are brought up in poverty and see little in life to offer them an opportunity to escape that. Of course Lisa did not report her rape to the police, but do we really imagine that she would have received any better treatment from them than Caroline received from PC Price?

THE SNATCHED AND THE SEDUCED

In the same way that we broke down the description 'runaway' so as better to understand the phenomenon of those young people who move away from home, so too we should see the Wests' victims as falling into two distinct groups. Whilst there are clear similarities between the two groups (most obviously that they were all murdered by the Wests), there were nonetheless differences between those victims who were abducted or snatched—usually from bus stops—and another group of young women who were seduced into voluntarily entering 25 Cromwell Street. In the abducted category are: Lucy Partington, Carol Cooper, Shirley Hubbard, Juanita Mott and Therese Siegenthaler; in the seduced group: Lynda Gough, Shirley Robinson and Alison Chambers. To this latter group we could also add 'Sandra Johnson' (not her real name) who survived an attack by the Wests. Sandra's story which has been carefully reconstructed by Gordon Burn (1998: 283-290) throws some light onto the lives of the other young women who did not escape and who as a result were murdered by the Wests.

Sandra Johnson

In 1977 Sandra was 15 and two years earlier had started a relationship with Rose West's brother, Graham Letts, who at the time was 18. Sandra, whose parents had separated, was in care at Jordan's Brook House in Gloucester, a former approved school which is described by Howard Souness as caring for 'delinquent girls, most of whom had already been expelled from other homes. They were vulnerable adolescents, often from deeply troubled families and easily corrupted by people like the Wests' (1995: 163). Burn notes that Jordan's Brook House held 'twenty-three of the most difficult and disturbed girls in the country' (Burn, 1998:284).

Sandra was indeed disturbed and may have been schizophrenic. She had been raped by her father, then suffered from further sexual assaults by her brother. Sandra found her way to 25 Cromwell Street, having absconded from Jordan's Brook House and after spending the first night sleeping rough, although she seems to have been unaware that Graham Letts was Rose's brother.[3] As ever Rose West was charm personified, offering a shoulder to cry on and listening to all Sandra's worries and problems over 'orange squash and biscuits' (Souness, 1995: 166). Sandra became a regular visitor during the summer of 1977, even after she had returned to Jordan's Brook House, until one day when Rose led her upstairs and then subjected her to a serious sexual assault, which culminated in her being raped by Fred West. Sandra ran out of the house and wondered who she could turn to so as to explain what had happened to her, but 'there was nobody now. Because you were in care you were bad. There was nobody.' (Burn, 1998: 287). A few weeks later Sandra returned to 25 Cromwell Street with a can of petrol, fully intending to pour some through the letterbox and set the place alight. She could not do it and threw the can away.

Throwing the petrol can away suggests something of Sandra's belief in the impossibility of changing her circumstances—it was what was to be expected, in much the same way that even after having been raped Caroline went back to hitch-hiking to and from Gloucester. There was nothing else to be done; that was all that there was. So too Sandra's observations that there was 'nobody' and 'because you were in care you were bad' underline an obvious theme which is common to many of the victims that the Wests seduced. In short, most came from very damaged backgrounds and had spent significant periods of time in care.

Shirley Robinson

Shirley Robinson, for example, was a 17-year-old who came from a broken home and had been in care in Wolverhampton since the age of 14. She was so badly nourished that when the Wests saw her they nick-named her 'Bones' and Burn describes how Shirley was in effect a 'friendless and homeless lemon to take home and put with Rose' (1998: 288). The idea of Shirley being 'friendless' seems perfectly to echo Sandra's observation that there was 'nobody' to turn to in a time of crisis. The Wests could fill that void—but for their own reasons—and you can almost hear West promising Shirley all manner of wonders at his house, in

---

[3] Fred West seems to have been a regular visitor to Jordan's Brook House—his transit van was often seen parked outside the gates and this may have been why several of the girls ended up at 25 Cromwell Street (see Burn, 1998: 307).

much the same way that he had previously promised Caroline Raine that she would be a 'nanny'. However, whilst Shirley might indeed have formed some form of relationship with Rose West, she would eventually become pregnant with Fred's child, which in all likelihood was why she was killed. Shirley disappeared in May 1978 and when her body was eventually uncovered in 1994 her unborn baby was found buried with her.

Alison Chambers

Alison Chambers was also a resident of Jordan's Brook House and has been described as 'the most tragic girl to visit Cromwell Street' (Souness, 1995: 182). Known to other residents as 'Al' or 'Ali', she was thought to be very insecure and had run away from various homes in South Wales after her parents had divorced. She had also managed to abscond from Jordan's Brook House and had got as far as Paddington in London before being found and brought back. She suggested to staff that she wanted to go 'on the game'—much like Lisa in Nottingham. She was not popular with the other girls and was a regular target for bullying, which is of course another form of friendlessness, or of there being 'nobody'. This in turn led to her absconding and almost inevitably she found her way to Cromwell Street and the home of the man who was often in his transit van at the gates of the home.

Burn captures all of this rather well when he imagines West in his van, with his 'jokes and banter. Roll-ups and offers of rides. Lightly, lightly. If it takes a year, it takes a year. He could be tirelessly patient' (Burn, 1998: 308). We now know through former residents at the house that West had told Ali he had a farm in the country and had promised her that when she left the home when she was 18 she could ride horses all day and walk in the fields. Rose even gave her a picture of the 'farmhouse' that they owned and Ali did not realise that in fact it was a picture from an estate agent's brochure (Souness, 1995: 183). Here is another version of the 'nanny' routine, tailored to meet the needs of the specific victim who had been targeted. Poor Ali even wrote her mother a long letter, in which she described living with a very:

> homely family ... I look after their five children and do some of their housework. They have a child the same age as me who accepts me as a big sister and we get on great ...the family own flats and I share with the oldest sister.
>
> (quoted in Souness, 1995:184)

This is a confusing letter, but suggests something of how the Wests must have been viewed by some of the girls who entered 25 Cromwell Street. They were a 'homely family', which is of course what Alison had never had and the idea of her progressing and bettering herself through her association with them is perhaps revealed in the remark that they have a 'child' who is the same age as

Ali, but who nonetheless thinks of her as a 'big sister'. In short, perhaps for the first time in her life, Ali has status; she has something to offer. So too the Wests 'own flats', which seems to suggest the wealth and entrepreneurship of the upwardly mobile and must have been meant to have impressed Ali's mother that she was with people of substance and probity.

Alison had been reported as missing to the police—having absconded from Jordan's Brook House yet again just four weeks short of her 18th birthday—but because of the letter that she wrote to her mother no further action was thereafter taken. Her decapitated and dismembered body was later found in a hole in the garden, next to a wall of the bathroom extension. A plastic leather belt was found strapped under her chin and another belt looped around her head to clamp her mouth shut and stop her from screaming.

Carol Cooper

Carol Cooper—known as 'Caz'—was not seduced by the Wests, but much of her background seems very similar to the lives of Sandra, Ali and Shirley. Since she was 13 she had been living at the Pines Children's Home in Worcester. Her parents had divorced when she was four and after her mother had died when she was eight she had tried to live with her father, but this did not work out. A life in children's homes followed. Caz was pretty, intelligent, tall and strong, but did not like the homes that she was sent to. She would regularly abscond, sleep rough and had been caught shoplifting. By November 1973, aged 15, she had a boyfriend called Andrew Jones and on Saturday 10 they went to the local cinema, had fish and chips afterwards, then went to a pub. Caz drank bitter orange. Andrew took Caz to the bus stop, but they had been arguing and when she asked him to kiss her he refused. Before the bus arrived they'd patched things up and Andrew gave his girlfriend eighteen-and-a-half pence to pay for her bus fare home. He never saw her again (all details taken from Souness, 1995: 145-146). Six weeks after Caz's murder, West snatched Lucy Partington.

Shirley Hubbard

Shirley Hubbard was also last seen getting on a bus in Worcester. Shirley had been in children's homes from the age of two, but was eventually fostered by Jim and Linda Hubbard who lived in Droitwich in the Midlands. At the age of 15 she ran away from home and was eventually found sleeping rough in a field with a soldier some five miles outside of Worcester. She had 'Shirl' tattooed on her forearm. She then seems to have taken up with a boy called Dan Davies, whom she met at a fair in Worcester. She managed to get herself some work experience at Debenhams. On 14 November 1974 she and Dan spent the afternoon walking around the town eating chips, until eventually he saw her onto the bus to Droitwich. She never returned home and when her decapitated body was discovered in 1994 her skull was still encased in a hood mask. The mask had two holes through which had been inserted plastic tubes in what had clearly been an attempt to keep her alive for as long as possible, but Souness (1995: 147) believes that she died of 'suffocation or strangulation'.

Juanita Mott

Juanita Mott's father was a US serviceman who returned to Texas without his wife or daughter. Juanita was dark and fiery, and her family found her difficult. On a number of occasions she had been taken into care and when she reached 15 she left home and found herself a flat in Stroud Road, Gloucester. By the age of 16 she had had an ectopic pregnancy, told friends to call her 'Nita' and found herself a new flat in Cromwell Street. Whilst she was there she was found guilty of stealing a pension book and sent to Pucklechurch Remand Centre in Gloucester. Eventually she received a sentence of two years' probation and found herself a job in a local bottling factory. By 1975 she was living with a friend of her mother's in Newent and would hitch-hike into Gloucester to socialise. Nita's remains would also be found in the cellar of 25 Cromwell Street in 1994.

Therese Siegenthaler and Lynda Gough

For different reasons, Therese Siegenthaler and Lynda Gough—two other victims of the Wests—more closely resemble Lucy Partington than Ali, Shirley, Caz or Nita. Most obviously Therese, who had been born and raised in Switzerland, was a 21-year-old student studying sociology at Woolwich College and was living in digs in Deptford in London. In April 1974 she had set out to hitch-hike to Holyhead so as to catch the ferry to Ireland and meet up with a friend. We do not know how, or where she was picked up by West, but we do know that her body was found in the cellar of 25 Cromwell Street adjacent to that of Lucy Partington.

Neither was Lynda Gough from a broken home, but lived at home with her mother and father in Gloucester. She seems to have been befriended by a few of the male lodgers who were living in Cromwell Street and over time became a regular visitor to the house. Lynda had a job working as a seamstress at the Co-op and when she hadn't returned home after several days her mother went in search of her. Eventually the search took her to 25 Cromwell Street and the woman who answered the door, Rose West, looked familiar. The Wests denied all knowledge of ever having seen Lynda. It was then that Mrs Gough noticed that Rose was wearing Lynda's slippers and that there were more of Lynda's clothes hanging on the washing line. Now the Wests did remember that they had seen Lynda, but they said that she had left and gone to Weston-Super-Mare. The Goughs tried to reach her there, but of course they could not find her, for by then she was dead and buried under the floor of the ground-floor bathroom area. Surprisingly the Goughs never reported their daughter's disappearance.

Heather West

The Wests' final victim was their own daughter, Heather, and the victim who would eventually bring their murderous world to an end as her brothers and sisters did everything that they could to find out what had happened to her (West and West, 1995). Heather disappeared four months before turning 17. Her awful childhood was characterised by gross sexual abuse by her father and by her uncle; by sleeping in the cellar where the bodies of the young women who had been murdered were buried; and by being routinely strapped into her bed at night to prevent her from running away. Heather had even reached an agreement with her elder sister that they would stand guard for each other outside their shower, so that they would know in advance if their father was trying to come into the bathroom. No wonder Heather wanted out of Cromwell Street and, like Ali Chambers, dreamed of living in the countryside. Even so and despite everything that was going on at home, Heather had done well at school and had achieved eight GCSEs. She had also found herself a job cleaning chalets at a holiday camp in Devon. This fell through, but the rest of the family was told that Heather had gone off to work and they never saw her again (all details taken from Burn, 1998: 315-334).

In retrospect it would seem that West killed Heather because he couldn't risk her describing what had been happening at 25 Cromwell Street. In short he and Rose had learned from their experience with Caroline Raine and whilst they could control Heather within the house, they were less certain that that would hold true when she ventured out beyond the world that they had created. In many ways Heather's desire to leave home and the appalling circumstances of her childhood echoes the lives of many of the other young women who were murdered by her father and mother. But for a twist of fate, it could easily have been Heather who found herself in care at Jordan's Brook House and fantasising about a life without a daily dose of gross physical and sexual abuse; one where she had something to look forward to, even if she had nothing to look back at.

AT THE END OF THE ROAD

This chapter has taken as its focus the murders committed by the Wests. However, in doing so it has also attempted to understand the vulnerability of young people who run away, stay away, or are thrown away from their home, by using the research conducted by the Children's Society and the investigative journalism of Nick Davies. In this way I have attempted to generalise beyond the individual circumstances of the young women who were murdered by the Wests and look more broadly at a far more widespread phenomenon. After all there were over 66,000 first-time runaways in England and Wales in 2005 and we now know that if they have nowhere to go and sleep rough, they are likely to develop survival strategies that will involve stealing, begging and, in extreme cases, prostitution. We also know that many will put themselves in danger as a consequence. Underlying this phenomenon are a variety of factors and not simply the 'rebellion' of young people against their parents, or carers. Rather we can see the physical and sexual abuse, the inadequacies of the care system and the poverty that have characterised their lives and from which they would like to escape. Who can blame them?

Thankfully this was not lost on the city of Gloucester and in 1997—three years after the discoveries in Cromwell Street, the ASTRA Project was set up (see www.astraproject.org.uk). 'ASTRA' stands for Alternative Solutions To Running Away and the project aims to reduce the incidence of persistent running away from family, foster home or care. As the website makes clear, 'few young people run away because they really want to. In the majority of cases a young person runs away because they feel that adults don't care, don't listen, or don't understand.' The ASTRA Project also interviewed many of the young people who had gone missing in Gloucester so as to give advice to those young people who were considering running away. One passage is concerned with 'What dangers could young people face if they run away?' The answer was:

> Loads! People could leave you hurt and no one would know where you are. People might offer you somewhere to stay, but you wouldn't know if they could be trusted. You might have to steal, beg or even sell your own body to get money for food—this could get you into trouble with the police. You could even be abducted and murdered—it DOES HAPPEN!

'Does happen' is in capital letters just to emphasise the point.

CHAPTER 6

Children

CHAPTER 6

Children

> Somebody on the ward was looking for a victim. They were looking for someone who wouldn't complain. That was easy. There were plenty to choose from. It hardly mattered who. Pick this little girl with the blonde hair and the wheeze? No. Pick this boy with brain damage? He's two but he can't speak. No. Pick this one—this baby boy with brown eyes like olives. Pick him. He's on his own. No one can see. Do him. It's easy, as easy as pulling petals off a daisy. Pick Patrick Elstone. (Davies, 1993: 143)

When people think about serial killers who have targeted children, by and large they think about the Moors Murderers—Ian Brady and Myra Hindley, who killed five children (two girls and three boys) between the ages of 10 and 17 in the early 1960s. Indeed the Moors Murderers, in particular Myra Hindley, have become emblematic of serial killing in Britain more generally, and their story and especially their images seem omnipresent within the true crime genre.

Their faces, for example, appear on the front cover of Fido's (2001) *A History of British Serial Killing*, with Hindley's police photograph displayed prominently in the centre, staring out at prospective readers. Indeed this same police photograph—when re-worked as a series of child's handprints by the artist Marcus Harvey—caused controversy at the 'Sensation' Exhibition at the Royal Academy of Art in 1997. Sensation was an exhibition of work by young British artists, much of which had been bought by the collector Charles Saatchi, and Harvey's 'Myra' proved to be controversial as soon as the exhibition opened. So much so that windows at the Royal Academy were smashed, and two demonstrators hurled ink and eggs at the picture, requiring it to be temporarily removed and repaired before being re-exhibited behind perspex, guarded by security men. Despite the controversy—or perhaps because of it—the exhibition attracted some 300,000 visitors between September and December, then went on an international tour.

Gekoski (1998: 109) suggests that the hold that the Moors Murderers have on our consciousness stems from the fact that their murders 'marked the end of an era of innocence.' She continues:

> After 1965 the streets were considered an unsafe place for children to play; parents began to walk their children to and from school, and were reluctant to let them out of their sight in the evenings, or at weekends. Their children were safe nowhere, and with no one. (Gekoski, 1998: 108)

This is, of course, utter nonsense. Quite apart from the quadrupling of the numbers of children who were placed on the Child Protection Register after 1965 because of the risks that they faced from their own parents or carers, and almost as big an increase in the numbers of children who were taken into care (Davies, 1997: 238)—all of which suggests that it is overwhelmingly the home and not the street which is unsafe for children—serial killers such as the paedophile Robert Black still targeted children much later in our time-frame. Black, for example, snatched his three young victims off the streets as they played, or walked to and from their homes between 1982 and 1986. Even so few people would be able to cite his name or describe the circumstances in which he came to kill. Whilst it is beyond the scope of this book to look for the source of the hold of the Moors Murderers on our collective imagination this would seem to lie not so much in the loss of innocence and what happened to childhood after 1965, but has probably more to do with the gender of Myra Hindley.

Whilst few people would know very much about Robert Black, even fewer, I would suggest, would recognise the serial killer who is being described at the start of this chapter—a serial killer who murdered four young children, and attempted to kill nine others in 1991. The person who is being described by Nick Davies is Beverly Allitt and she is the only female British serial killer over our time-frame who acted alone. Nonetheless she does not appear at all in Fido's history of British serial killing and her picture is certainly not on his front cover.

This chapter is concerned with child victims of serial killers, and as such uses 'childhood' as a context within which to link the victims of Brady, Hindley, Black and Allitt. In doing so it uses aspects of James and Prout's (1990) attempt to establish a 'new paradigm' in the development of childhood sociology, which emphasises that childhood should be seen as a social construction and that children are active in this construction, rather than the passive subjects of social processes and structures. The chapter employs this new paradigm so as to aid understanding of which children, and in what circumstances, become the victims of serial killers; in particular it discusses the 'discovery' of child sexual abuse over our time-frame. As such it builds on the materials presented in *Chapter 5,* where the phenomenon of runaways and throwaways was discussed. It also seeks to amplify James and Prout's (1990: x) assertion that children are not just 'natural, passive, incompetent and incomplete' or, as John Muncie (1999: 3) has put it, they are not just defined by what 'they lack' but they are also more positively agents in, as well as products of social processes.

The contribution of children to these social processes is rarely acknowledged, or if it is, this is merely as a prelude to their contributions being discredited for one reason or another. Thus, secondly, the chapter attempts to sketch more generally some of the emergent boundaries of yet another reconstruction of childhood that is taking place in late Modernity. Here it is argued that we are not just witnessing what Jenks (1996: 128) has described as the 'conceptual eviction' of those children who seriously offend from the category of 'children', but we are also beginning to see the blurring of the boundary between childhood and being an adult—in society as a whole and especially in relation to youth justice, where increasingly children are treated as if they are adults.

Whilst this reconstruction of childhood forms the backdrop to what is being considered at some length, the central focus of the chapter relates to describing those children who have been the victims of serial killers. So too, along the way, some time is also devoted to the circumstances in which Allitt came to murder at Grantham and Kesteven General Hospital and to looking at the organization of the National Health Service (NHS). In doing so I am attempting to uncover why it was that killing children was as easy as 'pulling petals off a daisy'. Finally the chapter attempts to broaden responsibility for these deaths beyond the personal responsibility of Allitt and therefore begins to question how 'vulnerability' is created in childhood by organizations such as the NHS specifically and the criminal justice system more generally. The chapter opens by investigating the moral panic about paedophiles—which is of relevance given the murders by Robert Black and the sexual abuse of children more generally–before sketching in some of the more recent developments related to youth and criminal justice.

CHILD SEXUAL ABUSE—RESISTANCE AND RECONSTRUCTION

One of the best places to view the social construction and re-construction of childhood over our time-frame is in the current moral panic about child sexual abuse. Kitzinger (1997: 184), for example, suggests that the sexual abuse of children is not an anomaly or an aberration, but rather part of the structural oppression of children and thus that the way to overcome that oppression is to fundamentally alter how we conceive of childhood. For Kitzinger it is 'childhood as an institution that makes children "vulnerable"'. Instead of viewing childhood in terms of 'vulnerability' and thus being in need of adult 'protection', we should talk openly about power, and think conceptually about 'liberation' and 'oppression'. Thus, rather than think of children as 'defenceless' in relation to sexual abuse we should instead build on 'children's existing sense of self-protection and their ability to kick, yell and run'. Adults have consistently ignored the strategies that young people have evolved to defend themselves against sexual abuse, which has resulted in 'children's successful defences rarely com[ing] to public/adult attention' (Kitzinger, 1997: 173, 175). Such defences include: children sleeping with the family dog by their bed; deliberately making themselves look unattractive by refusing to bathe or wear make-up; and establishing relationships with other young people so as to be able to 'gain comfort, information and assistance from each other rather than from adults' (Kitzinger, 1997: 170).

For the moment it is also important to acknowledge that the 'discovery' of paedophilia and child sexual abuse has been one of the dominant drivers in the reconstruction of childhood that is taking place at the end of the book's time-frame. Jenks (1996: 86), for example, notes that the discovery of sexual abuse does not have anything to do with any alteration in the levels of abuse by adults of children, but is rather 'because of the changing patterns of personal, political and moral control in social life more generally which have, in turn, affected our vision of childhood.' More than this, as the child itself and childhood more generally have become emblematic of the social structure at a time which Jenks characterises as 'late Modernity', child sexual abuse too becomes a 'device for constituting reality' and a 'way of making sense' (Jenks, 1996: 98). Thus late Modern society has:

> re-adopted the child. The child in the setting of what are now conceptualised as post-modern cultural configurations, has become the site or the relocation of discourses concerning stability, integration and the social bond. The child is now envisaged as a form of 'nostalgia', a longing for times past. (Jenks, 1996: 106-107)

Thus to:

> Abuse the child today is to strike at the remaining, embodied vestige of the social bond and the consequent collective reaction is, understandably, both resounding and vituperative. The shrill cry of 'abuse' is a cry of our own collective pain at the loss of our social identity. (Jenks, 1996: 109)

This is a very insightful analysis and whilst one might wish to question aspects of how Jenks pushes his argument theoretically, we would do well to remember that the re-discovery of sexual abuse has in practical terms simply afforded greater degrees of control and surveillance over the lives of children, 'problem families' (who were initially viewed as the only source of sexual abuse) and increasingly other adults, who have come to attention through their internet usage.

Paradoxically, the discovery of child sexual abuse and the paedophile has gone hand-in-glove with other aspects of late Modern life that have increasingly coveted and sought to sexualise and ultimately market the promise of young people and their bodies (Silverman and Wilson, 2002). Thus, for example, we could look to the music, fashion and cosmetics industries which use young people in sexual ways and who seem to have decided that there is little difference between children and adults. The British pop group S Club 7 morphed seamlessly into S Club Juniors, and small girls, for example, have increasingly come to dress like adult women, who in turn come to look like young girls, blurring the line between 'child' and 'adult'.

Perhaps this process was at work in September 2002, when the British Board of Film Classification (BBFC) replaced the 12 certificate with the 12A rating, which allowed children to view 'adult' films from which they had previously been excluded. Thus, for example, recent James Bond films, *The Mummy* and especially *Spider Man* were rated at 12 and indeed the latter was described by the BBFC as 'possibly the most violent film aimed at a young audience' (reported in the *Guardian*, August 30 2002). However *Spider Man* was heavily marketed to children via toys and breakfast cereals with the result that several local councils overturned the BBFC's initial rating and let in children under 12. With the introduction of the 12A rating, *Spider Man* was immediately re-released by Columbia TriStar Films and became one of the highest-grossing hits of that year while the Hollywood thriller *The Bourne Identity* became the first film to be released under the 12A rating.

THE DIONYSIAN VERSUS THE APOLLONIAN CHILD IN CRIME AND PUNISHMENT

In discussing the blurring of the boundaries between child and adult we would also do well to remember that as long ago as 1962 Philippe Aries, using paintings as his primary source, argued that up to and including the Middle Ages there was no collective perception of children being different from adults and that as soon as children were physically able they went 'straight into the great community of men' (1962: 412). Constructions and reconstructions of childhood are thus a relatively recent phenomenon, with various tours and detours along the way, albeit largely reflecting what Jenks (1996: 70-81) describes as the two dominant ways of talking about children, which he represents through the two different and competing images of the Dionysian and the Apollonian child. The former see the child as essentially a wilful, impish force, capable of evil and thus needing adult control and surveillance, whilst the latter sees the child as angelic, innocent, unpolluted by the world and thus needing adult protection, facilitation and encouragement. Of course, power in both images of the child is vested with adults, who are able to dispense with the construction of childhood altogether—should they wish to do so. Indeed some have argued that what we are currently witnessing, for various reasons is the 'disappearance' of childhood (Postman, 1994). We do not need to go this far, especially since there are now various legal attempts to set parameters around the concept of childhood—including children in jail. However, I would argue that we are beginning to see the boundaries between 'child' and 'adult' becoming blurred and indistinct and that these blurrings are particularly apparent in relation to those young people who commit crime, which like childhood, is also a social construction.

The attempt to 'do something' to prevent young people from committing crime, or how best to respond to them after they have committed a crime are two of the perennial issues at the heart of youth criminal justice systems. As Muncie and Hughes (2002: 1) have argued, what is done is essentially a 'history of conflict, contradictions, ambiguity and compromise' with an amalgam of rationales that seeks 'the compromise between youth as a special deserving case and youth as fully responsible for their own actions'. For Muncie and Hughes a compromise is eventually reached between these competing rationales—which echo Jenks's images of the Dionysian and Apollonian child—by expanding the remit of the youth justice system both in terms of sentencing powers and system reach. Thus the youth justice system is not simply interested in those who offend, but also those who are 'at risk' of offending, resulting in what it means to be young becoming 'increasingly tightly defined and regulated' (Muncie and Hughes, 2002: 2). The end product, as Rose (1989: 121) has argued, is that childhood has become the most 'intensively governed sector of personal existence.' More than this, Simon (2001) detects in the United States: a 'penality of cruelty', with the death penalty available for juveniles (up until 2006), shame sanctions and the resurgence of boot camps; and in this country: an inexplicable willingness to send young people to young offender institutions despite extraordinarily high levels of self-harm, suicide, brutality and a lamentable failure to actually change high rates of recidivism.

Obviously the willingness to send young people to prison is not prompted by 'evidence led practice' or 'what works'. It is perhaps best explained by reactions to young people in the wake of the murder of James Bulger in 1993 (c.f. Wilson and Ashton, 1998; Jenks, 1996; Muncie 1999) which have seen young people who commit crime become the 'human equivalent of dangerous dogs' and thus deserving the full weight of policing, sentencing and custodial initiatives. New Labour have been in the vanguard of these processes and whilst it is difficult to discern a fundamental philosophy underpinning the various initiatives that have taken place since 1997—which Newburn (2002: 454) describes as a 'frenzy' of activity—there have been overlapping and sometimes conflicting rationales, which in turn are related to the overlapping and conflicting conceptualisations of childhood itself.

However, one clear feature of the youth justice landscape has been what Muncie and Hughes (2002: 4) have characterised as 'adulteration'. Thus, for example, the ancient legal presumption of *doli incapax* (lack of criminal capacity) was abolished for 10-to-14-year-olds in 1998. Furthermore Anti Social Behaviour Orders (ASBOs) which can be applied to children as young as ten (the age of criminal responsibility in England and Wales), were introduced by section 1 Crime and Disorder Act 1998. Whilst the Home Office did not initially view young people as the primary targets for ASBOs, strong lobbying by various local councils saw to it that young people were eventually seen as central to the 'anti-social paradigm'

(Burney, 2005). Allied to these, children—whether they have committed an offence or not,—can now be subject to curfews and their parents to parental responsibility orders if their children truant, are school excluded or get into trouble with the police. Thus children and their families, directly in this latter respect and indirectly through, for example, child safety orders, have become the focus for New Labour's criminal justice policies, which seem to be based on conceptions of what 'normal' children and families are like (Muncie and Hughes, 2002: 9). Nonetheless, those young people who do come persistently to the attention of the youth justice system have very complex lives and often experience systematic patterns of disadvantage which are not going to be solved by New Labour's appeals to morality and responsibilisation.

Finally, before discussing Brady, Hindley, Black and Allitt, we should also remember that childhood has always been iconic of broader social anxieties and as a result children have always been the subjects of the adult gaze, whether in the guise of protection and empowerment, or control and regulation. In this respect what I am suggesting is that late Modernity is reconstructing childhood by blurring the boundary between childhood and adulthood, so as to achieve outcomes that suit adult needs. Thus these outcomes may be about developing new markets and commercial opportunities, or simply to permit and facilitate adult sexual fantasy. In youth justice terms this blurring provides a semblance of control—of 'something being done' about crime and punishment—by treating young people as if they were adult and punishing them accordingly. Overall, the line between being a 'child' and being an 'adult' becomes less and less obvious, whilst at the same time strenuous efforts are maintained to proclaim childhood as precious and worth protecting—especially when society confronts a high-profile crime involving the murder of a child or children.

BRADY, HINDLEY AND BLACK

Given the extensive coverage of the crimes of the Moors murderers I do not intend to dwell too long on the individual victims of Ian Brady and Myra Hindley (for a general introduction see Fido, 2001: 121-141). However, given the relative lack of knowledge about Robert Black and his victims I will spend some greater time covering the circumstances in which Black—a convicted paedophile—came to kill and what this might or might not reveal about the changing nature of childhood. Above all I will try to compare and contrast the child victims of these serial killers— and in doing so use several of the more established, academic descriptions of serial killing, before then considering the victims of Beverly Allitt.

Brady and Hindley were 'indiscriminate' serial killers. The description 'indiscriminate' is meant to convey that they killed both boys and girls and they did not seem to be particularly worried if these boys and girls were roughly of the same age. Thus, for example, their final victim was 17-year-old Edward Evans, whom they murdered on 6 October 1965, whilst their first victim was Pauline Read— whom they killed some two years previously on 12 July 1963, after she was enticed into Hindley's car as she walked to a dance at the Railway Workers' Social Club in Manchester. Pauline was 16 years old and whilst her age was similar to that of Edward's, other victims of Brady and Hindley's include 12-year-old John Kilbride, 12-year-old Keith Bennett and 10 year-old Lesley Ann Downey.

The murder of their youngest victim—Lesley Ann Downey, on Boxing Day 1964—was particularly heinous, although her disappearance at the time did not provoke any widespread police interest (Gekoski, 1998: 92). Her body was eventually found on 10 October 1965, after the police had been alerted to Brady and Hindley's activities through Hindley's brother-in-law, David Smith, and after the murder of Edward Evans. Lesley Ann's body was found buried in a shallow grave on Saddleworth Moor. As if that was not bad enough, the police also discovered two suitcases in a locker at Manchester Central Station which contained pornographic photographs of Lesley Ann and a harrowing tape of her begging for her life.

Whereas Brady and Hindley were indiscriminate in their choice of victim, Robert Black was only interested in very young girls aged between five and 12. His preference for young girls reflected his fixed paedophilic personality. Thus, for example, he killed Susan Maxwell in July 1982, Caroline Hogg in July 1983 and Sarah Harper in March 1986. All three girls were aged under 12, with Susan and Sarah the oldest at eleven and five-year-old Caroline the youngest. Like most serial killers, Black is suspected of having killed many more than the three young girls whom he was convicted of murdering and Ray Wyre (1995: 12), for example, who interviewed Black at some length, believes that he molested 'hundreds' of young girls, abducted 'dozens' and 'at least eight may have died'.

Like the Wests, Brady and Hindley may have enticed their victims into a car on the promise of a lift and they may well have benefited from the fact that a lift was more likely to have been accepted by a child given Hindley's gender. Hindley also seems to have used a ruse to entice the children into the car so, for example, she asked John Kilbride to help her move some boxes and Pauline Reade to help her find a glove that Hindley claimed she had lost on Saddleworth Moor (all details from Fido, 2001: 126). When they arrived at the moor Brady would be waiting, having ridden there on his motorbike. There is also some evidence that Brady may have known one of their victims (Edward Evans) previously (Gekoski, 1998: 92).

Black did not know any of his victims and simply 'snatched' them as they walked or played in the streets, before bundling them into his van. Indeed we know something of his *modus operandi* precisely because a few victims survived an attack by Black. Teresa Ann Thornhill, for example, was attacked on 28 April 1988. Teresa was 15 at this time—outside Black's normal target range—but she was slight, small and looked much younger than her age. She was walking back to her house in Nottingham when a blue transit van passed her:

> I saw the driver get out and open the bonnet of the engine. As I walked level with the van the man shouted, 'Oi' to me. I looked towards him to make sure he was talking to me. I couldn't see anybody else about. I ignored him, looked away and carried on walking. Then he shouted 'Can you fix engines?' I replied 'No, I can't' ... I suddenly felt the man grab me from behind. I screamed and tried to struggle free. He picked me up and carried me across the road to the big blue van. I was till screaming and fighting to get away ... he then put his big hand over my mouth, covering my nose. With his hand over my face I felt as if I was going to pass out, so I bit him on his hand. This forced him to release his hand from my face. I then bit him on the arm and screamed again ... I think that it was at this point that I knocked his glasses off. As he held me he opened the driver's door of the van and tried to bundle me inside. I fought with all my strength and used ... my feet to push backwards and stop him from getting me inside. I think he said something like 'Get in, you bitch,' as we were struggling. (Quoted in Wyre, 1995: 116-117)

This attack is very interesting for several reasons. Firstly it suggests that Black had planned what he was doing and that he had developed a method for overcoming a child that he saw as a suitable victim. For example, he believed—incorrectly as it happens—that Teresa was younger than she was and crucially that she was alone. In fact a boyfriend heard Teresa's screams and came to her aid.

Secondly we can see that Black tried to engage Teresa's sympathies (a technique also used by Hindley) and have her help him overcome a problem—his broken engine—although this was merely an excuse to get her closer to the van so that he could bundle her inside.

Finally it reveals something of the bravery of Teresa and her strategy for overcoming her assailant. She screamed, she bit, she knocked his glasses off, she used her feet and her strength to prevent Black getting her inside his van and we can see in Black's response to her—'Get in, you bitch', his frustration at his inability to overcome her and achieve his objective. Indeed, Teresa's behaviour is almost a perfect example of what Kitzinger (see above) has described as children's 'existing sense of self-protection and their ability to kick, yell and run' (1997: 173). So too, when Teresa did get help it was another child, a boyfriend, rather than an adult who came to her aid.

Of course Teresa was relatively old at 15 and as has been suggested she was outside Black's normal target range. However, his final intended victim was a six-year-old girl called Mandy Wilson. Mandy was very much within Black's preferred age range and he attempted to abduct her on 14 July 1990 from the village of Stow in the borders between Scotland and England, as she walked to a friend's house to play. Black's attack on Mandy bears striking similarities to the attack some two year's earlier on Teresa and is recounted by Mandy's neighbour, David Herkes, who witnessed the abduction as he cut his grass:

All I could see were her little feet standing next to the man's. Suddenly they vanished and I saw him making movements as if he was trying to stuff something under the dashboard. He got into the van, reversed up the driveway that the child had just come from and sped off towards Edinburgh. (quoted in Gekoski, 1998: 200)

Herkes noted down the van's registration number and immediately called the police, who fortunately were on the scene in a matter of a few minutes. As he was briefing the police as to what had happened, Black's van reappeared and Herkes shouted, 'That's him!' (Gekoski, 1998: 201), which prompted one police officer—Mandy's own father—to step into the road, causing Black to swerve to a halt. Thus Mandy was saved—although by this stage she had already been sexually assaulted by Black (Gekoski, 1998: 201). Black was given a life sentence for the abduction of Mandy in August 1990 and then further life sentences in May 1994 for the attempted abduction of Teresa Thornhill and the murders of Susan Maxwell, Caroline Hogg and Sarah Harper.

Given that Susan Maxwell had been murdered in July 1982, Gekoski (1998: 212) asks, 'Why had it taken eight years for Black to be apprehended, three years longer than it had taken to catch Peter Sutcliffe?' Indeed her question seems particularly pertinent given the development of various police computer packages such as HOLMES in the aftermath of the Sutcliffe investigation which were supposed to be of assistance in investigations of this kind. Ray Wyre (1995: 227) is even more scathing and suggests, for example, that 'Black's life and, with it, his career as a sex offender illustrated an almost complete failure by every part of the investigative and penal system in Britain.' In short the penal system had failed to stop Black from offending and the police had then failed to catch him.

Part of this investigatory failure that Wyre draws attention to can be attributed to the fact that Black, unlike Brady and Hindley, was a geographically transient serial killer. In other words he did not kill his victims and dispose of their bodies in one area, but rather in several areas which would mean that, for example, he would cross from one police jurisdiction into another. Black thus used his work as a delivery man for Poster Dispatch and Storage (PDS)—a company he had joined in 1976 and where he was responsible for the Scottish run—to create opportunities to locate both suitable victims and also sites where he could later discard their bodies.

Working for PDS, at that time based in London, his deliveries took him through the Midlands and the north of England to the Scottish borders, Edinburgh, Glasgow and as far north as Dundee. In July 1982—the month that Susan Maxwell disappeared after walking back to her home in Cornhill-on-Tweed, near Coldstream after a tennis match—Black was on the Scottish run delivering posters related to a new high profile campaign for Kestrel lager, a brand being promoted by Scottish and Newcastle Breweries as 'the thinking man's lager'. No doubt Susan was abducted in much the same way that Black had attempted to abduct Teresa and Mandy and her body was eventually discovered on 13 August 1982 in a shallow ditch beside a lay-by on the edge of the A518 at Loxley, two miles outside Uttoxeter and some 250 miles away from Coldstream.

Caroline Hogg was five when she was murdered on 8 July 1983. She lived in the seaside resort of Portobello, on the outskirts of Edinburgh, and on the day in question had been to a friend's house for a birthday party. On her return at around 7p.m., she asked her mother Annette if she could have five minutes to play on the swings in the park and when her mother agreed, she slipped off her party shoes to put on her pink trainers. Less then 15 minutes later Annette went in search of her daughter and 30 minutes after that she called the police station in Portobello High Street. Caroline's body was found ten days later, dumped on the edge of a lay-by near Twycross in Leicestershire, which was again a considerable distance from where she had been snatched.

Sarah Harper lived in Morley in Leeds with her mother Jacki, her nine-year-old sister Claire and her five-year-old brother David. On the evening of 26 March 1986, just as the popular evening TV 'soap' *Coronation Street* was starting, Jacki asked Sarah to go and fetch a loaf of bread from a traditional corner shop which was about 100 yards away from their home. On her way out of the door Sarah grabbed two empty lemonade bottles, which would have been worth about 20 pence in terms of refunds to hand in at the shop. She reached the shop, but never returned home. Her body was found in the River Trent at Wilford on the outskirts of Nottingham on April 19. She had been sexually assaulted, bound and gagged. Sarah had been alive when she had been thrown into the river and her cause of death was recorded as drowning.

What should we make of the abductions and murders of Susan, Caroline and Sarah? In particular do the circumstances of their murders reveal anything about the changing nature of childhood? Despite what is claimed by Gekoski after the Moors murders (see above) the answer would appear to be 'no'. Young girls still ran errands for their parents; walked by themselves to play tennis matches against friends; went to birthday parties and then ran out of the house to the park to play on the swings. In doing so they were let out of the sight of their parents—not because their parents didn't care about their welfare, or because they calculated that the chances of their children being abducted and murdered by a stranger were extremely small[1], but simply because this was and remains part of the normal process of gaining independence, taking responsibility and growing up. As such, our response to these awful murders should not be to place even more controls and still greater surveillance on children and childhood because we believe that children are constantly at risk of attack, but rather to question how it was that Robert Black came to kill and why it took so long to stop him.

---

[1] Frank Furedi (2001: 10-11), for example, has calculated that the numbers of children murdered between 1988-1999 actually decreased.

We have already discussed the difficulties of investigating cases of this kind when police borders are crossed by geographically transient serial killers, but we should also note that Black had first come to the attention of the courts as a result of an assault on a young girl in Scotland in the summer of 1963, when he was 17 years old. In this assault Black had enticed the girl to go with him to a disused building on the promise of showing her some kittens. Once in the building he held her by the throat—almost strangling her—whilst he sexually assaulted her. The girl was later found walking the streets bleeding, confused and crying. Black duly appeared at Greenock Juvenile Court charged with lewd and libidinous behaviour against a seven-year-old girl. He was found guilty, but given an admonishment—which is in effect a warning to be of good behaviour in the future. He walked away from court a free man and not a single paragraph was reported about the case in any newspaper (details taken from Wyre, 1995: 93-120).

Black continued to molest young girls and as a result of another sexual assault on a six-year-old girl was sent to borstal in 1967. On his release he moved from Scotland to England—probably to both escape the attention that he had created in his home area through his past offending and also to create the opportunity to offend in the future—before eventually joining PDS in 1976. Ray Wyre, who has interviewed Black extensively, is in no doubt that during this time Black continued to offend and became an obsessive collector of child pornography. In one particularly interesting passage, Wyre describes Black as 'slipp[ing] through the gratings of the urban streets in which he existed: another grimy worker in a part of the city crumbling away, a loner, a man with no girlfriend, wife, or family and no apparent prospects of finding any one of them' (1995: 60). This description is meant to suggest the anonymity of Black's work with PDS—delivering posters to sites on the outskirts of our towns and cities—and also something of his isolation from other people and normal family life. Perhaps we should also note that two of his victims, Caroline Hogg and Sarah Harper, lived with their families in those parts of the city which Wyre characterises as 'crumbling away' and that his description also captures a sense that Black had slipped through the gratings of the criminal justice system too.

We might see the criminal justice system as also 'crumbling' and elsewhere I have suggested that 'if your gas central heating system worked like our criminal justice system, you would long ago have had to switch to oil, or frozen to death' (Wilson and Ashton, 1998: xi). After all Black had been offending for some 35 years before being caught with Mandy Wilson in the back of his van, had been to court on at least two occasions and had served a custodial sentence for a sexual assault on a child. At no point was he ever offered counselling or treatment for his offending, he was simply released back into the community, in all probability more dangerous than when he had first been sentenced. Even so, as record-keeping stood at that time his name did not appear on any police database, which is why luck played such a major role in his arrest and it explains why he was never a suspect in any of the three murders for which he was eventually convicted.

PULLING PETALS OFF DAISIES—BEVERLY ALLITT

Claire Peck was 15 months old when she was admitted to Ward Four of Grantham and Kesteven General Hospital (hereafter referred to as Grantham General Hospital) on 22 April 1991 at 4.15 p.m. She was no stranger to the ward, having been in and out of hospital since her birth, with breathing problems related to asthma. Claire's worried parents, Sue and David, accompanied her, but they put their faith in the hospital staff to look after their little girl who was learning to walk and had blond, wavy hair and a 'cheeky way of blinking both eyes when she laughed' (Davies, 1993: 151). Claire was having a bad asthma attack and wheezing quite badly. One of the ward's two consultant paediatricians, Dr Nelson Porter, arrived at the treatment room to assess her condition at 5.10 p.m. and ordered some X-rays. He also decided to give Claire an injection of aminophylline by intravenous drip, which was a delicate procedure and had to be done slowly over 15-20 minutes, so as to avoid damaging her heart.

Dr Porter left the treatment room to calculate the correct dosage and another nurse went to find David and Sue, who were waiting in the parents' room, to appraise them of the situation. Claire was left alone in the treatment room with Beverly Allitt and when another nurse arrived only a few minutes later Claire's face was dark blue, her back arched up off the bed and she had stopped breathing. She was immediately given oxygen through a face mask and Dr Porter also injected into her some of the aminophylline. Quite quickly Claire recovered and she started to breathe again. The crisis seemed to be over and Dr Porter left once more to advise David and Sue of the situation.

The Allitt Inquiry (Clothier, 1994) takes up the story from this point and simply suggests that whilst Claire seemed to be improving:

> an hour later Allitt raised the alarm again. Claire was dark blue and not breathing. The other nurses and the consultant, Dr Porter returned to the room just as her heart stopped beating. The team made vigorous attempts to resuscitate her. They were successful in restoring circulation and oxygen saturation of the blood, but her heart would still not restart. Claire was declared dead later that evening. (Clothier, 1994: 36)

Whilst all of this might be factually correct, it hardly captures the appalling drama that was unfolding and the dreadful circumstances that Claire's parents were having to face. Indeed, the inquiry's version ignores the fact that when Dr Porter was returning to the treatment room at about 6.30 p.m. he had brought David and Sue with him (and Sue's parents too) and that Allitt had appeared and shouted, 'Quick, quick, she's gone blue again!' (Davies, 1993: 154). So too it was obvious on entering the treatment room that Claire was dead, or as the inquiry rather quaintly puts it—'her heart had stopped beating'. Dr Porter and his team nonetheless did indeed work for another hour-and-a-half attempting to resuscitate Claire, but it is Davies who advises us that Sue and David leaned over Claire, touching her arms and legs, stroking her wavy blond hair and cradling her in their arms before kissing her goodbye. She was pronounced dead at 8.25 p.m.—just over four hours after having been admitted to the ward.

The differences between the inquiry's account and that provided through primary research by the campaigning journalist, Nick Davies, are marked. It is also clear that there was no love lost between the official inquiry—which reported in 1994 after Davies had published his book and what he had uncovered—and Davies himself. Indeed, a footnote on p. 88 of the inquiry report draws attention to 'a journalist's account of the matter', but in disputing what Davies had said in relation to the inquiry's terms of reference it airily dismisses the rest of his book with the comment, 'there seems no need to deal any further with the rest of the book' (Clothier, 1994: 88-89).[2]

Here I am attempting to blend carefully the 'official' account of the inquiry with those issues uncovered by Davies. In doing so it is abundantly clear that Claire Peck need not have died and that Ward Four should have been shut down at least two weeks earlier when, on April 12, conclusive evidence emerged that there was a killer in the hospital. Even after Claire's death on April 22 the hospital was to wait a further eight days before they called in the police so between April 12 and 30 Allitt killed one child and attacked three others—Patrick Elstone, Christopher Peasgood and Christopher King. Indeed by the time Claire was admitted to Ward Four there had been 24 occasions when the hearts or lungs of children had mysteriously stopped in the previous two months and three children who had died in circumstances that at first no one could explain.

An explanation became clearer on Friday April 12, so it would appear, when Dr Porter was advised that one child who had been attacked, Paul Crampton, had a large quantity of exogenous insulin in his blood, which pointed in the direction of there being a killer on the loose on the ward. Yet, again it seems, neither Dr Porter nor any administrator at the hospital called in the police to investigate, nor were any new security procedures introduced onto the ward to control, for example, the issue of drugs; there was no multi-disciplinary case conference to review the chain of events that had unfolded over the previous two months, and children continued being admitted onto the ward, as if it was a safe place for sick children to recover.

---

[2] Of note, the copy of *Murder on Ward Four* by Nick Davies has been stolen from the Radzinowicz Library in Cambridge, and if one wants to read the only copy that now exists in the University Library this must be done within the Reading Room of the library in the sight of the librarian. There were no such problems in getting hold of the the Allitt Inquiry, or indeed of being able to borrow a copy.

Indeed he and a fellow paediatric consultant both, so it appears, left the ward the following week to attend the annual conference of the British Paediatric Association. No wonder Allitt found killing children in her care as easy as pulling 'petals off a daisy'.

How are we to explain what happened at Grantham General Hospital and crucially to what extent should we see the murder there of four children and the attempted murder of nine others as the personal responsibility of Allitt? Was she solely to blame for repeatedly attacking and killing children in her care, or are there other responsibilities too? Specifically, was how she was recruited, trained and supervised also responsible for these deaths and then, more generally, were there responsibilities related to the organization, financing and management of the NHS? As ever Davies and the Allitt Inquiry were at odds on where responsibility should lie. Davies, for example, concluded:

> Ward Four was trapped by habit and lack of supervision, by low morale and lack of funds, staked out and helpless, the perfect victim. The problems which the Health Service inflicted on the hospital conspired together to set the scene for Nurse Allitt's crimes and then enabled her to get away with them. (Davies, 1993: 345)

On the other hand, the Allitt Inquiry concluded:

> The main lesson from our Inquiry and our principal recommendation is that the Grantham disaster should serve to heighten awareness in all those caring for children of the possibility of malevolent intervention as a cause of unexplained clinical events.
> (Clothier, 1994: 130).

To find the balance between these essentially competing conclusions we need to look a little more closely at how Allitt came to be employed on Ward Four and how she was supervised. We also need to look at the various responses, by different people at a number of stages, as events unfolded between February and April 1991. In particular we need to assess what steps were taken—or not taken—after April 12, when Dr Porter was advised about Paul Crampton's blood sample.

Recruitment, supervision and April 12

Allitt attended Grantham College to complete a pre-nursing course, as she was too young and did not have sufficient O-levels to enter nursing training directly (all details taken from Clothier, 1994: 12-23). The course at the college was two years long and whilst there were some difficulties in her first year, more pressing problems emerged during her second year. For example, Allitt always seemed to have a number of illnesses and injuries and would show these to her tutors as a way of drawing attention to herself.[3] In fact she missed 52 days out of a possible 180 in

---

[3] We now know that Allitt was suffering from Munchausen Syndrome—a term coined in the 1950s to describe a particular form of hospital addiction, and which involves the sufferer often presenting

her second year. Even so, she applied to South Lincolnshire School of Nursing to train for a further two years as a pupil nurse, with a view to becoming an enrolled nurse. On her application she did not name anyone from Grantham College as a referee—who might conceivably have commented on her sickness absences which thus might also have flagged up her lack of suitability as a nurse.

During her pupil nurse training there were some unexplained incidents at the nurses' home (involving mysterious fires and so forth), but of greater concern was Allitt's continued record of sickness. She missed a total of 126 days' training during her 110 week course and even the official inquiry noted that 'such a high level of sickness was unusual' (Clothier, 1994: 16). Although she was never referred by the school, Allitt actually attended the Accident and Emergency Department of Grantham General Hospital on at least ten occasions, but the school of nursing was never informed of these attendances. Eventually Allitt passed her exams to become an enrolled nurse, but due to her sickness record she had not completed the required number of days on a ward and therefore needed to undertake a further ward placement before qualifying as an enrolled nurse. She undertook that placement on Ward Four.

In December 1990 Allitt was interviewed in the general recruitment round for nurses at Grantham General Hospital, but she failed to impress the interviewers and was not offered a job. Thus by February 1991 she was nearly at the end of the time that she needed to spend to complete her practical experience and her formal training was due to end on February 18. She had no job to go to, but the Clinical Service Manager, Moira Onions, made inquiries on her behalf about training courses to become a qualified childrens' nurse or a registered sick children's nurse (RSCN). Such a course was available at Pilgrim Hospital in Boston, but when Allitt was interviewed with a view to joining the course she again failed to impress and was not offered a place.

However, given that Grantham General Hospital was short of RSCNs and had just lost two from Ward Four in December 1990, Moira Onions decided to create an enrolled nurse post on Ward Four and interview Allitt for the job. Allitt was interviewed by Moira Onions and Sister Barbara Barker, the ward manager, on February 15 and offered a six month contract on Ward Four. Thus she began work as an enrolled nurse on Ward Four on 19ᵗFebruary 1991, even though there had been no satisfactory health screening of her, nor any police check as was required. Even the official inquiry is moved to conclude that 'virtually none of the procedures in the hospital's recruitment policy was followed when Allitt was appointed'

at hospital with stories of medical disorder and which can be supported by pathological evidence which has often been falsified. So too there is Munchausen Syndrome by Proxy—a term introduced in 1977 by Professor Roy Meadow, whereby the fictitious injury or manifestation of illness is inflicted on others—usually a child. This should be seen as a form of child abuse. Of note, about a quarter of those who are subsumed under the label Munchausen Syndrome by Proxy have themselves Munchausen Syndrome.

(Clothier, 1994: 22). Five days after she started work, Allitt killed her first victim—seven-week-old Liam Taylor.

Here we might do well to consider why it was that none of the hospital's normal recruitment procedures were followed and why managers at the hospital almost fell over backwards to recruit an enrolled nurse with an appalling sickness record who had actually been turned down for a post in the hospital's normal recruitment round. Was this just kindness on the part of hospital managers for a student nurse with no job to go to or were there other forces at work? The answer seems to be more to do with practicalities than with kindness.

Ward Four at this time was supposed to have 10.66 whole time equivalents (WTEs), or, in other words, the number of nurses employed—whether full-time or part-time—should have been equivalent to 10.66 nurses working full-time (all details taken from Clothier, 1994: 89-94). The actual number of nurses in post was far lower than 10.66 WTEs and during the months in question there were only three full-time nurses and one part-time nurse on Ward Four who held the qualification of RSCN, which is the equivalent of 3.53 WTEs. As a result Ward Four was understaffed and regularly had to make use of a 'bank' of nurses to make up the shortfall. Even so, only one of the 'banked nurses' was a RSCN.

All of this meant that often there was no RSCN on duty at all on Ward Four and that, as the official inquiry rather obliquely notes, 'indeed on some shifts an enrolled nurse was left in charge of the ward' (Clothier, 1994: 92). Of course one of these enrolled nurses was Beverly Allitt, who as a consequence was given responsibilities and power that she in other circumstances would not have been given due to her inexperience and lack of qualifications. This is no small matter, for it meant that, for example, Allitt would have had access to the drugs cabinet. It also meant that as the only qualified nurse on duty she would have been expected to 'special' a sick child, in effect giving that child her undivided attention, which thus created for her the opportunity to be alone with that child and to do with him or her as she pleased.

We might also reasonably have presumed that as a recently qualified nurse Allitt would have been subject to regular supervision by more senior nurses. Sister Barbara Barker, the Ward Manager, was the most experienced nurse at the hospital who held the qualification of RSCN and, it should be remembered, interviewed Allitt for the post on Ward Four. It is therefore reasonable to assume that she would have taken some responsibility for overseeing Allitt's work, but as the official inquiry puts it, 'we have heard evidence that Sister Barker did not function well in her role as leader,' and 'she did not take an interest in the training of learners' (Clothier, 1994: 99-100). In other words Allitt, once in post, was very much left to her own devices, with little supervision, guidance or questioning about what was happening to children under her control. Indeed, this becomes all the more apparent when we investigate what steps were taken to assess a large number of mysterious emergencies with children in Allitt's care, when their hearts or lungs stopped working and she was the only person present. In particular, further light is thrown onto the management and oversight of Ward Four in considering what action was taken when Dr Porter became aware of the results of Paul Crampton's blood test.

Paul Crampton was five months old when he was admitted onto Ward Four on Wednesday 20 March 1991, with a history of wheezing. He was diagnosed as suffering from either a moderate chest infection or mild asthma. However, when nurses—including Allitt—came to give Paul medication on Saturday March 23rd they noticed that he was cold, clammy and showing signs of low blood sugar—although he was not diabetic. Paul was put on a glucose drip and soon recovered. On the Sunday morning the drip was taken down, but later replaced when Paul's father found him once again cold and clammy. A blood sample was taken from Paul and this demonstrated that his blood glucose was low. Paul was fine for another three days, but then had a further attack on the Thursday 28, when Allitt returned from three days' leave. Following this episode Paul was transferred to the Queen's Medical Centre in Nottingham where he gradually recovered. One of Ward Four's two consultants, Dr Porter, could not understand why Paul's blood sugar kept dropping so dramatically so he had blood samples taken which were then sent off to a laboratory in Cardiff for analysis.

On Friday April 12 Dr Porter received a telephone call from the Cardiff laboratory explaining that Paul Crampton's blood sample contained a large quantity of exogenous insulin which thus suggested that he had been injected with insulin. This was very significant information. Nonetheless Dr Porter hesitated—a hesitation compounded by the fact that he was not given too much support by the Queen's Medical Centre in Nottingham, whom he had telephoned to discuss the result (all details taken from Clothier, 1994: 59-61 and 111-113). Dr Porter was suspicious and relayed some of those suspicions to staff on Ward Four, but in any event he and a fellow consultant went off to the annual conference of the British Paediatric Association which began on April 15. In doing so he was downplaying the information that he had been given and whilst there may very well have been a heightened awareness as to what was going on within the ward, no changes to the ward's procedures were introduced, no case conferences were held, no new security arrangements were initiated and nor were the police contacted.

We might reasonably have expected that if these results had been taken seriously then the ward would have had to have been closed—at least temporarily. This would have been catastrophic for the hospital more generally. Although not something commented upon by the official Allitt inquiry, Davies notes that Grantham General Hospital was £200,000 overspent and whilst it was 'a tiny faction of the budget … the money had to be found and the hospital could not afford to go creating a public panic, driving valuable patients away' (Davies, 1993: 163). More than this, if they closed Ward Four they would not have the funding to pay for the two consultants, which in turn meant that they would not be able to run the special baby care unit. If they lost the special baby care unit, then they would not be able to run the maternity ward and in this NHS funding 'house of cards':

> If they lost that, they would have lost one of their 'core services' and they would then lose their status as a District General Hospital. In other words, in the brave new world of the NHS market, if they created a public scare when none was necessary, they could lose the hospital. (Davies, 1993: 163)

In short, there was a great deal going on behind the scenes to play down what was happening on Ward Four and it would be two weeks after first hearing the results of Paul Crampton's blood test before Martin Gibson, the hospital's manager, finally decided to call in the police.

RESPONSIBILITY AND WHERE DOES IT LIE?

I have gone into the history of Beverly Allitt in some detail for her case seems to stand as a paradigm more generally for the thesis at the heart of this book. In short, were the murders of the four young children in her care her sole responsibility, or did responsibility rest more broadly on the circumstances that conspired to have her recruited, trained, appointed and supervised on Ward Four—factors which were in turn related to the broader organization, financing and management of the NHS?

So too: is the responsibility for the serial murders of the other children in this chapter the individual responsibility of Hindley, Brady and Black, or just as likely to be related more generally to, for example, how childhood is socially constructed (and which is predicated upon a child's 'weakness' and 'vulnerability'), or to the failings of the criminal justice system which allowed a paedophile to walk free from court with only an admonishment? In trying to answer these questions we need to remember that all serial killers need to gain access to suitable victims so as to be able to kill and kill again without being detected. As such they operate in circumstances where there are weak social arrangements, where people do not look out for each other and in which they are able to gain not only the access that they need, but also the opportunities to create the conditions in which they come to kill.

These opportunities are created by many things. For example, in Allitt's case a lack of vigilance is obvious as is a failure to act when it became clear that someone on Ward Four was killing patients. That failure to act was a product of many factors and whilst it is impossible to determine precisely which factor was pre-eminent, there is little doubt that given how the hospital was funded closing the ward would have had a disastrous effect on the hospital's finances. In any event it seems fair to conclude that Allitt was not solely responsible for the deaths of her four victims. Whilst she might have succeeded in other circumstances to have been recruited as a children's nurse and to have gained access to a sick child that she might have wanted to injure or kill, a suitably robust clinical environment with an appropriate level of qualified staff offering regular supervision and prepared to act upon a series of unexplained medical events would have prevented her from injuring as many children as she did and from killing four of her patients. Above all, appropriate action after April 12 would certainly have saved the life of Claire Peck.

But what of the victims of Hindley, Brady and Robert Black? As far as Black is concerned it is difficult not to agree with Wyre's conclusion that 'Black's life and, with it, his career as a sex offender illustrated an almost complete failure by every part of the investigative and penal system in Britain' (1995: 227). In short and as has been described in this chapter, the failures of the police and the penal system allowed Black the opportunity to gain access to his victims and, in failing to stop him, helped to create the circumstances in which he was able repeatedly to target and kill young girls.

Yet there is more going on here too, for Wyre also draws attention to Black's 'life', as well as to his offending behaviour. By this he is referring to the fact that Black was abandoned as an infant then adopted by an elderly couple, who both unfortunately died which meant that Black was taken into care. Of course many people have difficult childhoods and are taken into care, but they do not all go on to become serial killers and thus we should not push this analysis too far. However, what does seem to be of more relevance—both in relation to Black and to Hindley and Brady—is that the opportunities that they exploited to kill children were socially structured, albeit at different points in our time-frame and for different reasons.

In Black's case these social constructions are centred on his paedophilia and more generally by the growing fetishising of young people's bodies. This can be seen most obviously at work in the music, fashion and entertainment industries, where there appears to be a relentless commercial ethic to sexualise children and young people. This in turn feeds into a cultural and social paedophilia that uses children and childhood for financial gain and in doing so blurs the line between what it means to be a child and what it means to be an adult. Black's use of children was of course simply sexual, but do we seriously doubt that his paedophilic tendencies are replicated more generally within society and that his knowledge of that replication was used by him to facilitate his offending?

At first glance broadening the responsibility for the murders committed by Hindley and Brady seems to be a much more difficult task—a difficulty not eased by their status within the pantheon of evil in the British true crime genre. Yet, there is a case to be made for broadening that responsibility, if only to underscore that how we conceptualise 'childhood' creates the conditions in which people like Brady and Hindley are able to operate. For if children are not valued and if the adult world does not take seriously the fears and anxieties of children, then they in turn will look elsewhere for support and protection and in doing so will not necessarily make the right decisions. (And look again, for example, at some of those young people who fell victim to the Wests in *Chapter 5*)). However, this is not meant to imply that the child victims of Hindley and Brady were not valued or loved by their parents, or that they looked to Brady or Hindley for protection. Indeed it is obvious that their young victims were loved and it is also clear that Brady and Hindley often exploited a child's willingness to trust adults who asked for help. Rather what I am suggesting is that childhood is a space that is fraught with difficulties for children—difficulties that are more often than not created and exploited by adults—and that negotiating and overcoming those difficulties remains part of what it means to 'grow up', whether at the start of our time-frame or at its close. Whilst the adult world has responded by placing greater controls on children towards the end of that time-frame (and has also evicted some children from 'childhood' altogether) — where for example a child is more likely to be driven to school than to walk there—we have to remember that similar controls were also present when Brady and Hindley were looking for victims.

However the point here is not to debate whether there are now more controls on children than at the start of our time-frame, or whether those controls are more effective or appropriate, but rather to acknowledge that the vulnerability in childhood that allows serial killers to target children is created and then maintained by adults who define what it is to be a child and which then keeps children powerless by defining how the space that we call 'childhood' is occupied and experienced.

CHAPTER 7

Conclusions

CHAPTER 7

Conclusions

I agree with Professor Wilson that the roads are important in this case. Look at the fact that the A12 and the A14 lead to ports—Felixstowe and Harwich. I think that this is crucial—they are used by foreigners. Lorry drivers and so forth. I think that this is significant, as I just can't see an Englishman being involved with these murders.

(E-mail sent to me via *Sky News*)

THE IPSWICH KILLINGS 2006

On 30 October 2006 19-year-old Tania Nicol left the house that she shared with her mother, Kerry, and her younger brother, Aaron, and went to work in the small red-light area of Ipswich clustered around Portman Road—better known outside the town as the home of the local football team, Ipswich Town. Tania's mother claimed that she did not know that her daughter was involved in prostitution and her friends also preferred to remember her as a 'lovely girl who was always giggling at the back of the class' at the local comprehensive, Chantry High School.[1] After leaving school Tania drifted into a variety of unskilled jobs, including working as a chambermaid in a local hotel, but quite quickly her drug use meant that she needed to earn more money so she started to work in some of the town's massage parlours—including one where her mother worked as a cleaner, although presumably not at the same time. Tania was last seen on October 30 and her naked body would eventually be found on December 8, in a stretch of Belstead Brook near the village of Copdock, close to a disused stretch of the A12.

Tania's body was found six days after the body of Gemma Adams had been discovered. Gemma too had been found naked and in Belstead Brook, but over a mile away as the crow flies from where Tania's body had been discarded, near the village of Hintlesham. It now seems likely that their bodies had been dumped together and that Tania's had simply drifted further downstream after days of torrential rain. Gemma was 25 years old when she disappeared on November 15, described by her father as a 'loving daughter', who was 'good company, bright and intelligent'. Gemma had grown up in the village of Kesgrave, where she had enjoyed going to Brownies, playing the piano and riding horses. Like Tania—

---

[1] All of these quotes are taken from interviews that I either conducted or was privy to at the time with various parties involved in events surrounding the Ipswich murders, or from interviews conducted by Paul Harrison, of *Sky News*. I have also attempted to triangulate these interviews with accounts reported in the *Guardian*, in particular.

whom Gemma knew—she had a drug habit and had been using heroin for eight years. As a result she had lost contact with her family and over time had become involved in prostitution.

The discoveries of the naked bodies of two young women in a space of a few days started to elevate this local story into one of national and eventually international interest. However, before the media descended on Ipswich—making it impossible to find a hotel room in the town and when it became commonplace for some of our best-known broadcasters to present the news live from outside Suffolk Police Headquarters—I was asked to go down to Copdock to see what I made of the locations where the bodies of Gemma and Tania had been found for *Sky News*.

It was immediately apparent that the killer must have had some local knowledge of the roads and had been quite careful about how he (I assumed) had disposed of the bodies. For example, the disused roads near both Hintlesham and Copdock gave him plenty of opportunity to park a vehicle which might have contained two bodies and it was also noteworthy that these locations were isolated, lacked street-lighting in the dark and there was therefore very little chance that he would be interrupted as he went about his business. So too, by leaving the bodies in water, the killer was—perhaps inadvertently, perhaps by design—limiting the amount of forensic evidence that the police would be able to gather. He was also quite plausible as a 'punter' and I quickly 'Googled' 'dogging sites Suffolk' to see if these locations were listed. But there was something else that nagged away at me; something that I remain only partly convinced of, but was nonetheless prepared to say on camera. The murders of Tania and Gemma and how their bodies had been disposed of reminded me of the murder in Norwich of Natalie Pearman—'the walking portrait of an ordinary girl' whom I described in *Chapter 3*.

Over the next few days the bodies of three other young women would be discovered. Anneli Alderton, 24, Paula Clennell, 24 and Annette Nichols, 29, were all involved in prostitution too and, inevitably, all had serious drug habits.

Anneli's body was found on December 10, near the village of Nacton, which www.swingheaven.co.uk describes as a 'good dogging site—go through Nacton village, past the school and then follow signs for the picnic area. The bottom two car parks are best for couples.' Anneli, who was three months pregnant when she disappeared, was described by her friends as 'a bright soul [who] always made us laugh at school' and was last seen on the 5.53 p.m. train from Harwich to Colchester on December 3. Her body was discarded in woodland and found relatively quickly. Thus there was more opportunity for the police to gather forensic evidence where she was discovered and also CCTV footage of her last journey on the train which they could release to the public. At the police press conference that followed the discovery of Anneli's body women in Ipswich were warned to 'stay off the streets. If you are out alone at night, you are putting yourself at risk,' which caused one journalist to comment, 'We could have been right back to 1977, when police effectively put a curfew on women during Sutcliffe's killing spree' (Bindel, 2006). This might have been their intention in Ipswich too and the police seemed more than a little on the 'back foot', especially as Anneli had been murdered after there were supposedly more police patrols on the ground. Finally, the bodies of Paula and Annette were found, which—like those of Tania and Gemma—were dumped close together, on waste ground near the village of Levington. Paula left behind three young children and Annette, perhaps hoping to leave prostitution behind, had recently completed a four-year course at a local college to become a beautician.

Over the next few days the local drugs economy of Ipswich was opened up for public consumption. As such we discovered that the price of a bag of heroin was £15 and how drugs were at the root of the local sex industry. So too we learned how the young women involved in prostitution had responded when the local authority ringed the red light area with CCTV cameras in the hope that it would dissuade them from soliciting. It did not. In fact all that this had done was encourage the women to use their mobile phones to arrange meetings with their 'punters' (which will no doubt mean that mobile phone records could provide some vital clues as to the identity of the killer). However, not every woman was pleased with this development and more than one explained that since the introduction of CCTV they had less time to assess a punter—as they were simply eager to jump into a car and get away from the cameras. So too, we learned that ASBOs, fines and 'zero tolerance policing' had done little to put a stop to prostitution and more than one talked about being arrested as an 'occupational hazard' and of the tension that existed between the local police and the prostitutes. Then, after one false start, there was an arrest on 19 December 2006 and at the time of writing a man is currently awaiting trial for all five murders.

The story of the Ipswich murders reminds us of one of the dominant themes that has appeared in this book and which is worth re-stating within the conclusion. Namely, the persistence of the vulnerability of young women involved in prostitution, whether from the start or the end of our time-frame.

I pursued this theme at some length in *Chapter 3*, where I discussed policing failures and the public's attitude towards the murders of young women involved in prostitution—which seemed to me to be more sympathetic in 2006 than it had been in the 1970s—and I do not intend to dwell on this matter further. However, it is also worth noting that my e-mail correspondent whom I quote at the start of this conclusion had clearly never heard of Peter Sutcliffe, Paul Brumfitt or 'Jack the Stripper' and I was struck by how many people—quite sincerely—wanted to e-mail me with their theories as to who they thought the killer was and why they believed he was targeting prostitutes. These theories ranged from 'religious motives'—given that the first two bodies were found in water and 'the killer is still living at home with his mother, who disapproves of sex'—to more fanciful theories based on the KGB organizing the murders. The 'medical-psychological' tradition would seem to have seeped deep into the public's consciousness, which suggests that it is important to re-state what this book has set out to demonstrate. This is, namely, that serial killing should be seen from the perspective of the victims—those who are killed—rather than from the perspective of the serial killer and his or her motivation. As such I have sought to determine why it is that serial killers have targeted just five main groups in this country since 1960 and why women and girls dominate all but one of these groups.

So too I have sought to question whether serial killing can be seen as a form of 'homicidal protest' or if other factors, such as the move from Britain being an 'inclusive' to an 'exclusive' society are related to these groups—the 'left behind' falling victims to the attentions of serial killers. I will return to these themes shortly, but I would also like to pose other questions within this conclusion which link these five groups and which I hope will create a suitable ending to the book. Namely, is the rate of serial killing in Britain increasing, or slowing down; which groups are likely to remain vulnerable to the attentions of serial murderers in the future; and why did 1986 produce more serial killers than any other year in our time-frame?

THE RATE OF SERIAL MURDER—1960-2006

The graph in *Chapter 1* demonstrates the year in which people, as far as we are able to determine, fell victim to serial killers and this is reproduced overleaf for ease of reference. Overall there were—based on my strict categorisations about who qualifies as a serial killer for the purposes of this book and whether they were British born and raised—some 326 victims of 19 serial killers over our time-frame. As I have argued, this is almost certainly an underestimate of the numbers of people who have been killed by serial killers in this country during this period, as I have excluded, for example, those people who were murdered by a serial killer who has never been caught. I have also (with the exception of Harold Shipman) only counted the number of victims that the killer was tried and convicted for at court, although it is clear that most of the serial killers who have been imprisoned are suspected of having killed many more than those whom they were convicted of killing. I have also excluded the Ipswich murders from this graph given that the case is still ongoing. However, based on these numbers and bearing in mind the caveats that I have drawn attention to, we can quickly make one or two superficial statistical points.

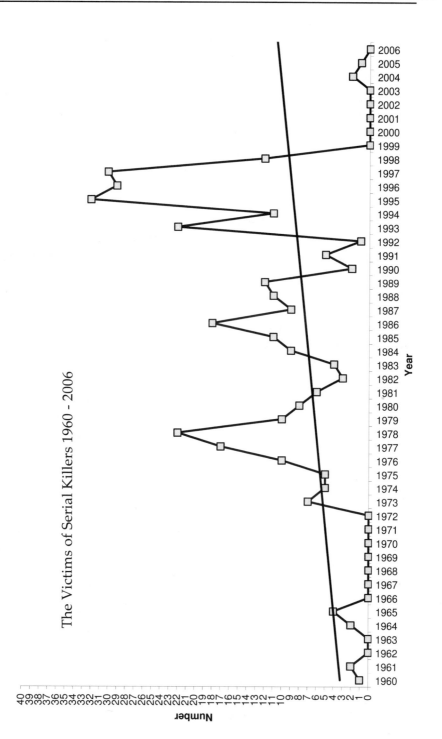

The Victims of Serial Killers 1960 - 2006

The average number of people killed by a serial killer each year in this country is seven and there would appear to be on average two serial killers active at any one time. These averages obviously hide peaks and troughs both in relation to the number of victims and the number of active serial killers. For example, there were large numbers of victims in the mid-1990s, when in particular Harold Shipman (this country's most prolific serial killer) was active, whereas during the late 1960s and early 1970s no one seems to have fallen victim to a serial killer. So too, the year when there were most serial killers active was 1986. It was during this year, for example, that Duffy and Mulcahy killed three victims, Kenneth Erskine killed seven, Shipman murdered eight and Robert Black killed one. There was also an Italian-born serial killer active in London in 1986, but he has been excluded from the graph. I will discuss the significance of 1986 more fully below, but for the moment I want to continue to look at the rate at which people were murdered over the time-frame, by considering the significance of the trendline that is introduced within the graph.

A rising trend

Trendlines are a common way to analyse the general direction—up, down, or sideways—of prices, securities or commodities. For example, the value of a stock can move in one of these three ways and whilst it might be subject to various highs and lows, depending on, for example market forces, it is nonetheless still possible to discern the stock's general direction and to predict the trend into the future. Using a trendline in this graph helps us to determine whether the rate of serial killing has gone up or down over the time-frame and whether this trend might continue.

As is obvious the trendline in the graph suggests that the rate of serial killing has increased and would appear to predict that it will continue to rise, despite significant gaps after Shipman was arrested and even allowing for the fact that the most recent murders in Ipswich have been excluded. This would suggest that the underlying factors that have produced a trendline of this type remain strong—despite the peaks and troughs that the figures produce. Yet, why should this be so and what groups in particular might still be vulnerable to attack?

Throughout the book—whether within the 'inclusive' or 'exclusive' society, as Young (1999) has described Britain over the time-frame—I have argued that certain factors have remained constant, which helps us to identify which groups are vulnerable to attack by serial killers. For example, I have argued that the persistence of homophobia over the time-frame, despite recent legislative initiatives related to civil partnership agreements between gay couples, has been the driving force behind the victimisation of gay men by serial killers. I have further suggested that this homophobia has impacted upon the way in which attacks on gay men and women are policed, based on primary research related to

The Pink Shield Project in Birmingham. So too I have discussed policing in relation to attacks on young women involved in prostitution and then more broadly how public moralising about the lifestyles associated with prostitutes, or indeed with gay men, contributes to a culture whereby it is easier for serial killers to create both the opportunities to gain access to individuals from within these groups and then the opportunities that they need to kill them. As for the elderly I have argued that their 'silence' within society, and more broadly their lack of power, creates circumstances in which they become marginalised and excluded which also creates the opportunities needed for serial killers to kill and kill again. I have talked about the phenomenon of 'runaways' and 'throwaways'—young people leaving home for one reason or another and what happens to them when they try to make their way in the world. Finally, for children I have described the reconstruction of childhood that is currently taking place and the conceptual eviction of some children from the category of 'childhood' altogether—blurring the line between what it means to be a 'child' and an 'adult'.

Looking at the underlying forces that I have described above helps us to begin to determine why the rate of serial killing might continue to rise in the future, as predicted by the trendline. After all, these forces seem to be persistent, albeit that there are often glimmers of hope in the opposite direction in relation to, for example, new regulations regarding the management of the performance of general medical practitioners, or the relative lack of moralising that I detected in relation to the murders in Ipswich of five young women who worked in prostitution. So too it might be argued that the reconstruction of childhood could serve to create fewer opportunities for serial killers to target children, especially as more and more children seem to be spending greater amounts of their spare time in the home, rather than playing outside. However, we have to be careful not to exaggerate this process and we should also remember that there are some significant numbers of young people who continue to leave home for various reasons and in doing so make themselves vulnerable. Gwyther Rees (2001: 9), for example, Head of Research for the Children's Society and co-author of much of the research that I alluded to in *Chapter 5*, identifies that 77,000 young people run away for the first time each year in Britain and most of these children are aged between 13 and 15. This would seem to be a group that would remain a prime target for serial killers. But are there other groups too, that might be vulnerable in the years to come?

Simon Winlow and Steve Hall (2006) have recently published their ethnographic research with over 40 young people, between the ages of 18 and 25, in a northern city in Britain to investigate the night-time economy, or as they characterise it, 'the rather grim reality of life in the post-industrial pleasure-dome' (Winlow and Hall, 2006: 9). In doing so they are eager to try and understand how young, working class people have responded to nearly 30 years of the 'exclusive society' and how they continue to respond to the replacement of Britain's traditional, manufacturing economic base, with one based on job insecurity, out-sourcing and increased consumption. For whilst the old industrial work of the past had an 'exploitative certainty'—where workers tended to stay in the same job, in the same location—the economic basis for work now done by young people demands both 'geographical and sector mobility,' (Winlow and Hall, 2006: 19). So too they are interested in investigating how old manufacturing towns and cities have re-branded themselves as places where young people come to eat, drink and spend, reflecting an economic base that has moved from production to consumption. As such, Winlow and Hall (2006: 8) uncovered a picture of extreme anxiety, precariousness, atomisation, social division and hostile interpersonal violence—'without doubt the most spectacular and disturbing feature of the night-time economy.'

The violence that they uncovered in the night-time economy was of a different kind to the violence that has traditionally been described when lots of young people who know each other get together and go out drinking. Specifically, Winlow and Hall (2006: 120) argue that 'unpredictable stranger violence is becoming more common'—a consequence, they conclude, of the 'inevitable by-product of the ineffectually regulated cultures of transgression and hedonism that support the logical demand of the continuous economic growth of the night-time leisure scene' (Winlow and Hall, 2006: 108). By this they mean that the night-time economy is not controlled by the police, or by private security firms who simply do not have enough resources to cope, and as a result 'frequent incidents of alcohol-triggered violence teeter on the verge of unmanageability' (Winlow and Hall, 2006: 188). Finally they conclude that 'the night-time economy is now the primary site for interpersonal violence in Britain' (Winlow and Hall, 2006: 193).

In this rich and provocative account Winlow and Hall have begun to try to look into the future of Britain and in doing so have given us cause for concern. Specifically, their suggestion that stranger violence is becoming more common and that the site of that violence is within the night-time economy of our major towns and cities suggests an emerging problem that will have to be managed. So too they have identified a group of vulnerable young people, in a situation and space which lacks police regulation. As such the possibility that someone might use their vulnerability within that situation and space to kill is obvious—especially given the opportunities that the lack of police regulation affords to someone so minded.

The exclusive society and 1986

These persisting, underlying forces that I have been describing might be seen as simply the outcome of much broader social and particularly economic forces that I have already drawn attention to (which were also the basis for what was being argued by Winlow and Hall) and which have been characterised in various ways throughout the book, especially in *Chapter 1*. So, for example, we can see Britain becoming over the time-frame an 'exclusive society'; a '40/30/30' society (below); or a society of 'us and them', where the rich have got richer since 1979 and the poor have become the 'left behind' or, as Bauman (2005: 2) has recently described the poor, 'flawed consumers'. Perhaps Davies captures this best when he describes the poor as being the 'reject list of the new welfare state' (Davies, 1997: 179) and 'looking back into the history of the country of the poor, it turns out that it was created quite deliberately, rather like the great penal colony of Australia was planned and created by politicians in London two centuries earlier' (Davies, 1997: 285-286).

The planning that Davies is alluding to is clearly related to the market, or as Will Hutton (1995: 82) has described it, planning that leaves 'capitalism to its own devices'. By this he means that Britain has become a low-cost, deregulated producer, with correspondingly low social overheads and a minimalist welfare state. Thus, for example, supplementary benefit for the unemployed as a proportion of full time earnings dropped from 26 per cent in 1979 to 19 per cent in 1993; union membership was discouraged and fell dramatically from 13.3 m to 9 m over the same period; and Hutton argues that the state was also trying to 'wash its hands of future generations of old people' (1995: 199). So too Davies draws attention to the 3m people who were unemployed by 1993 and the fact that, while between 1966 and 1977 wages of all men in all social classes grew at the same rate, from 1979 they started to diverge. Between 1979 and 1992 those already on the highest wages saw their income grow by 50 per cent, whilst those on the lowest wages were actually worse off than they had been in 1975 (Davies, 1997: 174).

Hutton characterises the consequences of these processes as Britain becoming a '40/30/30' society. By this he means that only 40 per cent of the workforce is in full-time, secure employment; 30 per cent are insecurely self-employed or working casually; and the remaining 30 per cent—the 'marginalised' are unemployed or working for 'poverty' wages. Young (1999) takes this basic outline, adds to it in his own way as a criminologist and suggests that a society based on these economic divisions leads to separation and exclusion, where there are fewer collective values and greater individualisation. This in turn produces 'material and ontological precariousness' (Young, 1999: 26) and as such the values and relationships that are necessary to sustain a stable social order are undermined. As a result crime more generally rises and, as I have tried to demonstrate, I believe that it is also possible to apply these same arguments to explain the rise of serial killing in this way too.

Young, Hutton and Davies were all writing in the mid to late 1990s and only Young's work appeared after the coming to power of New Labour in the General Election of 1997. There are two points to be made here—the first related to New Labour and their tenure in power; the second as to when these trends could first be discerned.

Looking at this first point from a criminological perspective and whilst this is a favourite topic of debate, the coming to power of New Labour does not seem to have particularly altered the course that was being pursued by their Tory predecessors. Indeed, I have already drawn attention to the changes and continuities in youth and criminal justice under New Labour in *Chapter 5*. Those changes which they did initiate would not have been out of place had they been introduced by a Conservative government. So too there would seem to have been a continuation of the social and economic policies of their predecessors, albeit that these have been characterised as being a 'Third Way'—bringing together social justice and a dynamic economy. Nonetheless, New Labour has drawn directly from neo-liberal discourses in its analysis of the global economy. Indeed 'globalisation' has become a favourite justification of the New Labour 'project' and thus the British economy, it is argued has to continue to make itself as attractive to investors as possible by maintaining a deregulated economic approach and limiting any interventionist strategies (Hay, 1999. For a general introduction to changes and continuities after 1997 see McAnulla, 2006). All of this again helps us to explain why the trendline in the graph predicts that serial killing will continue to rise—a prediction also given some substance by Winlow and Hall's (2006) research.

With regards to the second point, it is of course difficult to suggest when these trends could first be discerned. Whilst Hutton was writing in 1995, Davies in 1997 and Young in 1999, it is clear that what they were describing had to predate their published work. Looking backwards we can of course suggest that the coming to power of Mrs Thatcher in 1979 ushered in a period when a 'new right' ideology—based on ideas popularised by Friedrich von Hayek (1944), Milton Friedman (1953) and Robert Nozick (1974), which are now characterised as 'Thatcherism'—gained the ascendancy. This 'new right' ideology emphasised that the British state had become involved in too many areas and specifically that too many national resources were being spent on welfare. In turn the demands on government were increasing and as a consequence taxes on business had become too high, limiting the private sector's profit-making and wealth-creating potential. As a result, it was argued, there should be less government regulation and intervention in the economy, and far less provision for those who were poor and unemployed, from the fear that this would create 'welfare dependency'.

Whilst this broad outline seems fair enough, we should not push this analysis too far and we have to remember that, for example, much of the welfare state did survive Thatcherism. Nonetheless, it is scarcely controversial to suggest that Britain did change after 1979 and that those changes are related to policy directions influenced by 'new right' thinking.

But when did all these changes begin to make an impact on people's 'material and ontological' sense of themselves? Danny Dorling (2005), in his analysis of murder in Britain since 1981, notes that the murder rate is increasing for one specific group of victims—those men who were born in or after 1964. He further suggests that this fact tells us something about society and how it is changing. More generally, for example, he notes that what makes one community more dangerous than another is poverty and then specifically he suggests that it is important to remember that men born in or after 1964 would leave school in 1980/81, depending on their birthdays. He sees this as significant, as we have to remember that:

> The summer of 1981 was the first summer for over 40 years that a young man living in a poor area would find work or training very scarce and it got worse in the years that followed. When the recession of the early 1980s hit, mass unemployment was concentrated on the young, they were simply not recruited. (Dorling, 2005: 37)

So, Dorling is suggesting that by 1981 the first generation that had reached maturity in the 'exclusive society' would have quickly become aware that the way that their grandfathers, fathers or elder brothers had graduated from school and into work had changed. That change would bring with it other changes too in relation to how this generation could put meaning into their lives and it was predicated upon 'new right' thinking which wanted a deregulated economy and no 'welfare dependency'. As Dorling has demonstrated, one of the by-products of these trends was an increase in the murder rate for this specific group and whilst murder is a different phenomenon from serial killing this insight perhaps also helps us to begin to understand why 1986 produced so many serial killers. In other words, these broad social and economic forces created the conditions in which those who wanted to kill and kill again were given the opportunities to do so. Here I am not suggesting some crude economic cause and effect, but rather—I hope—a more nuanced observation. In other words, in the same way that young men in 1981 first became aware that their world had changed, so too those killers who were active found it easier to kill their elderly, gay and child victims. But did they do this as a form of 'homicidal protest'?

LEYTON AND THE 'HOMICIDAL PROTEST'

As I have made clear, this book can be read as an extended argument with Elliot Leyton (1986) and in particular his suggestion that serial killing is a form of 'homicidal protest'. As I outlined in both the *Introduction* and *Chapter 1*, and pursued more closely in *Chapter 2* through my discussion of the victims of Harold Shipman, Leyton suggests that serial killers murder those who they believe are threatening their position in the social and economic structure. So too Leyton harnesses this argument to three broad time-frames and the period that most closely overlaps with the time-frame of this book is his post-1945 'modern period'. It is during this time, Leyton suggests, that serial killers will come from the working class or the lower middle class and their victims will be from the middle class. However, the victims of serial killers in Britain between 1960-2006 do not seem to have come from the middle classes at all, but instead are overwhelmingly individuals within groups that lack power, voice and agency. Indeed, following the arguments of Grover and Soothill (1999), I have suggested that serial killing in this country should only be seen as a form of 'homicidal protest' if we can extend that description to incorporate the sense that this implies a form of 'revenge' perpetrated on those who could be described as an economic 'burden' on society.

THE ROLE OF POVERTY

Of course this is to generalise about the victims of British serial killers over our time-frame in a way that is unfair to some of those who were murdered. It totalises their experiences and backgrounds and, as I have drawn attention to the label 'elderly', for example, can mask a range of backgrounds, situations and economic circumstances. Nonetheless, what does dominate any analysis of the majority of those who have been murdered by serial killers during this period is their poverty. (Here too remember that Dorling has already described how poverty is the key factor in making a community susceptible to an increased murder rate.) They are 'the left behind' of an economic structure that has moved inexorably from production to consumption.

This is significant, for all of this of course begs the question as to what role and function the poor have in a society that is characterised by the economic imperative to consume. After all, whilst the labour of the poor was once needed and valued in an economy that produced manufactured goods to sell to the world, in the out-sourced, deregulated, lean economy that has emerged since 1979, the ability of the poor to work no longer seems to guarantee them the protection of the state that their labour once commanded. As such they have become a burden, through their inability to consume in the same way or to the same extent as those who have power, status and money. As Bauman (2005: 113) has recently put it, the poor in these changed economic circumstances 'are totally useless.' He continues:

> No one—no one who truly counts, speaks up and is heard—needs them [the poor]. For them, zero tolerance. Society would be much better off if the poor just burnt their tents and left. The world would be much more pleasant without them. The poor are not needed and so they are unwanted. And because they are unwanted, they can be, without much regret and compunction, forsaken. (Bauman, 2005: 113)

Of course, if no one who 'truly counts' speaks up when someone is murdered and if the world is seen as much more 'pleasant' without the existence of that person—because of their age, gender, sexuality or the fact that they work in prostitution—then no one is either going to notice or care if more and more of the same type of person get killed. The poor have not so much 'burnt their tents and left', as had them burned for them. In this respect serial killing emerges as the ultimate form of 'forsaking': the ultimate form of abandoning and deserting the poor, in a culture that has increasingly come to place its primary value on consumption. In doing so it has left in its wake fractured communities, where individuals are now more and more cut off from each other, whilst all the time living precarious and anxious lives that no longer seem to be connected to the lives of anyone else. No wonder our trendline predicted that serial killing would continue to rise.

Bibliography

M Amis (2001), *Experience*, London: Vintage

P Aries (1962), *Centuries of Childhood*, London: Jonathan Cape

Z Bauman (2005), *Work, Consumerism and the New Poor*, Maidenhead: Open University Press

J Bennett and D Gardner (2005), *The Cromwell Street Murders: The Detective's Story*, Thrupp, Stroud: Sutton Publishing

M Bilton (2003), *Wicked Beyond Belief: The Hunt for the Yorkshire Ripper*, London: Harper Collins

J Bindel (2006), 'Terror on Our Streets,' *Guardian*, 13 December 2006

F Brookman and M Maguire (2003), *Reducing Homicide: A Review of the Possibilities*, London: The Home Office

A Buonfino and G Mulgan (2006) (eds), *Porcupines in Winter: The Pleasures and Pains of Living in Modern Britain*, London: The Young Foundation

G Burn (1998), *Happy Like Murderers: The True Story of Fred and Rosemary West*, London: Faber and Faber

E Burney (2005), *Making People Behave: Anti-Social Behaviour, Politics and Policy*, Cullompton, Devon: Willan

D Canter (2003), *Mapping Murder: Walking in Killers' Footsteps*, London: Virgin Books

The Children's Society (1999), *Still Running: Children on the Streets in the UK*, London: The Children's Society

T Clark and J Penycate (1976), *Psychopath: The Case of Patrick Mackay*, London: Routledge & Kegan Paul

N Davies (1993), *Murder on Ward Four: The Story of Bev Allitt, and the Most Terrifying Crime Since the Moors Murders*, London: Chatto & Windus

N Davies (1997), *Dark Heart: The Shocking Truth about Hidden Britain*, London: Chatto & Windus

S D'Cruze, S Walklate, and S Pegg (2006), *Murder*, Cullompton, Devon: Willan

Sir L Donaldson (2001), *Harold Shipman's Clinical Practice, 1974-1998*, London: Department of Health

D Dorling (2005), 'Prime Suspect: Murder in Britain,' in P Hillyard, C Pantazis, S Tombs, D Gordon and D Dorling (eds), *Criminal Obsessions: Why Harm Matters More than Crime*, London: Crime and Society Foundation

E Durkheim (1933), *Suicide*, London: Routledge

S Egger (1984), 'A Working Definition of Serial Murder and the Reduction of Linkage Blindness,' *Journal of Police Science and Administration*, 12 (3), pp. 348-357

M Fido (2001), *A History of British Serial Killing*, London: Carlton Books

B Fone (2000), *Homophobia: A History*, New York: Metropolitan Books

J Fox and J Levin (2005), *Extreme Killing: Understanding Serial and Mass Murder*, Thousand Oaks, Ca.: Sage

M Freidson (1970), Profession of Medicine: *A Study of the Sociology of Applied Knowledge*, New York: Harper and Rowooks

M Friedman (1953), *The Methodology of Positive Economics*, Chicago: University of Chicago Press

F Furedi (2001), *Paranoid Parenting: Abandon Your Anxieties and Become a Good Parent*, Harmondsworth: The Penguin Press

N Gerrard (2004), *Soham: A Study of Our Times*, London: Short Books

C Gilleard and P Higgs (2000), *Cultures of Ageing: Self, Citizen and the Body*, Harlow: Pearson Education Ltd

G Gresswell and C Hollin (1994), 'Multiple Murder: A Review,' *British Journal of Criminology*, 34 (1), pp. 1-14

C Grover and K Soothill (1999), 'British Serial Killing: Towards a Structural Explanation,' *British Criminology Conferences: Selected Proceedings*, Volume 2, http://wwwlboro.ac.uk/departments/ss/bccsp/vol02/08GROVEHTM

C Hay (1999), *The Political Economy of New Labour: Labouring Under False Pretences?* Manchester: Manchester University Press

F von Hayek (1944), *The Road to Serfdom*, London: Routledge & Sons Ltd.

E Hickey (1991), *Serial Murderers and their Victims*, Pacific Grove, Ca.: Brookes/Cole Publishing

R Holmes and S Holmes (1994), *Profiling Violent Crimes*, Thousand Oaks, Ca.: Sage

S Holmes and W de Burger (1988), *Serial Murder*, Newbury Park, Ca.: Sage

Home Office (2004), *Paying the Price: A Consultation Paper on Prostitution*, London: The Home Office

Home Office (2006), *A Coordinated Prostitution Strategy and a Summary of Responses to Paying the Price*, London: The Home Office

W Hutton (1995), *The State We're In*, London: Jonathan Cape Ltd.

I Jack (2006), 'Ian Jack Contemplates Lost Sundays,' *Guardian* 11 March 2006.

A James and A Prout (1997) (eds.), *Constructing and Reconstructing Childhood*, Basingstoke: Falmer

O James (1995), *Juvenile Violence in a Winner-Loser Culture: Socio-Economic and Familial Origins of the Rise of Violence Against the Person*, London: Free Association Books

P Jenkins (1988), 'Serial Murder in England, 1940-1985,' *Journal of Criminal Justice*, Volume 16, pp.1-15

C Jenks (1996), *Childhood*, London: Routledge

L Kelly and J Radford (1987), 'The Problem of Men: Feminist Perspectives on Sexual Violence,' in P Scraton and P Gordon (eds) *Causes for Concern: British Criminal Justice on Trial*, Harmondsworth: Penguin

J Kitzinger (1997), 'Who are you Kidding? Children, Power and the Struggle against Sexual Abuse,' in A James and A Prout *Constructing and Reconstructing Childhood*, London: Falmer 1997, pp. 165-189

E Larson (2003), *The Devil in the White City: Murder, Magic and Madness at the Fair that Changed America*, New York: Vintage Books

E Leyton (1986), *Hunting Humans: The Rise of the Modern Multiple Murderer*, Toronto: McClelland and Stewart

P Lilly (1993), *Benefits and Costs: Securing the Future of Social Security*, Mais Lecture

Sir W Macpherson (1990), *The Stephen Lawrence Inquiry: Report of an Inquiry by Sir William Macpherson of Cluny*, Cm 4262, London: HMSO

S McAnulla (2006), *British Politics: A Critical Introduction*, London: Continuum

J McManus and I Rivers (2001), *Without Prejudice: A Guide for Community Saefty Partnerships on Responding to the Needs of Lesbians, Gays and Bisexuals*, London: NACRO

A Masters (2005), *Stuart: A Life Backwards*, London: Harper Perennial

B Masters (1986), *Killing for Company: The Case of Dennis Nilsen*, London: Coronet Books

B Masters (1996), *'She Must Have Known': The Trial of Rosemary West*, London: Doubleday

J Matthews (2006), 'Ruchill: A Glasgow Housing Scheme,' in A Buonfino and G Mulgan (eds), *Porcupines in Winter: The Pains and Pleasures of Living Together in Modern Britain*, London: The Young Foundation

R Merton (1938), *Social Structure and Anomie*, New York: Irvington

M Midgley (1984), *Wickedness: A Philosophical Essay*, London: Routledge

J Muncie (1999), *Youth Crime: A Critical Introduction*, London: Sage

J Muncie and G Hughes (2002), 'Modes of Youth Governance: Political Rationales, Criminalization and Resistance,' in J Muncie, G Hughes and E McLaughlin (eds), *Youth Justice: Critical Readings*, London: Sage

C Murray (1990), *The Emerging British Underclass*, London: Institute of Economic Affairs Health and Welfare Unit

C Murray (1994), *Underclass: The Crisis Deepens*, London: Institute of Economic Affairs Health and Welfare Unit

T Newburn (2002), 'The Contemporary Politics of Youth Crime Prevention,' in J Muncie, G Hughes, E McLaughlin (eds), *Youth Justice: Critical Readings*, London: Sage

C Newman (1989), *Young Runaways: Findings from Britain's First Safe House*, London: The Children's Society

R Nozick (1974), *Anarchy, State and Utopia*, Oxford: Blackwell

C Peters (2005), *Harold Shipman: Mind Set on Murder*, London: Carlton Books

C Phillipson (1998), *Reconstructing Old Age*, London: Sage

K Plummer (2001), 'The Call of Life Stories in Ethnographic Research,' in P Atkinson, A Coffey, S Delamont, J Loffland, L Loffland (eds), *Handbook of Criminology*, London: Sage, pp. 395-406

N Postman (1994), *The Disappearance of Childhood*, London: W H Allen

M Presdee (2004), 'The Story of Crime: Biography and the Excavation of Transgression,' in J Ferrell, K Hayward, W Morrison, M Presdee (eds), *Cultural Criminology Unleashed*, London: Glasshouse Press, pp. 41-48

G Rees (2001), *Working with Young Runaways: Learning from Practice*, London: The Children's Society

G Rees and J Lee (2005), *Still Running II: Findings from the Second National Survey of Young Runaways*, London: The Children's Society

R Reiner (1992), *The Politics of the Police*, Hemel Hempstead: Harvester Wheatsheaf

N Rose (1989), *Governing the Soul*, London: Routledge

D Sandbrook (2005), *Never Had It So Good: A History of Britain from Suez to the Beatles*, London: Little, Brown

D Seabrook (2006), *Jack of Jumps*, London: Granta Books

M Seltzer (1998), *Serial Killers: Death and Life in America's Wound Culture*, London: Routledge

J Silverman and D Wilson (2002), *Innocence Betrayed: Paedophilia, The Media and Society*, Cambridge: Polity Press

J Simon (2001), 'Entitlement to Cruelty: Neo-Liberalism and the Punitive Mentality in the United States,' in K Stenson and R Sullivan (eds), *Crime, Risk and Justice*, Cullompton: Willan

K Simpson (1980), *Forty Years of Murder*, London: Grafton Books

Dame J Smith (2002-2005) all reports taken from www.the-shipman-inquiry.org

K Soothill (2001), 'The Harold Shipman Case: A Sociological Perspective,' *The Journal of Forensic Psychiatry*, Vol 12 No 2 (September), pp. 260-262

K Soothill and D Wilson (2005), 'Theorising the Puzzle that is Harold Shipman,' *Journal of Forensic Psychiatry and Psychology*, Vol. 16 No 4, pp. 658-698

H Souness (1995), *Fred and Rose: The Full Story of Fred and Rosemary West and the Gloucester House of Horrors*, London: Time Warner Books

T Thomas (2000), *Sex Crime: Sex Offending and Society*, Cullompton: Willan

P Waddington (1999), *Policing Citizens*, London: UCL Press

G Weinberg (1972), *Society and the Healthy Homosexual*, New York: St Martin's Press

S West and M West (1995), *Inside 25 Cromwell Street: The Terrifying True Story of Life with Fred and Rose West*, Monmouth: Peter Grose Ltd.

P Willis (2000), *The Ethnographic Imagination*, Cambridge: Polity Press

D Wilson (2003), ' "Keeping Quiet" or "Going Nuts": Some Emerging Strategies Used by Young Black People in Custody at a Time of Childhood Being Re-constructed,' *Howard Journal of Criminal Justice*, 42, December, 411-425

D Wilson (2004), ' "Keeping Quiet" or "Going Nuts": Strategies Used by Young, Black Men in Custody,' *Howard Journal of Criminal Justice*, 43, July, 317-330

D Wilson (2005), *Death at the Hands of the State*, London: The Howard League for Penal Reform

D Wilson and J Ashton (1998), *What Everyone in Britain Should Know About Crime and Punishment*, Oxford: Oxford University Press

D Wilson and B McCalla (2004), *The Last Respectable Prejudice: An Evaluation of the Pink Shield Project*, Birmingham: UCE

S Winlow and S Hall (2006), *Violent Night: Urban Leisure and Contemporary Culture*, Oxford: Berg

R Wyre and T Tate (1995), *The Murder of Childhood: Inside the Mind of One of Britain's Most Notorious Child Murderers*, Harmondsworth: Penguin

J Young (1999), *The Exclusive Society*, London: Sage

Index

Pit of Shame
THE REAL BALLAD OF READING GAOL
Anthony Stokes
With a Foreword by **Theodore Dalrymple**

This remarkable book looks at the **life and times of Reading Gaol** during the period that **Oscar Wilde** was a prisoner there and contains new insights concerning his classic poem, *The Ballad of Reading Gaol*. *Pit of Shame*, by senior prison officer Anthony Stokes, is based on upwards of ten years research and familiarity with the very fabric of Reading Gaol. It also tells of notorious and famous prisoners such as **Thomas Jennings**, **Amelia Dyer** (the 'Reading Baby Farmer') and **Stacey Keach** (the Hollywood actor); of all the hangings at Reading over the years, including of Trooper **Charles Thomas Wooldridge** - the 'C. T. W.' of Wilde's ballad (which is fully analysed); the chain of events that led to the rejection of capital punishment by the UK; and of escapes, brutality, corruption, incompetent criminals and other humorous and entertaining incidents. There are also chapters on internment in the wake of Ireland's Easter Rising, Reading's role as a local prison and borstal correctional centre (and later as a recall and correctional centre), and its use by the Canadian military for 'invisible prisoners'. All this is enhanced by **fascinating period detail from the archives, newspapers and records,** including the old Visiting Committee book, Execution Log, chaplain's journal, building plans and other, until, now largely hidden materials – making *Pit of Shame* a must for any reader interested in **crime, punishment, prisons** and **English literature.**

'Here is a detailed history of a single institution that is of wide philosophical significance and that could be read with great profit and enjoyment by the ... general reader ... If I had to recommend a single book about the history of imprisonment in this country, this would be it'. **Theodore Dalrymple** from the **Foreword**

> I know not whether Laws be right,
> Or whether Laws be wrong;
> All that we know who lie in gaol
> Is that the wall is strong;
> And that each day is like a year,
> A year whose days are long.
>
> Oscar Wilde (*The Ballad of Reading Gaol*)